Black Family
Violence

Black Family Violence

Current Research and Theory

Edited by

Robert L. Hampton
Connecticut College
Children's Hospital Center

Lexington Books
D.C. Heath and Company/Lexington, Massachusetts/Toronto

Library of Congress Cataloging-in-Publication Data

Black family violence : current research and theory
  edited by Robert L. Hampton.
      p.   cm.
    Includes index.
    ISBN 0-669-21858-8 (alk. paper)
    1. Family violence—United States.   2. Afro-Americans—Families.
  I. Hampton, Robert L.
  HQ809.3.U5B56   1991
  362.82'92'08996073—dc20   90-23280
                                                      CIP

Published simultaneously in Canada
Printed in the United States of America
International Standard Book Number: 0-669-21858-8
Library of Congress Catalog Card Number: 90-23280

The paper used in this publication meets the minimum requirements of
American National Standard for Information Sciences—Permanence of
Paper for Printed Library Materials, ANSI Z39.48-1984. ∞™

    92 93 94 95 8 7 6 5 4 3 2

*To my students for making teaching and learning
a mutually fulfilling exchange*

Contents

Tables and Figure

Tables

Figure

Preface

F amily violence in all its various forms is an ancient phenomenon. During the 1970s and 1980s a growing body of research has delineated the nature and scope of family violence; however, our understanding of the antecedents and consequences remains incomplete. This is especially the case when one looks at the paucity of research on violence among families of color.

The black population remains one of the fastest growing subgroups in the United States. Based on current projections, the black population is expected to increase dramatically over the next decade. Because the rate of growth among blacks is expected to remain almost twice as fast as the rate of growth for the total U.S. population, blacks would rise from 12.4 percent to 13.4 percent of the U.S. population between 1988 and 2000 (U.S. Bureau of Census, 1986).

Research on the family lives of black Americans has increased significantly over the past twenty-five years. There have been major divisions within this field concerning the extent to which black families differ from nonblack families as a function of the "culture of poverty," cultural deviance, or cultural variations based on different sociocultural environments. Regardless of the perspective used, given the critical importance of social relationships called families to adults and children, the emergence of black family life as a specialized research field is not surprising. Even with this growth in research and the use of competing conceptual orientations, many critical areas of black family life remain underresearched.

This book is intended to fill two needs: a need for further research in the area of family violence and a need for more research on black families. Both previously published and unpublished materials are included. The contributors were carefully selected from a variety of disciplines and reflect different approaches. The diverse perspectives brought to bear on the subject by professionals from many disciplines adds to the richness of this book.

There have been few systematic studies of family violence based on representative samples of a single city, state, or the entire country. There are even fewer studies that attempt to measure changes in the rates of violence. In "Is Violence in Black Families Increasing? A Comparison of 1975 and 1985 National Survey Rates," Robert Hampton, Richard Gelles, and John Harrop compare rates of physical violence in black families from the First National Family Violence Survey, conducted in 1975, with the rates from the 1985 replication. They found that the rate of severe violence toward black women declined 43 percent—a statistically significant change. The rate of parent-to-child and wife-to-husband violence did not decline. The authors discuss several explanations for these differences.

Chapter 2 also uses data from the Second National Family Violence Survey. As the largest survey based on a true cross section of black families the data presented here probably come closer to describing the real situation of violence toward black children than data derived from clinical or official sources. Based on rate of very severe violence reported in the survey Hampton and Gelles estimate that 379,000 children were severely assaulted by their parents in 1985.

Susan Zuravin and Raymond Starr, Jr., address the question of racial difference in the psychosocial characteristics of mothers of physically abused and neglected children. After a careful review of the literature, they find some important differences between black and white mothers in three of the four categories of characteristics—growing up experiences, social functioning, and emotional well-being. They explore the implication of this study for future empirical research and prevention strategies.

Chapters 4 through 6 describe three different studies on violence toward women. Using data from a hospital-based child abuse sample, Linda McKibben, Edward De Vos, and Eli Newberger found that the medical records of 59 percent of the mothers were diagnostic or highly suggestive of current or previous victimization. The rate of violence against single mothers of child abuse victims was four times the rate of violence against mothers who were married. The authors conclude with suggestions for improving clinical practice with families in which child abuse has occurred.

Chapters 5 and 6 are comparative studies. Lettie Lockhart found no significant differences among two racial groups in rates of violence toward women. Edward Gondolf, Ellen Fisher, and J. Richard McFerron found that income- and marital-related variables differed among their sample of Anglo, black, and Hispanic shelter residents.

Chapter 7 is a conceptual overview of elder abuse with specific reference to black families. Oliver Williams and Linner Griffin explore some of the barriers to research in this field and recommend several programmatic responses to elder abuse.

In part V we address studies of family homicides. Coramae Richey Mann compares black women who kill their loved ones to black women who kill strangers, friends, or acquaintances. Ann Goetting compares men and women arrested in Detroit, Michigan, for killing their spouses. She notes several important differences between male and female subjects. These differences have major implications for the study of context of lethal and nonlethal family violence.

It has been argued for some time that practitioners must go beyond the limited boundaries of patient-provider relationship to be effective in many minority communities. In chapter 10, Carl Bell discusses the principle of community development as practiced by a community psychiatrist, in preventing black-on-black violence.

Robert Pierce and Lois Pierce address the issues of culturally sensitive and appropriate protective services interventions. They feel that the child welfare system frequently fails to adequately serve thousands of children of color. Recommendations are offered to correct this situation.

Students will find the book a fundamental introduction to family relationship issues in the study of black family life. Experienced practitioners will find the book helpful in expanding their knowledge base and thinking about the implications of race for their work.

Acknowledgments

Many people were involved in the development of this book. The authors of the chapters were the key contributors. They represent diverse points of view and professional orientations. This is consistent with current scholarship on family violence and on African-American families.

This book owes much to my previous work and research on family violence. I thank the following people for their special contributions: Eli and Carolyn Newberger and the entire Family Development Study at Children's Hospital Center in Boston have been supportive colleagues for more than a decade; Richard J. Gelles, with whom I have collaborated over the past four years, Thomas Gullotta and the staff of Child and Family Agency of Southeastern Connecticut with whom I have worked closely for the past few years, and members of the Ethnic Minorities Section of the National Council of Family Relations.

I want to express my thanks to my colleagues in the Department of Sociology and the entire student life staff at Connecticut College; to the many research assistants who helped with data acquisition, review, and library work: Emily Cusic, Naida Snipas, Alisa Kreger, Sarah Robson; to my assistant and project manager Beverly Kowal who quietly suffered through countless drafts, missed deadlines, and day-to-day disruptions; and to the others who assisted in the production of this volume: Barbara Johnson, Diane Birmingham, and Lynn Monihan. I would like to thank Margaret Zusky, senior editor at Lexington Books for her continued support. Finally, I want to thank Cathy, Robyn, and Conrad, my wife, daughter, and son, for their critical social and emotional support.

Part I
Overview

1

Is Violence in Black Families Increasing?
A Comparison of 1975 and 1985 National Survey Rates

Robert L. Hampton
Richard J. Gelles
John Harrop

T his chapter compares the rates of physical violence against black children and spouses found in the Second National Family Violence Survey conducted in 1985 with the rates found in the First National Family Violence Survey conducted in 1975 (Straus, Gelles, and Steinmetz, 1980). It extends an earlier analysis conducted by Straus and Gelles (1986) in which they compared the results of the 1985 survey on family violence to the 1975 survey. In examining rates of severe, very severe (children only), and overall violence Straus and Gelles (1986) found that rates of severe and very severe ("child abuse") toward children declined 23.6 percent and 47.2 percent, respectively, and that the rate of severe violence ("wife beating") toward women declined 21.1 percent in the previous decade (although the change in violence toward women was not statistically significant). The rates of other measures toward men remained essentially unchanged.[1]

The report that rates of severe assaults against women and children were lower in 1985 than in 1975 raised considerable controversy (for example, Berliner, 1987; Cohn, 1987; Schene, 1987; Stocks, 1988). Straus and Gelles (1986) argued that the decrease, at least in part, was due to a change in the family structure, improved economic conditions, and the growth in treatment and prevention services. In view of the

Reprinted with permission from *Journal of Marriage and the Family* 51 (November), 969–80.

An earlier version of this chapter was presented at the 1988 annual meeting of the American Sociological Association, Atlanta, Georgia. The study reported here is a product of the Family Violence Research Project at the University of Rhode Island. Reprints and a bibliography listing other papers available for distribution will be provided on request to the second author. The research was carried out with funds provided by the National Institute of Mental Health, Grant MH 40027.

important policy implication of these findings, as well as the controversy surrounding the data, further investigation of the differences between 1975 and 1985 rates is needed.

One important means of extending the analysis of changes in rates of family violence is to examine changes among specific social and economic groups. One benefit of this analysis will be to add to the discussion of whether changes are due to actual changes in behavior, changes in willingness to report family violence, or methodological artifacts. A second benefit will be to determine whether the declines occur in minority as well as majority families.

Violence in Black Families

It has been argued that black Americans, as a group, are considered more violent than white Americans (Comer, 1985). Although the media and the public have shown an increasing interest in violence recently, relatively little attention has been given to violence in black families. As a result, a substantial deficit exists in our current knowledge about violence in black homes.

Child Abuse in Black Families

Black children have been overrepresented in the national tabulation of official child abuse and neglect reports since their inception. According to the 1980 census, black children account for about 15 percent of all children in the United States. From 1976 to 1980, however, the proportion of child abuse and neglect reports involving black children remained fairly constant at about 19 percent. Further, in 1982 black children constituted 22 percent of all child maltreatment reports. This figure declined to 20.8 percent in 1984 (American Association for Protecting Children, 1986), then rose to 26.8 percent in 1985 (American Association for Protecting Children, 1987).

Since the poor and racial minorities are typically overrepresented in official reports of deviant behavior (Gelles, 1975; Newberger et al., 1977), it is risky to draw conclusions from the official reports of child maltreatment about the rate and changing rates of child maltreatment in black families. Several research studies have found that children from poor and minority families are more likely to be labeled *abused* than children from more affluent and majority homes with comparable injuries (Gelles, 1975; Hampton, 1986; Hampton and Newberger, 1985; Katz et al., 1986; Nalepka, O'Toole, and Turbett, 1981; Turbett and O'Toole, 1980). Stated differently, factors such as race and social class are as (or more) important in determining which cases will be labeled child abuse than is the nature of the injury or incident.

Survey data have not supported the contention derived from official child abuse and neglect report data that black parents are more violent and abusive than white parents. Data from the First National Family Violence Survey (Straus, Gelles, and Steinmetz, 1980) found little difference between blacks and whites in the rate of severe violence toward children (15 percent in black families, 14 percent in white families). This finding was similar to an earlier observation made by Billingsley (1969). Given the association between unemployment, low income, and violence toward black children, black families were expected to report higher rates of violence because black families reported higher unemployment rates and lower incomes than white families. Cazenave and Straus (1979) found that aid and support, especially child care provided by black extended family members, seemed to reduce the risk of abusive violence in black families. Further, when they controlled for income and husband's occupation, they found that blacks were less likely than whites to engage in acts of severe violence toward their children.

Violence between Spouses in Black Families

The literature on battered women tends to overlook the experiences of nonmajority women (Asbury, 1987). The battered-wife literature typically addresses the issues of ethnicity and abuse in one of three ways: (1) by failing to mention the race of the women studied (e.g., Flynn, 1977; Roy, 1982); (2) by acknowledging that only majority women are included (e.g., Bowker, 1984; Steinmetz, 1977); or (3) by including some women of other nonmajority groups but not in proportions comparable to their number in the national population (e.g., Hofeller, 1982; Walker, 1984). There are no national official reporting statistics on wife battering. Because of this, and because most studies of battered women are based on small, nonrepresentative samples drawn from shelters, clinical populations, or advertisements, researchers have yet to investigate whether there are any issues unique to black women in violent relationships, and, if so, what they are and how they can be addressed (Asbury, 1987).

To date, there have been no papers or analyses on the issue of violence toward black men except for the First National Family Violence Survey (Straus, Gelles, and Steinmetz, 1980), discussed below. This is not surprising, given the controversy surrounding the issue of violence toward men (see, for example, Gelles and Straus, 1988; McNeely and Robinson-Simpson, 1988; and letters to the editor in *Social Work* 33 (1988):189–191).

The First National Family Violence Survey (Straus, Gelles, and Steinmetz, 1980) is generally cited as the primary (and sole) source of data on the prevalence and incidence of spousal violence in black families. Straus and his colleagues reported that black husbands had higher rates of overall and severe violence toward their wives than white husbands. The rate of severe violence toward wives, or wife abuse, in black families was 113 per 1,000, while the rate was 30 per 1,000 in white households. Black wives were twice as likely to engage in acts of severe violence against their husbands (76 per 1,000) compared with white wives (41 per 1,000).

Methods

A complete definition of violence and abuse, and a detailed description of the measurement of violence and abuse and the sampling methodology for the 1975 and 1985 National Family Violence Surveys, can be found in Gelles and Straus (1988); Straus, Gelles, and Steinmetz (1980); and Straus and Gelles (1986). Here we provide a brief summary.

The First (1975) and Second (1985) National Family Violence Surveys comprise national probability samples of 2,143 and 6,002 households, respectively.[2] In order to make an appropriate comparison between the two surveys, it was necessary to compare the same types of families surveyed. Therefore, the more restrictive 1975 categories were used, that is, households with a current couple and/or with a couple and at least one child three to seventeen years living at home.[3] The 1975 sample includes 147 black current couple households, of which seventy-five had at least one child three to seventeen years of age at home. The 1985 sample had 576 couples, 277 of which had at least one child three to seventeen years of age living at home.

For the purpose of both national surveys, violence was nominally defined as "an act carried out with the intention, or perceived intention, of causing physical pain or injury to another person." The injury could range from slight pain as in a slap, to murder. The motivation might range from a concern for a person's safety (as when a child is spanked for going into the street) to hostility so intense that the death of the person is desired (Gelles and Straus, 1979). Abuse was defined as those acts of violence that had a high probability of causing injury to the person (an injury did not actually have to occur). Violence was measured by the violence or "physical aggression" items of the Conflict Tactics Scales that are listed in table 1–1. The items are grouped into various indexes, which provide a more reliable measure. This study uses the Overall and Severe Violence indexes or scales (Straus, 1979; 1981; 1989) as used by Straus and Gelles (1986), but not the Very Severe Violence Scale, which they had used also.[4]

Table 1–1
Parent-to-Child Violence: Comparison of Rates in 1975 and 1985

Type of violence	Rate per 1,000 Children Aged 3 through 17[1]			
	1975 (n = 75)	1985 (n = 277)[2]	Z for 1975–85 Differences	Percent Change
A. Minor violence				
1. Threw something	41	54	———[3]	+31.7
2. Pushed/grabbed/shoved	187	301	−1.958	+61.0
3. Slapped or spanked	517	601	−1.309	+16.2
B. Severe violence items				
4. Kicked/bit/hit with fist	14	4	———[3]	−71.4
5. Hit, tried to hit with something	135	217	−1.576	+60.7
6. Beat up	27	11	———[3]	−59.3
7. Threatened with gun or knife	0	0	0	0
8. Used gun or knife	0	0	0	0
C. Violence indexes				
Overall violence (Items 1–8)	541	652	−1.756	+20.5
Severe violence (Items 4–8)	149	221	−1.361	+48.3

1. For two-caretaker households with at least one child 3 to 17 years of age at home.
2. A few respondents were omitted because of missing data on some items, but the n is never less than 74.
3. No valid Z value because $n_1 P_0$, $n_2 P_0$, $n_1 q_0$, or $n_2 q_0$ is not greater than 5 as required for use of the normal approximation.

Results

Violence toward Black Children

Table 1–1 presents the comparison for each violent act as well as the summary indexes. The data in part A show that the occurrence of each form of minor violence toward black children increased in the ten years. The data in part B show a decrease in two forms of severe violence and an increase of one form. None of these changes are statistically significant.[5] The individual indicators are included in the tables for the record and to show what went into the summary tables. The most important and reliable results are those for the summary indexes or scales (Straus and Gelles, 1986; Gelles, Straus, and Harrop, 1988).

The Overall Violence Index in part C indicates whether a parent used any of the eight forms of violence at least once in the past year. There was a 20 percent increase in the rate of overall violence toward black children between 1975 and 1985. In 1975 black parents were reporting at least one act of violence toward their children during the survey year at the rate of 541 per 1,000. In 1985 the rate rose to 652 per 1,000. Table 1–1 also shows that the rate of severe or "abusive" violence increases from 149 per 1,000 to 221 per 1,000, an increase of 48 percent. The change is entirely due to the increase in item 5, that is, in parents hitting or trying to hit their children with something. Neither the increase in overall violence nor in severe violence is statistically significant.

One possible reason why severe violence toward black children stayed the same statistically while violence toward children in the general sample decreased is that black families did not gain from the low inflation and low unemployment of the decade between 1975 and 1985. Given the relationship between poverty, unemployment, and violence toward children (Baron and Straus, 1988; Hampton, 1987; Sampson, 1987), we hypothesized that the lack of decrease in severe violence toward black children might be the result of an increase in violence among poor black families balancing a decrease in violence among the rest of the families. We tested this notion by examining the changing rates of violence toward black children, controlling for income. The rate of severe violence increased by only 5 percent for the lowest-income families (the bottom 15 percent of the income distribution, with income less than or equal to $10,000), while it increased 53 percent among those in the higher-income group (the upper 85 percent). Thus, our hypothesis about an increase in violence toward children in poor black families balancing a decline in violence in the rest of families was not supported.

Violence between Spouses

Table 1–2 summarizes the findings on violence between married or cohabitating couples. The rate of overall violence by husbands toward their wives was the same in 1975 and 1985 at 169 per 1,000. The rate of severe violence by husbands, a measure of "wife beating," declined 43.4 percent from 113 per 1,000 couples in 1975 to 64 per 1,000 in 1985. This is both a statistically and substantively significant decrease in the rate of wife beating by black husbands.

The overall violence rate for black women toward black husbands increased 33.3 percent from 153 per 1,000 in 1975 to 204 per 1,000 in 1985. Similarly, the rate of severe violence against black men increased 42.1 percent from 76 per 1,000 in 1975 to 108 per 1,000 in 1985. These changes were not statistically significant.

Table 1–3 presents the rates for each of the husband-to-wife and wife-to-husband violence items used in computing the Overall and Severe Violence indexes reported in table 1–2. With the exception of throwing something, or using guns or knives, the occurrence of every act of violence toward black wives declined in the previous ten years. The 55.9 percent decline in the rate of "slapping" from 118 per 1,000 in 1975 to 52 per 1,000 in 1985, and the 60.9 percent decline in the rate of "hitting or trying to hit with something" from 69

Table 1–2
Marital Violence Indexes: Comparison of 1975 and 1985

	Rate per 1,000 Couples		Z for the 1975–85	Percent
Violence Index	1975	1985	Differences	Change
A. Husband-to-wife indexes				
Overall violence (1–8)	169	169	0	0
Severe violence (4–8) ("Wife beating")	113	64	2.03*	−43.4
B. Wife-to-husband indexes				
Overall violence (1–8)	153	204	−1.38	+33.3
Severe violence (4–8)	76	108	−1.14	+42.1
C. Couple indexes				
Overall violence (1–8)	190	247	−1.43	+30.0
Severe violence (1–8)	113	129	−.52	+14.2
Number of cases[1]	147	576		

1. A few respondents were omitted because of missing data on some items, but the n is never decreased by more than 5.

* $p < .05$

per 1,000 in 1975 to 27 per 1,000 in 1985, are the only statistically significant changes. Four of the wife-to-husband violence items increased and four decreased. None of these changes were statistically significant.

Table 1–3
Marital Violence: Comparison of Specific Acts, 1975–1985

	Husband-to-Wife		Wife-to-Husband	
Types of Violence	1975	1985	1975	1985
A. Minor Violence				
1. Threw something	35	45	83	77
2. Pushed/grabbed/shoved	146	141	110	148
3. Slapped	118	52**	54	64
B. Severe violence items				
4. Kicked/bit/hit with fist	69	38	48	61
5. Hit, tried to hit with something	69	27*	48	75
6. Beat up	35	24	14	14
7. Threatened with gun or knife	7	1	35	12
8. Used gun or knife	0	2	7	2
Number of cases[1]	147	576	147	576

1. A few respondents were omitted because of missing data on some items, but the n is never decreased by more than 5.

* Significant Z test for 1975–85 difference, $p < .05$
** Significant Z test for 1975–85 difference, $p < .01$

*Comparing the Rates of Violence in Black
and White Families*

For comparison purposes, table 1–4 provides a summary of the 1975
and 1985 violence rates and changes in the rates for black and white
families. The table also summarizes black-to-white ratios for both
years.

Ten years ago the rates of both overall and severe violence toward
children by black parents were essentially the same as for whites. In
1985 the rates of overall violence were about the same in white and
black families; however, the rate of severe violence toward black children has become more than twice the rate of severe violence toward
white children. Ten years ago the rate of severe violence toward black
women was nearly four times greater than the rate of severe violence
toward white women. In 1985 the rate of severe violence toward black
women dropped substantially to slightly more than twice the rate of
severe violence against white women. Ten years ago black women's rate
of severe violence against their husbands was twice the rate for white
women, but in 1985 the rate of abusive violence by black women rose

Table 1–4

**Comparison of Rates of Violence (per 1,000) in Black and White Families for
1975 and 1985**

Type of Violence	Black			White			Ratio: Black to White	
	1975	1985	Percent Change	1975	1985	Percent Change	1975	1985
	Current Couples with Children Aged 3 to 17							
	(n = 75)	(n = 277)		(n = 980)	(n = 1,761)[1]			
Parent-to-child								
Overall	541	652	+20.5	637	646	+1.4	.8	1.0
Severe	149	221	+48.3 *	138	103	−25.4 **	1.1	2.1
	Current Couples							
	(n = 147)	(n = 576)		(n = 1,834)	(n = 4,313)[1]			
Husband-to-wife								
Overall	169	169	0	112	107	−4.5	1.5	1.6
Severe	113	64	−43.4	30	28	−6.7	3.8	2.3
Wife-to-husband								
Overall	153	204	+33.3	106	116	+9.4	1.4	1.8
Severe	76	108	+42.1	41	39	−4.9	1.9	2.8
Couple								
Overall	190	247	+30.0	147	150	+2.0	1.3	1.6
Severe	113	129	+14.2	54	51	−5.6	2.1	2.5

1. These are weighted n's.

 * p < .05
** p < .01

to nearly three times greater than the rate for white women. These changes are not only substantively important in their own right, but they also complement the changes (or lack thereof) when blacks are compared with the general population.

Discussion

The comparison of the rates of violence toward black children and between black spouses reveals differences from the patterns found by Straus and Gelles (1986), although the exact nature of the differences is not clear because of the issue of statistical versus substantive significance. Given the relatively small black samples, it took substantial changes in the rates of violence for differences to be statistically significant. Thus, although some of the changes in the rates of violence appear substantial, only the rate of wife abuse declined significantly. If we rely on traditional measures of statistical significance, our conclusion must be that there has been no change in the rates of overall violence or severe violence toward children and men in black families and in the rate of overall violence toward black women. Compared with the Straus and Gelles (1986) data, this means that the only differences are that (1) severe violence toward black children remained stable in comparison to the statistically significant decline found among the entire sample; and (2) violence toward black women declined significantly, while it remained unchanged among women in the entire sample.

If, however, we assume as did Straus and Gelles (1986) that the substantive differences are as important as statistical significance, then we find that (1) severe violence toward black children increased, in contrast to the decline in the entire sample; (2) severe violence toward black wives decreased, as it did among the overall sample; and (3) overall and severe violence toward black husbands increased, while it was essentially stable in the entire sample. We continue our discussion using the more conservative, statistical significance to interpret our findings, except in certain instances in which we use both interpretations and identify them clearly.

Explaining the Changes

Straus and Gelles (1986) noted three plausible explanations for the changes they report: (1) differences in the methodology used in the two surveys; (2) changes in respondents' willingness to report violence to researchers; and (3) actual changes in behavior. Irrespective of whether one relies on statistical or substantive significance, it is clear that there were different changes among black families compared with nonblacks.

At least with regard to violence toward children, we know of no theory or data that would explain why white and other nonblack parents were less likely to report violence toward their children in 1985 than 1975 while black parents either reported the same levels (statistical significance) or higher levels (substantive significance). Similarly, we know of no theory or evidence that would explain why telephone interviewing or telephone sampling frames would produce those results. We conclude, as did Straus and Gelles (1986), that the patterns of change and stability are due to actual changes in behavior and not to methodological or attitudinal factors.

Straus and Gelles (1986) suggested that changes in family structure and economic status may explain declines in rates of violence toward women and children. Specifically, they noted that structural changes in the American family, such as a rise in the age at first marriage, increase in the average age for having a first child, and a decline in the number of children per family, may result in reduced risk of violence in the home. In addition, lowered inflation, lowered unemployment, and greater economic prosperity may also have reduced the risk of domestic violence.

Table 1–5
Comparison of Family and Economic Characteristics of Parents
of Children Aged 3 to 17, by Race, 1975–1985

Category	1975	1985	Change
All Parents			
n	1,147	1,430[1]	
Mean age of respondent	37.7	37.5	− .2
Mean age of respondent at time beginning current marriage or relationship	22.8	23.9	+ 1.1
Mean number of children living at home	2.5	2.0	− .5
Median family income	$17,500	$27,500	+ $10,000
Percentage of husbands unemployed	4.3	3.4	− .9
Black parents			
n	75	277	
Mean age of respondent	39.2	37.5	− 1.7
Mean age of respondent at time beginning current marriage or relationship	23.2	24.7	+ 1.5
Mean number of children living at home	2.6	2.0	− .6
Median family income	$11,000	$27,500	+ $16,500
Percentage of husbands unemployed	8.0	7.9	− .1

1. This number excludes respondents from the black, Hispanic, and state oversamples, and thus is the same sample that Straus and Gelles (1986) used to make their comparisons.

If the decline in the rate of violence toward children in the entire sample was due to changing family structure and better economic conditions, then black children may have failed to gain from the benefits of economic prosperity and changing family structure. Black women, however, appear to have gained a measure of safety from 1975 to 1985 that could be due to economic and family changes.

Tables 1–5 and 1–6 present data from the First and Second National Family Violence Surveys that bear on selected aspects of family structure and economics. Although we did not measure age at first marriage or age when the first child was born, we do have data on age, age when the current relationship began, number of children living in the home, family income, and husband's rate of unemployment. Data are presented for the entire sample as reported on in Straus and Gelles (1986), and for the black sample reported on in the present study.

Parents

Table 1–5 indicates that the family and economic changes for parents in the entire sample were similar to those experienced by black parents of children three to seventeen years of age. Age of respondent actually

Table 1–6
Comparison of Family and Economic Characteristics of Couples by Race, 1975–1985

Category	1975	1985	Change
All couples			
n	2,143	3,520[1]	
Mean age of respondent	41.0	42.6	+1.6
Mean age of respondent at time beginning current marriage or relationship	23.6	25.0	+1.4
Mean number of children living at home	1.8	1.9	+.1
Median family income	$13,500	$27,500	+$14,500
Percentage of husbands unemployed	4.4	2.9	−1.5
Black couples			
n	147	576	
Mean age of respondent	42.6	42.0	−.6
Mean age of respondent at time beginning current marriage or relationship	24.1	26.0	+1.9
Mean number of children living at home	1.9	1.9	0
Median family income	$9,000	$22,500	+$13,500
Percentage of husbands unemployed	6.8	6.4	−.4

1. This number excludes respondents from the black, Hispanic, and state oversamples, and thus is the same sample that Straus and Gelles (1986) used to make their comparisons.

declined slightly from 1975 to 1985, although the mean age when the current relationship began did increase. The average number of children declined similarly in the entire sample of parents and among blacks. Median income increased for both groups, but much more so for black parents, who earned the same median income as the entire sample of parents in the study in 1985, compared with earning $6,000 less in 1975. Unemployment declined for both groups, although the decline was slight among black husbands. Thus, the absence of a significant decline in the rate of severe violence toward children is not explained by economic or family structure factors.

Straus and Gelles (1986) also speculate that the decline in violence might be due to increased public awareness and more prevention and treatment programs. It is possible that black children have not benefited from increased awareness or more prevention and treatment programs. We have no data, nor do we know of any available data, that would support speculation about the effect of protective services for black children on the violence rate.

Another explanation for the lack of a significant decrease in the rate of severe violence toward black children has been raised. As we noted earlier, the nonsignificant increase in the rate of severe violence toward black children is entirely due to the fact that the rate of "hitting or trying to hit children with something" increased between 1975 and 1985. Some of the initial reaction to a preliminary version of this chapter attributed this to the notion that the use of objects to discipline children is considered appropriate in many black homes.[6] Others (Lassiter, 1987; Peters, 1981) also support this concept of the cultural appropriateness of using objects to strike children in black homes. This alone, however, does not explain why the rate of hitting or trying to hit children with an object increased by 61 percent between 1975 and 1985 in black families, compared with a statistically significant decline of 28 percent in the entire sample. In addition, we need to use caution in using the "hit or tried to hit with an object" item, since the item does not distinguish between straps and belts and hammers and bats. Clearly, however, we have identified differing behaviors among black families and families in general with regard to hitting children with objects.

Couples

Table 1–6 reveals that some of the family structural changes and economic changes suggested by Straus and Gelles (1986) did in fact occur among the population they surveyed. The mean age of respondents rose, as did age when the current relationship began. Similarly, median family income rose, while the rate of unemployment among the husbands declined. The mean number of children in the home did not change—which negates Straus and Gelles's assumption about family size—although the number of children at home is not the same as the number of children a couple has. Black couples surveyed in 1975 and 1985 experienced some of the same changes, except that the mean age of black respondents declined slightly instead of rising slightly, and black men's rate of unemployment declined more modestly than for all men. The data on family and economic changes support some of Straus and Gelles's (1986) speculation about the source of the declines in wife abuse. However, since the changes were similar for blacks and the entire sample of couples, we gain no insight as to why the rate of wife assault declined more among blacks than among the overall sample of families.

The data on violence by black women are as controversial as are all the data on violence toward men. It has been pointed out elsewhere (Gelles, 1979; Greenblat, 1983; Straus, 1977; Straus, Gelles, and Steinmetz, 1980) that the data on wife-to-husband violence can be easily misunderstood. The Conflict Tactics Scales provide no information about the sequence of violence or the outcomes of the violent acts. Given the gender differences in size, strength, and aggressiveness, it is likely that violence by men does more damage than violence by women (Steinmetz, 1977). Far more important, a great deal of violence by women is done for self-defense, self-preservation, or retaliation (Straus, Gelles, and Steinmetz, 1980). As there is virtually no social consciousness and social programing for violence toward men, it is difficult to even begin to comment about what the changes we found mean. Women use violence in self-defense, as instigators of mutual violence, or as the sole perpetrators of violence (Shupe, Stacey, and Hazelwood, 1986). Perhaps the increased consciousness about wife abuse has emboldened black women to fight back. Perhaps black women feel less subordinate to and dependent on black men than they did a decade ago, and the economic and social costs of striking back have declined. Some evidence for this explanation can be found in the data on the status of black women.

Between 1975 and 1985 the proportion of black families headed by women increased from 35.3 percent to 43.7 percent. There is abundant evidence that black women are willing to fill socially prescribed family roles. On the other hand, there are indications that many black men are unable to fulfill the prescribed roles of economic provider and family leader (Staples, 1985). The same cultural and economic forces that undermine the black male's ability to enact the provider/father role might contribute to both the growth of female-headed black families and the increase in wife-to-husband violence. Another plausible explanation for the increase is that the increase in the status of black women may reduce the costs of their using violence toward their husbands. Since 1970, black women have nearly caught up with white women in school enrollment and educational attainment (Farley, 1984). Black women have also gained relative to black men in educational attainment, occupational status, and earnings. Most black marriages involve a wife who is more highly educated than her husband (Spanier and Glick, 1980). In one out of five black marriages, the wife earns a higher income than her husband (Bureau of the Census, 1983). This status incompatibility may partially explain the increase in violence by black women, although, according to other research on family violence (Gelles, 1974; Hornung, McCullough, and Sugimoto, 1981; O'Brien, 1971), this should also have resulted in an increase in violence by men.

Conclusions

If child protective advocates were angered by the earlier report of a decline in child abuse, they should be distressed by the findings presented here. Although these results do not imply that two decades of public and private funding have been wasted, the results do suggest that black children have not enjoyed the benefits of reduced risk of severe violence. While the rates of severe violence were nearly the same in black and white homes in 1975, the rate of severe violence toward black children was double the rate toward white children in 1985. We found no evidence to link the lack of progress to adverse social or economic conditions or to inadequate access to prevention and treatment programs. Perhaps, as we discussed, the lack of progress is due to differing and perhaps changing cultural attitudes about which acts of violence are appropriate to use on children.

Our data indicate that the forces that produced an overall decline in violence toward women from 1975 to 1985 have benefited minority women to a greater degree than majority women. Black women experienced nearly four times more abusive violence compared with white women in 1975. The gap narrowed so that the rate of abusive violence toward black women in 1985 was slightly more than twice the rate of severe violence toward white women. Perhaps, also, the major prevention and treatment programs are actually more effective for minority women than for majority women. Although data on shelter use are limited, two studies suggest that black women make up a disproportionately high percentage of shelter residents (Asbury, 1987; Taylor and Hammond, 1987). In addition, it has been shown that community outreach efforts are highly successful in increasing participation of black women in shelter services (Wilson, Cobb, and Dolan, 1987). Perhaps the increased status of black women has served to protect them from abusive violence. The situation of men seems much more complex, however, and the perceptual blackout about battered husbands remains. We have few insights into the nature of violence by women toward men and even less insight into how to explain changes in the rates of violence toward men.

Future research will extend the analysis of violence in black families by examining the data from the Second National Violence Survey. The large sample and the availability of data on children under 3 years of age and on single parents will allow us to further illuminate the nature of violence in black families.

Notes

1. In comparing the 1975 and 1985 data, Straus and Gelles (1986) reported that the rate of overall violence toward children declined 1.6 percent, from 630 per 1,000 children to 620 per 1,000. The rate of severe violence declined 23.6 percent, from 140 per 1,000 to 107 per 1,000. The rate of very severe violence declined 47.2 percent, from 36 per 1,000 to 19 per 1,000. The rate of overall husband-to-wife violence declined 6.6 percent from 122 per 1,000 to 113 per 1,000. The rate of severe husband-to-wife violence declined 21.1 percent, from 38 per 1,000 to 30 per 1,000. The rate of overall wife-to-husband violence increased 4.3 percent from 116 per 1,000 to 121 per 1,000, while the rate of severe wife-to-husband violence declined 4.3 percent from 46 per 1,000 to 44 per 1,000. Only the declines for severe and very severe parent-to-child violence were statistically significant.

2. Straus and Gelles (1986) 1985 sample size was 4,032 households. This was the main cross-section sample of the Second National Family Violence Survey. The state, Hispanic, and black oversamples were not included in the Straus and Gelles (1986) article. Of the 4,032, there were 3,520 current couples and 1,428 current couples with at least one child aged three to seventeen living at home in their analysis.

3. Straus and Gelles established the "current couples" criterion for inclusion in the study in order to assure that they would have enough cases of marital violence for statistical analysis. The inclusion criterion of one child from three to seventeen years of age was established similarly for the purposes of studying sibling violence.

4. The Severe Violence Index contained the item "hit or tried to hit with something," while the Very Severe Violence Index excluded this item. The Very Severe Violence Index is not computed for spousal abuse. There were too few cases of very severe violence toward children in black families to allow for a reliable analysis of change from 1975 to 1985; as was the case with the First National Family Violence Survey, we are using the Severe Violence Index as our measure of child abuse for the black sample.

5. Marascuilo and McSweeney (1977) give the following large-scale Z approximation to the Irwin Fisher Exact Test of the significance of the difference between two uncorrelated proportions:

$$Z = \frac{P_1 - P_2}{P_0 Q_0 \dfrac{n_1 + n_2}{n_1 n_2}}$$

where:

P_1 and P_2 are measures of a variable expressed as a proportion from a Group 1 and a Group 2, respectively, and

n_1 and n_2 are the respective sample sizes,

$$P_0 = \frac{n_1 P_1 + n_2 P_2}{n_1 + n_2}, \text{ and}$$

$$Q_0 = 1 - P_0$$

6. Dennis Langely, deputy director of the Urban League of Rhode Island, responded to an earlier draft of our chapter by noting that many blacks are brought up to consider striking a child with a belt as proper discipline.

Part II
Child Maltreatment:
Incidence and Severity

2

A Profile of Violence toward Black Children

Robert L. Hampton
Richard J. Gelles

ew studies have addressed the issue of violence, abuse, and maltreatment in families of color or minority families. Gil (1970), in
his classic study of national child abuse reporting data in the late
1960s, concluded that families reported for physical child abuse were
drawn disproportionately from the less educated, the poor, and ethnic
minorities. Similar examinations of data on official reports of child
maltreatment also find that low income, less educated, ethnic minority
families are disproportionately reported for abuse and neglect (American Humane Association, 1979; American Association for Protecting
Children, 1985; 1986; 1987). On the other hand, the national surveys
of recognition and reporting of child maltreatment, sponsored by the
National Center on Child Abuse and Neglect (Burgdorf, 1980; National Center on Child Abuse and Neglect, 1988), failed to find a
significant difference between blacks and whites in the rates of maltreatment recognized and reported by professionals.

Conclusions drawn from examinations and analyses of official
abuse and neglect reporting data must be viewed carefully because the
data are subject to a labeling bias inherent in all official reports of
deviant or criminal behavior (Gelles, 1975). Newberger and his colleagues (1977) and Gelles (1987) suggest that lower-class and minority
children seen with injuries in a private hospital are more likely than
middle-class and upper-class children to be labeled as *abused*. There is
empirical support for this proposition, particularly with respect to
abuse cases seen in medical settings (Gelles, 1982; Hampton, 1986;
Hampton and Newberger, 1985; Turbett and O'Toole, 1980).

One source of data that is free from labeling bias are self-report
surveys. The First National Family Violence Survey (Straus, Gelles, and
Steinmetz, 1980) collected data on violence between family members
from a nationally representative sample of 2,146 households. Cazenave
and Straus (1979) reported on the incidence rates of violence by ethnic
group. They found that, overall, black respondents were less likely than
whites to slap or spank their children in the year prior to the survey.

When income and husband's occupation were controlled, blacks were less likely to use abusive violence toward their children. Cazenave and Straus (1979) explained that the aid and support, especially child care, that black families receive from neighbors, friends, and extended family members seems to reduce the risk of violence toward children in black families.

The examination of violence toward children in black families in the First National Family Violence Survey was constrained by the small sample of black families (n = 147) and the sampling frame was limited to two-caretaker households with children between the ages of three and seventeen years, thus omitting the approximately 35 percent of black households headed by single women. Nevertheless, the survey data did provide some important insights concerning violence toward children in black families. Specifically, it revealed that the rates of violence toward children vary by family income, social class, and degree of social network embeddedness.

The Second National Family Violence Survey involved a larger sample (6,002 households), an oversample of black households, and included single parents and children under the age of three years (Gelles and Straus, 1988). A comparison of the data from the two surveys revealed that the rate of abusive violence toward black children in two-caretaker households had increased between 1975 and 1985. Furthermore, black children were more likely to experience violence and abusive violence than white children in 1985, compared with the "no difference" finding in 1975 (Hampton, Gelles, and Harrop, 1989).[1]

This chapter extends the examination of violence toward children in black families and examines the incidence of violence toward children and risk factors for violence and abusive violence in a representative sample of black families.

Methods

A complete definition of violence and abuse, a detailed description of the measurement of violence and abuse, and the sampling methodology for the Second National Family Violence Survey can be found in Gelles and Straus (1988) and Straus and Gelles (1990). Here we provide a brief summary.

Sample and Administration

A national probability sample of 6,002 households comprised the Second National Family Violence Survey. The same was drawn using a Random Digit Dial procedure and was made up of four parts. First,

4,032 households were selected in proportion to the distribution of households in the fifty states. Then, 958 households were oversampled in twenty-five states. This was done to assure that there would be thirty-six states with at least one hundred completed interviews per state. Finally, two additional oversamples were drawn—508 black and 510 Hispanic households. The procedure for identifying the black and Hispanic oversamples was almost identical to the procedure for developing the main sample.

The data analyzed for this chapter are based on responses from black respondents selected through both the main and black oversample. This procedure yielded a sample of 797 black families of which 520 had children between the ages of zero and seventeen living in the household.

To be eligible for inclusion in the sample, a household had to include adults eighteen years of age or older who were: (1) *currently coupled* (married or unmarried cohabiting opposite sex couples); or (2) *previously coupled* (previously married or unmarried cohabiting opposite sex couples separated for less than two years); or (3) *single parents* with a child under eighteen years of age living in the same household. When more than one eligible adult was in the household, a random procedure was used to select the marital status of the respondent. If a couple was selected, a random procedure was used to select the gender of the respondent. When there was more than one child under the age of eighteen years old in the home, a random procedure was used to select a "referent child." Questions about violence toward children referred to violence between the respondent and the "referent child."

Telephone interviews were conducted by trained interviewers employed by the national survey firm, Louis Harris and Associates. When telephones were busy or there was no answer, three call-backs were made prior to substituting a new household. If contact was made and subjects refused to be screened or to participate, trained "refusal conversion" interviewers were assigned to the household.

The response rate, calculated as "completes as a proportion of eligibles" was 84 percent. Interviews lasted an average of thirty-five minutes.

Operationalizing Violence and Abuse

Violence was operationalized through the use of the Conflict Tactics Scales (CTS) (Straus, 1979; 1990).[2] First developed at the University of New Hampshire in 1971, this technique has been modified extensively in many studies of family violence. The items of the Conflict Tactics Scales are presented to respondents who are asked how often they used each technique when they had a disagreement or were angry with a family member during the previous year and, if not, at any other time in the course of the relationship with the family member. The Conflict Tactics Scales (CTS) contain eighteen items that comprise three factorially separate variables (Jorgensen, 1977; Schumm et al., 1982; Straus, 1979; 1990): (1) *use of rational discussion and agreement* (discussed an issue calmly; got information to back up your side of things; brought in or tried to bring in someone to help settle things); (2) *use of verbal and nonverbal expressions of hostility* (insulted or swore at the other; sulked or refused to talk about; stomped out of the room or house or yard; did or said something to spite the other; threatened to hit or throw something at the other; threw or smashed or hit, or kicked something); and (3) *Use of physical force or violence* (threw something at the other; pushed, grabbed, or shoved the other; slapped or spanked the other—spanked used for children only; kicked, bit, or hit the other with a fist; hit or tried to hit the other with something; beat up the other; choked the other—for adults only; burned or scalded—for children only[3]; threatened the other with a knife or gun; used a knife or fired a gun). Response categories were: once, twice, 3–5 times, 6–10 times, 11–20 times, more than 20 times. The "never" response had to be volunteered by respondents.

There are various scoring methods for the Conflict Tactics Scales (Straus, 1990). This chapter uses three indexes: (1) overall violence, which includes all the physical violence items; (2) severe violence, which includes the items that have a high probability of causing an injury—kicked,[4] bit, or hit with a fist; hit or tried to hit the child with something; beat up the child; burned or scalded the child; threatened the child with a knife or gun; used a knife or gun; and (3) very severe violence, which includes all the severe violence items with the exception of hit or tried to hit the child with something.

Reliability and Validity. The reliability and validity of the Conflict Tactics Scales have been assessed over the twenty-year period of their development. A full discussion of their reliability and validity can be found in Straus (1979; 1990) and Straus, Gelles, and Steinmetz (1980). There is evidence of adequate internal consistency, reliability, concurrent validity, and construct validity.

Results

Incidence

Sixty-four percent of the black respondents reported that they used some form of violence at least once toward the referent child in the preceding twelve months (1985). The proportion of parents who reported using some form of violence at least once while raising the child was 76 percent (table 2–1).

As has been found in previous studies of violence toward children (Gelles, 1978) the milder forms of violence were the most common. Nearly three-fifths (59 percent) of the children in black families were spanked or slapped during the study year. Slightly less than one in five children (18 percent) had parents or caretakers who hit or tried to hit with objects.

The rate for overall violence varies by age of the child (see Wauchope and Straus, 1990, for an analysis of the 1985 survey data). Among black children aged two to six years, 84 percent experienced at least one act of violence each year. The rate declines among children seven years old and older (see figure 2–1).

Projecting the rate of very severe violence toward black children (40 per 1,000) to the 9.4 million black children in the United States in 1985 yields an estimate of 379,000 severely assaulted children per year. Applying the rate of very severe violence *ever experienced* by black children yields an estimate of 480,000 very severely assaulted children. Using the broader measure of abuse, the severe violence measure, which

Table 2–1
Incidence of Types of Parent-to-Child Violence

	Rate Per 1,000 Children Under 18 Years Old $(n=519)^1$				
	Occurrence in the Past Year				Ever
	Once	Twice	More than Twice	Total	
(1) Threw something at the child	15	12	23	50	52
(2) Pushed, grabbed, or shoved child	73	66	137	276	291
(3) Slapped or spanked child	83	103	404	590	730
(4) Kicked, bit, or hit with a fist	10	2	12	24	27
(5) Hit with something	35	29	116	180	221
(6) Beat child up	6	6	12	24	29
(7) Burned or scalded	0	0	2	2	4
(8) Threatened with knife or gun	0	0	0	0	2
(9) Used knife or gun	0	0	0	0	0
Indexes					
Overall Violence (Items 1–9)				644	758
Severe Violence (Items 4–9)				197	238
Very Severe Violence (Items 4; 6–9)				40	52

1. A few responses were omitted because of missing data, but the n is never decreased by more than 5.

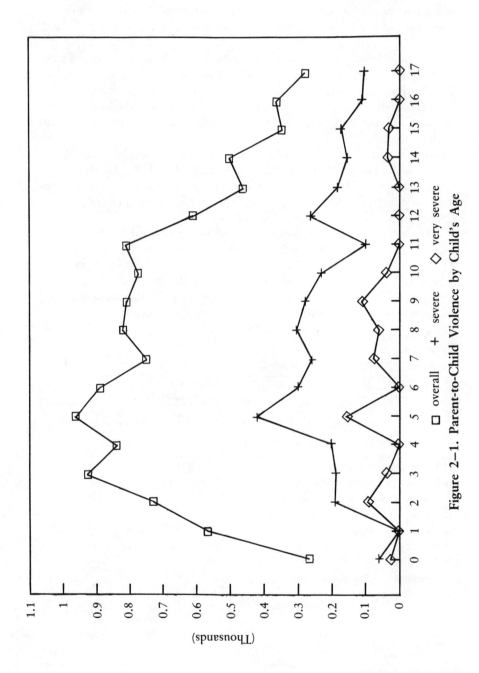

Figure 2–1. Parent-to-Child Violence by Child's Age

includes hitting or trying to hit with an object, yields estimates of 1.86 million severely abused children each year.

Comparing Blacks and Whites

Comparing the rate of violence used by black parents to violence used by white parents, we find that black parents are more likely to report throwing things at their children and hitting or trying to hit with an object. This is consistent with other studies of disciplinary techniques in black families that report black parents using belts, cords, switches, sticks, and straps to discipline their children (Hampton, 1987; Johnson and Showers, 1985; Lassiter, 1987; Peters, 1981; Showers and Bandman, 1986). As reported earlier (Hampton, Gelles, and Harrop, 1989), black parents are more likely to use severe and very severe violence toward their children (table 2–2).

Child Factors

As we noted earlier in this chapter, younger children are more likely to experience overall violence. Younger black children are also more likely

Table 2–2
Comparison of Rates of Parent-to-Child Violence in Black and White Families

	Rate Per 1,000 Children	
Type of Violence	White $(n=1,691)^1$	Black $(n=519)^2$
(1) Threw something at the child	27	50*
(2) Pushed, grabbed or shoved child	304	276
(3) Slapped or spanked child	558	590
(4) Kicked, bit, or hit with a fist	13	23
(5) Hit or tried to hit with something	91	180**
(6) Beat child up	4	23
(7) Burned or scalded child	4	2
(8) Threatened with knife or gun	2	0
(9) Used knife or gun	3	0
Overall Violence (1–9)	632	644
Severe Violence (4–9)	101	197**
Very Severe Violence (4; 6–9)	19	40**

1. A few responses were omitted because of missing data, but the n is never decreased by more than 5.
2. This number excludes respondents from Hispanic and state oversamples.
* p < .05
** p < .001

to experience severe violence (table 2–3). Examinations of official report data on child maltreatment find that females are more likely than
males to be victims of physical abuse (American Association for Protecting Children, 1987; Hampton, 1987; National Center on Child
Abuse and Neglect, 1988). Our self-report data reveal no statistically
significant differences between male and female children for the three
measures of violence.[5]

Social Factors

Analyses of official report data and self-report data on child maltreatment find a consistent link between poverty and physical violence and

Table 2–3
Rates of Parent-to-Child Violence by Selected Demographic Factors

	Rates Per 1,000		
Variable[1]	Overall Violence	Severe Violence	Very Severe Violence
Sex of child			
Female (261)	674	211	50
Male (258)	612	182	31
Age of child			
0–5 years (172)	698***	174***	52
6–12 years (205)	780	254	49
13–17 years (142)	380	141	14
Sex of respondent			
Female (377)	676**	188	40
Male (142)	556	218	42
Area of residence			
Central city (294)	697**	197	44
Suburb of central city (143)	559	196	49
Small town and rural (82)	598	195	12
Years lived in the community			
Less than two years (91)	725	242	88**
More than two years (428)	626	187	30
Number of children in household			
One (231)	554*	173	56
Two or more (288)	715	215	28
Family structure			
Two-parent household (331)	622	202	21***
Single-parent household (185)	676	178	70
Income			
Less than $10,000 (133)	707	188	60
Greater than $10,000 (360)	628	206	33

1. A few responses are omitted because of missing data, but the n is never decreased by
   more than 5 unless noted.
   * p < .05
   ** p < .01
   *** p < .001

abuse of children (Baron and Straus, 1988; Burgdorf, 1980; Curtis, 1975; Gelles, 1990; Gil, 1970; Sampson, 1987).

We examined the relationship among education, income, and occupation and violence toward black children. Neither educational attainment nor occupation yielded a discernible pattern. Black respondents who reported annual incomes below the poverty line reported higher rates of overall violence and very severe violence, although the differences were not statistically significant (table 2–3).

Community and Household Structure

Both the 1975 and 1985 National Family Violence Surveys found that the highest rates of family violence were reported to the study by respondents in central cities. The pattern for black families is modestly different. The rate of overall violence toward children is significantly higher in the central cities. The rates of severe violence do not vary by community, and although the differences are not significant, the rate of very severe violence is highest in suburbs of central cities and lowest in small towns and rural communities.

The length of residence in a community is associated with rates of family violence. Black parents who have lived in their community for less than two years report the highest rates of parent-to-child violence. This pattern is consistent across all three measures of violence. The difference is statistically significant for the rate of very severe violence, the rate of which is nearly two times greater among respondents who have lived in their community for less than two years, compared with respondents who had resided in the same community for more than two years.

Both official report data and self-report data find that the risk of child abuse is greater in single-parent households (Gelles, 1989; Gil, 1970; Sack, Mason, and Higgins, 1985). The data for black households are consistent with Gelles's (1989) analysis of the entire sample from the Second National Family Violence Survey. The rate of very severe violence is significantly greater in single-parent black households than in two-caretaker households. Two-caretaker black households were more likely to report using forms of severe violence toward their children, and this difference is almost entirely due to the higher rate of hitting or trying to hit children with objects in two-caretaker households compared with single-parent homes.

Intergenerational Transmission of Violence

There is abundant evidence from both clinical observations, analyses of official report data, and survey research that individuals who have experienced violence are more likely to use violence toward their own children as adults, although the relationship is far from perfect (Egeland, Jacobvitz, and Papatola, 1987; Egeland, Jacobvitz, and Sroufe, 1988; Herrenkohl, Herrenkohl, and Toedler, 1983; Kaufman and Zigler, 1987; Straus, Gelles, and Steinmetz, 1980; Widom, 1989). Kaufman and Zigler (1987) estimate that approximately 30 percent of individuals who experience abuse as children will be abusive as adults.

Black respondents who reported being hit by their mothers or fathers as teenagers were more likely to report using overall violence, severe violence, and very severe violence toward their own children (the difference for being hit as a teen by a father and using overall violence as an adult is not statistically significant—see table 2–4). Respondents who report being hit as teenagers by their fathers or mothers were nearly three times more likely to say they used some form of very severe violence more than once toward their children.

Witnessing violence in the family of orientation also is related to the likelihood of using violence toward one's children. Those respondents who witnessed a father hit a mother or mother hit a father were more likely to report higher rates on all three measures of violence (the differences for respondents who witnessed a father hit a mother and used overall and very severe violence toward their children were not statistically significant—see table 2–4).

The Relationship between Marital Violence and Violence toward Children

One important finding from the First National Violence Survey was that couples who did not hit each other report the lowest rate of abusive violence toward their children (Straus, Gelles, and Steinmetz, 1980). Violent husbands and wives are likely to be violent parents. Our data on black households also indicate that high rates of spousal violence are associated with higher rates of abusive violence toward children.[6] As can be seen in the bottom panel of table 2–4, the differences are both substantial and significant. The rate of very severe violence in homes where the husband has used severe violence toward his wife is nearly four times greater than the rate of very severe violence in homes where husbands do not abuse their wives.

Income

Total family income level was not significantly associated with any of the three measures of violence toward children. Examining the relationship between respondent's experience with violence in his or her family of orientation and controlling for current total family income, however, yields some important insights. The rate of all three measures of vio-

Table 2–4
Rates of Parent-to-Child Violence by Family Background

	Rates Per 1,000		
Variable	Overall Violence	Severe Violence	Very Severe Violence
Respondent hit as teen by mother			
Never (260)	573***	123***	23*
Once (56)	661	214	18
More than once (170)	741	306	71
Respondent hit as teen by father			
Never (348)	609	164*	32*
Once (52)	654	288	38
More than once (71)	746	282	99
Respondent's father hit mother			
Yes (90)	689	333***	67
No (408)	627	164	37
Respondent's mother hit father			
Yes (63)	778**	317**	127***
No (437)	618	176	37
Respondent could approve of husband slapping wife in some situations			
Yes (44)	773	386***	136***
No (473)	634	180	32
Respondent could approve of wife slapping husband in some situations			
Yes (89)	775**	303**	56
No (429)	615	175	37
Husband-to-wife severe violence in home			
Yes (26)	846*	385***	77*
No (304)	602	184	16

* $p < .05$
** $p < .01$
*** $p < .001$

lence is significantly lower among respondents who report never being hit as a teenager by their mother and whose current family income is above $10,000 per year compared with those respondents who were struck by their mothers (see table 2–5). The same pattern occurs for those whose current income is below the poverty line, but the relationships, except for overall violence, were not significant.

The original statistically significant association between witnessing maternal violence toward a spouse is maintained in families with incomes of $10,000 or more in 1985. The rates of abusive violence were higher among the higher income families in which the respondent had witnessed maternal violence compared with poverty income families. With one exception, all of the relationships were in the expected direction.

Table 2–5
Level of Parent-to-Child Violence by Family Background by Total Family Income

	Rates Per 1,000		
Variable	Overall Violence	Severe Violence	Very Severe Violence
Income < $10,000			
Respondent hit as teen by mother			
Never (59)	610*	136	51
Once (16)	813	125	—
More than once (43)	814	279	116
Income > $10,000			
Respondent hit as teen by mother			
Never (188)	559**	122*	11*
Once (37)	622	243	27
More than once (119)	731	328	59
Income < $10,000			
Respondent hit as teen by father			
Never (89)	663	146	45*
Once (8)	750	125	—
More than once (21)	810	333	190
Income > $10,000			
Respondent hit as teen by father			
Never (244)	594	172*	25
Once (43)	651	326	47
More than once (46)	717	283	65
Income < $10,000			
Respondent's father hit mother			
Yes (25)	800	280	120
No (99)	677	162	51
Income > $10,000			
Respondent's father hit mother			
Yes (61)	639	377***	49
No (288)	622	167	31
Income < $10,000			
Respondent's mother hit father			
Yes (20)	800	100	100
No (106)	689	208	57
Income > $10,000			
Respondent's mother hit father			
Yes (41)	805**	439**	146***
No (309)	599	172	11
Income < $10,000			
Gender of respondent			
Male (19)	474*	53	53
Female (114)	746	211	61
Income > $10,000			
Gender of respondent			
Male (119)	588	252	42
Female (241)	647	183	29

* $p < .05$

** $p < .01$

*** $p < .001$

When we examine the relationship between gender of the respondent and violence, by income level, we see that lower income women had higher rates of violence toward children. The rate for overall violence was 746 per 1,000 for females compared with 474 per 1,000 for men (the difference was statistically significant). The rate of severe violence for poverty income female respondents was 298 percent greater than for poverty income male respondents.

For families with incomes of $10,000 or more, we observe a slightly different pattern. Female respondents tend to have a slightly higher rate of overall violence. Male respondents, however, reported higher rates of severe and very severe violence.

Discussion

The Second National Family Violence Survey and this chapter were designed to examine the prevalence, nature, and risk factors for parent-to-child violence in black families. As the largest survey based on a true cross section of black families, the data presented here probably come closer to describing the real situation of violence toward black children than data derived from clinical or official sources.

As expected the milder forms of violence were the most common. The sex of the child, age of the child, and the number of years the family lived in the community were related to all three measures of violence. Our data clearly indicate that either experiencing violence as a teen or witnessing violence in the family of orientation is significantly associated with violence in the family of procreation. Furthermore, the child abuse rate was significantly higher in households where wife battering occurred than in nonwife-battering households.

In an earlier paper we found that the rates of severe violence toward black children were higher in 1985 than in 1975 (Hampton, Gelles, and Harrop, 1989). Using a sample of current couples with children age three to seventeen years at home, that study also reported that the rate of severe parent-to-child violence was 114 percent greater in black families than in white families (221 per 1,000 compared with 103 per 1,000). This finding argues for the need for continued basic research that can shed light on group differences in the risk of violence, and for the study of factors that create special vulnerability or resistance to particular forms of maltreatment (Garbarino and Ebata, 1983).

Future research with these data must systematically address group differences for the entire sample of black and white families. In addition, given the growth of female-headed households among blacks, additional analyses should be done comparing the rate of violence in single-parent and two-parent households.

Notes

1. The comparison was limited to two-caretaker households with children between the ages of three and seventeen years living in the household.

2. A complete discussion of the Conflict Tactics Scales items can be found in Straus (1979; 1981; 1990).

3. Burning and scalding were included in the 1985 version of the Conflict Tactics Scales but were not included in the 1975 version.

4. In most instances the outcome from being kicked, although painful, does not result in an injury. The absence of an injury does not remove it from the category of an abusive violence.

5. Our research on family violence often poses the problem of statistical versus substantive significance (Gelles, 1988; 1989; Hampton, Gelles, and Harrop, 1989; Straus and Gelles, 1986). When examining the low base-rate phenomenon of child abuse and other low base-rate variables such as pregnancy or single parenthood, we often find substantial percentage differences between categories. Yet, as a result of the skewed distributions of the main variables, the differences are not statistically significant. The dilemma of achieving statistical significance when studying low base-rate phenomena has been discussed by Goodman and Kruskal (1959) and by Finley (1884). We resolve the dilemma here as we have in previously published work—while we attempt to be appropriately conservative in using measures of statistical significance, we do not overlook substantively significant percentage differences.

6. We report rates for husband-to-wife severe violence as one measure of interspousal violence. A similar association between parent-to-child violence and couple violence exists in this sample for wife-to-husband overall violence and husband-to-wife overall violence.

3

Psychosocial Characteristics of Mothers of Physically Abused and Neglected Children: Do They Differ by Race?

Susan J. Zuravin
Raymond H. Starr, Jr.

C ulture, ethnicity, and race have received relatively little attention in the child maltreatment literature. Garbarino and Ebata (1987) have observed that cultural and ethnic differences have received a treatment that might best be described as benign neglect. Hampton (1987) has noted that "little attention has been given to violence against black children" (p. 3). Pierce and Pierce (1987) have emphasized "the need to consider more seriously the aspect of race in research and practice with sexually abused children and their families" (p. 67).

Reviews of the literature (e.g., Hampton, 1987; Garbarino and Ebata, 1987) reveal that when culture, ethnicity, and/or race have been addressed by researchers, it is usually with respect to matters of incidence, type, nature, severity, and attitudes toward maltreatment. Few investigators have focused on determining if the context of maltreatment or the characteristics of maltreating families, parents, and children differ by these factors. Yet such studies are extremely important for clinicians and program planners. They provide the type of information that has meaning for the development of effective treatment and prevention strategies. Given this belief in the potential importance of culture, race, and ethnicity for guiding the development of interventions, the purposes of this chapter are:

- to review existing knowledge about the effect of race on the contextual, familial, and parental correlates of physical abuse and neglect.
- to present some data from a study that focuses on identifying whether Afro-American and white mothers who physically neglect and/or abuse their children differ with respect to selected psychosocial characteristics.

Review of the Literature

This section has two objectives: (1) to identify the research design characteristics that are necessary to demonstrate an ethnic effect and (2) to review the findings and critique the methodology of studies that have examined ethnic effects.

Desirable Design Characteristics for Studies Examining Ethnic Effects

Studies of reported child maltreatment that are likely to provide the best information about whether the correlates of maltreatment differ by ethnicity should have, at least, the following three design characteristics.

1. They should include samples of families (or, in the case of aggregate studies of contextual correlates, samples of maltreatment rates) from all of the racial or ethnic groups that are being compared. Findings from such research—all other things being equal—are likely to lead to clearer conclusions than studies comparing results from different investigations, each of which studied a different ethnic group. Research using the former strategy provides more control over such potentially compromising factors as (1) drawing samples from populations that differ with respect to the time period when the maltreatment was reported or the jurisdiction in which the maltreatment was reported and/or (2) collecting data in different ways or with different types of measures.

2. They should include samples of both maltreating and non-maltreating families from each ethnic group and identify whether there are differences between groups by statistically analyzing data with ethnicity held constant. If a particular characteristic significantly discriminates between maltreaters and controls of one ethnic group but not the other, there is an interaction between ethnicity and the particular characteristic. In other words, such a finding suggests differences by ethnicity with respect to the relationship between the characteristic and maltreatment. Findings from studies that identify differences by directly comparing maltreaters of two ethnic groups are confounded by race. In other words, it is conceivable that the presence or absence of a specific characteristic is typical of the particular ethnic group as a whole rather than just the maltreaters.

3. They should conduct separate analyses for physical abuse and physical neglect. A number of recent studies (Wolock and Horowitz, 1977; Zuarvin, 1988a, 1988b) suggest that the correlates of the two types of maltreatment differ. Thus, findings from efforts that include a

mix of maltreatment types are likely to produce idiosyncratic results, ones that are highly dependent on the proportion of abusive versus neglectful families typical of the sample.

Review of Knowledge about Ethnic Effects

As might be expected, a search of the child maltreatment literature identified very few studies that met the above criteria. We found only one that met all three criteria (Giovannoni and Billingsley, 1970) and three that met at least the first criterion (Hampton, 1987; Spearly and Lauderdale, 1983; Wolock and Horowitz, 1977). Despite many design differences among these studies—for example, use of different measures, methods of collecting data, and data analytic procedures—all four of the efforts did identify some correlates of child maltreatment that differ by ethnicity. *However,* and at least in part because of the difference in study methodology, findings from the studies are frequently contradictory.

Contextual Correlates

Only one study has focused on examining ethnic differences in contextual correlates of maltreatment (Spearly and Lauderdale, 1983). Spearly and Lauderdale attempted to predict, from a variety of different population characteristics, ethnic-specific rates of reported child maltreatment for Texas counties. The major limitation of this study is that separate analyses were not performed for each of the three types of maltreatment: physical abuse, physical neglect, and sexual abuse. However, it is likely that the combined results are more apropos to physical neglect than physical or sexual abuse since 59 percent of the reports (21,837 and 36,945) were for neglect.

Two different sets of analyses, each using different county population characteristics, identified some possibly meaningful differences between the contextual correlates of Anglo, African-American, and Mexican-American maltreatment rates. The first set of analyses included community characteristics that were selected on the basis of theory that suggests that maltreating behavior is more likely to occur in socially and economically impoverished neighborhoods—ones where individuals and families are not embedded in social networks and families are economically stressed (Garbarino, 1981). Findings revealed ethnic-specific differences in the community correlates of child maltreatment. Anglo rates were very much related to economic stress; they declined as the proportion of affluent Anglo families increased and the average AFDC expenditure per child increased. On the other hand, African-American and Mexican-American rates were associated with social impoverishment. For the former, rates increased as the proportion of African-American female-headed families with children increased, and, for the latter, rates increased as the proportion of Mexican-Americans living in the county for less than five years increased.

The second set of analyses also focused on testing the social impoverishment hypothesis but with different community characteristics. The two variables that were included in the analysis were the ethnic-specific proportion of the total county population and the degree of urbanization (operationalized as rural, moderately urban, and highly urban). The researchers expected that counties characterized by small proportions of a particular ethnic group would have higher rates of maltreatment because there would be fewer sources of informal social support. With respect to urbanicity, they hypothesized that high proportions of individuals living in an urban as opposed to rural area would be associated with higher rates of maltreatment because of the breakdown in support and alienation that is often associated with urban living. Findings support those from the first set of analyses. Anglo rates were not affected by either characteristic while African-American and Mexican-American rates were. The former increased as the population became more urban while the latter increased as the population became more urban and the proportion of the population that was Mexican-American decreased. Spearly and Lauderdale (1983) interpret these results in terms of the hypothesis that African-American and Mexican-American families may be more dependent on informal networks of support for childrearing while Anglo families may "rely upon (their) relatively increased access to economic resources in the labor force and formal agencies" (p. 101).

Maternal and Family Characteristics

This section reviews findings from three studies (Giovannoni and Billingsley, 1970; Hampton, 1987; Wolock and Horowitz, 1977) with respect to five maternal or family characteristics that have been found to be important correlates of child maltreatment by studies that *did not* take ethnicity into account (Parke and Collmer, 1975; Polansky, Hally, and Polansky, 1976; Wolfe, 1985). The characteristics are number of children, mother's education, mother's childhood experiences, maternal social isolation, and maternal emotional well-being.

The Giovannoni and Billingsley (1970) study compared forty-five low-income, neglectful mothers (twenty-four African-American and twenty-one white), who were known to child protective services for physically neglecting their children, to forty comparison mothers (twenty-two Afro-American and eighteen white). None of the neglecting mothers was known to have a physically abused child. All analyses were bivariate in nature and used the chi-square statistic to determine statistical significance. As noted earlier, this study met all the criteria specified above.

The Wolock and Horowitz study (1977) compared 380 very low-income (AFDC recipients), physically neglecting, and/or abusing mothers known to child protective services to 144 comparable nonmaltreating mothers. Ethnic analyses were multivariate rather than bivariate in nature (i.e., white neglectors were compared with white controls) and five of the seven variables used in the analyses were indexes derived by combining several related variables (i.e., social isolation index, emotional well-being index, growing-up experiences index, etc.). As a result of the use of indexes it is not possible to look at the relationship between individual variables and neglect as did Giovannoni and Billingsley (1970) and Hampton (1987). The limitation of this study is that separate analyses were not performed by type of maltreatment; however, because only 28 of 380 maltreators were known to abuse but never neglect, the results can be interpreted as predominantly reflective of neglect or both neglect and abuse.

The Hampton (1987) study, a reanalysis of data from the First National Study of the Incidence and Severity of Child Abuse and Neglect (NIS-1) (U.S. Department of Health and Human Services, 1981), directly compared 205 Afro-American and 734 white abusive families who had been reported to CPS with respect to individual variables (no indexes were used). No statistical analyses were performed. Data were presented in the form of frequencies. The main limitation of this study is that the NIS-1, an examination of the prevalence of maltreatment, obviously included no control group; consequently, it is impossible for Hampton to control directly for race. As a result, findings may not be indicative of differences between maltreators but differences between individuals of different ethnic origins. In addition, the white families from the NIS-1 had higher incomes than the African-American families, leading to a possible confounding of the findings by income. Results of the three studies are detailed below.

With respect to *number of children* (living at home when the family was interviewed or came to the attention of CPS), findings from the three studies conflict. Giovannoni and Billingsley (1970) found no differences by race; African-American and white neglectors had more children than their controls but they did not differ from each other. They did find, however, some differences with respect to childbearing patterns. Afro-American mothers, even though they were older than their controls, were more likely to have had a child during the last year, while white mothers, who were the same age as their controls, were less likely to have had a child during the last year. Wolock and Horowitz's (1977) study of neglect did find differences by race. Results of their discriminant function analysis revealed that number of children was the most powerful of four predictors of child maltreatment for Afro-American families while it was the third most important of four predictors of maltreatment by white families. The more children the more likely the mother was to be among the maltreating group. Hampton, too, found differences by race. Afro-American families were three times more likely (31.5 percent versus 9.9 percent) to have five children than white families.

With respect to mother's *educational achievement,* findings also conflict. Giovannoni and Billingsley (1970) found no differences for any group; neglectors, regardless of race, were less likely to have completed fewer grades than their controls. On the other hand, both Wolock and Horowitz (1977) as well as Hampton (1987) found differences by race. The former study identified education (having completed few grades) as an important predictor of maltreatment among Afro-American but not white mothers. The latter study similarly found that Afro-American mothers were three times more likely (17.5 percent to 4.8 percent) than white mothers to have completed fewer than nine grades of school.

With respect to mother's *growing-up experiences,* two of the three studies found differences. Giovannoni and Billingsley's (1977) examination of family structure (being reared by one parent versus two) and family instability (number of major changes in family composition) found no differences between neglectors and their controls for either racial group. On the other hand, Wolock and Horowitz (1977), using an index of eleven items that tapped such constructs as physical neglect, feelings of psychological satisfaction with growing-up experiences, being severely beaten, family structure (being raised in an intact family), the presence of a heavy drinker in the home, and parents' education achievements found that having poorer quality experiences was a more powerful predictor of neglect among Afro-American than white mothers. Hampton (1987) found that being abused during the growing-up years, while not a prevalent phenomenon, was over three times more common (11.0 percent to 3.3 percent) for white than Afro-American mothers.

With respect to *social isolation,* both studies (Giovannoni and Billingsley, 1970; Wolock and Horowitz, 1977) that examined this factor found differences; however, their findings are somewhat contradictory. Giovannoni and Billingsley (1970) note that "overall relationships with kinship systems were more important than those with neighbors and friends. There were no significant differences between neglectors and controls for either ethnic group in either qualitative or quantitative aspects of relations to friends" (p. 200). With respect to degree of psychological attachment to kin and type of activities kin shared there were differences between white and Afro-American neglectors. While controls for both ethnic groups were more likely to be attached than neglectors, all Afro-American mothers regardless of maltreatment status showed a higher degree of attachment than white mothers. Additionally, Afro-American neglectful mothers differed from their controls in that the controls were significantly more likely to engage in mutual aid activities like baby-sitting and housecleaning while both groups of white mothers were equally likely to be low with respect to these types of shared activity. The researchers interpret their findings by explaining that "for Afro-American adequate mothers an active, supportive instrumentally oriented contact is as integral as more affectively oriented ones while for white adequate mothers the latter only appeared crucial" (p. 201).

On the other hand, Wolock and Horowitz (1977) found that their social isolation index—one that included five items that tapped frequency of contacts with friends (two items) and kin as well as number of memberships in formal organizations but no measures of psychological attachment or shared activities—was the most important for four predictors for neglect by white mothers, but it was not a predictor at all for neglect by Afro-American mothers. For white mothers, the fewer the contacts with friends and kin the more likely they were to be among the neglectful mothers.

With respect to *emotional well-being*, neither of the two studies (Wolock and Horowitz, 1977; Hampton, 1987) found very substantial differences. Wolock and Horowitz's emotional well-being index, one that included fourteen items that basically tapped degree of depression, was *not* a predictor of neglect for either ethnic group. Hampton's reanalysis of the NIS-1 data on abuse found that alcohol and drug problems were somewhat more characteristic of white than Afro-American mothers (16.8 percent of the white mothers had substance abuse problems compared with 12 percent of the Afro-American mothers), while emotional problems (operational definition not identified) were somewhat more characteristic of Afro-American mothers (13.1 percent compared with 9.1 percent of the white mothers).

In summary, this review of the very meager literature on ethnic differences in the correlates of child maltreatment leads to one important conclusion: More systematic research is definitely in order. Notwithstanding contradictions among findings—to be expected given the diverse methodologies used by the studies—differences were identified between Afro-American and white neglectful as well as abusive mothers.

Because relevant research is expensive and time-consuming, prior to launching into efforts aimed at examining ethnic differences, it is important to carefully think through two important considerations—the design of future efforts and the characteristics to be examined. Above we have outlined the design aspects that we believe to be important for studies that are exploring ethnic differences. Below we explore the characteristics that might be important to examine.

Currently, there is no theory about ethnic-specific causes of maltreatment that can direct us to the most important variables to examine. Consequently, our choices have to be based on clinical impressions, theories about child maltreatment in general, findings from the above studies, and results from research on child maltreatment that did not take race into consideration. Of the constructs examined by the studies reviewed above, at least three should be targeted for reexamination—family childbearing patterns (number of children is one marker), maternal growing-up experiences, and maternal social functioning (isolation). A fourth variable, education, is more appropriately included under maternal growing-up experiences. All three should be operationalized by a wide variety of different characteristics, including those used by the existing studies.

While our review does not indicate that *emotional well-being* was an impressive correlate of neglect or abuse for either ethnic group, recent studies (Famularo, Barnum, and Stone, 1986; Kaplan et al., 1983; Zuravin, 1988a) of child maltreatment that did not analyze their data by ethnic group have shown this to be an important construct when it is operationalized in terms of maternal depression and substance abuse. In addition, clinical observations suggest that both depression and substance abuse are very prevalent among maltreating mothers, particularly those who are neglectful. Conceivably, findings from the studies reviewed are not substantial because of the measures used. Use of improved methods of operationalizing depression and substance abuse may well lead to a better test of whether these characteristics are uniquely associated with specific ethnic groups. Given the importance for intervention of knowing whether maternal depression and/or substance abuse is associated with maltreatment by one ethnic group or another further examination is definitely indicated.

The study reported in this chapter was structured according to the design recommendations outlined above and examined four categories of maternal psychosocial characteristics—childbearing patterns, growing-up experiences, social functioning, and emotional well-being. The questions addressed by the study are:

1. Do any of the psychosocial characteristics discriminate between the two ethnic groups for child neglect? For child abuse?

2. Do the characteristics that discriminate between the two ethnic groups for child neglect differ from those that discriminate between the two groups for child abuse?

Study Methodology

Study Site

The geographic context of this study is Baltimore, Maryland, the central city of the Baltimore Metropolitan statistical area. With a population of 764,000 residents (U.S. Bureau of the Census, 1987) it is the eleventh largest city in the United States. Similar to other non–sun belt cities—Chicago, Detroit, Philadelphia, and Washington, D.C.—Baltimore has lost population since 1970 (U.S. Bureau of the Census, 1983). Statistics (U.S. Bureau of the Census, 1983) on the ethnic composition of Baltimore's population reveal that the majority are Afro-American (55 percent); 44 percent are white and 1 percent are of Spanish origin. With respect to ethnic demographics, Baltimore is similar to two other large U.S. cities, Washington, D.C., and Detroit, Michigan.

Currently, the city contains a disproportionate share of Maryland's poverty population. While only 17 percent of all Maryland families live in Baltimore (U.S. Bureau of the Census, 1984), 45 percent of all poor families and 55 percent of all poor, female-headed families are city residents. Comparison of per capita income statistics for cities with 100,000 or more population reveals that Baltimore, with its per capita income of $7,673, is the sixth poorest city in the United States. Poorer than Baltimore are Newark, Cleveland, Detroit, El Paso, and San Antonio (U.S. Bureau of the Census, 1984). As might be expected given such a large poverty population, Baltimore generates a disproportionate share of Maryland's child abuse reports. For the study years—1983 and 1984—approximately 35 percent of the 24,332 child abuse reports in the state central registry were from Baltimore.

Subjects

Five hundred and eighteen very low-income, single-parent mothers participated in the study. During the sampling month (January 1984), all respondents were residents of Baltimore, Maryland, received Aid to Families of Dependent Children (AFDC), and were the natural mother of at least one child twelve or under. Respondents were restricted to single parents and AFDC recipients because prior research (Park and Collmer, 1975; Wolfe, 1985) suggests that such parents may be at increased risk for child maltreatment. The 518 women were sampled from three different populations of clients known to the Baltimore City Department of Social Services (BCDSS).

Child Abuse Sample

The sample of 152 child-abusing mothers was selected from a sampling frame of 281 female-headed AFDC families who were receiving child protective services from Baltimore City Department of Social Services during January 1984 for having one or more physically abused children. To be included in the sampling frame a family had to meet the general study criteria—that is, be headed by a single parent, female AFDC recipient with at least one natural child twelve or under—and include one child who had sustained injuries at a minimum severity level of 4 on the Magura-Moses Physical Discipline Scale (Magura and Moses, 1986). Relevant injuries include bruises, welts, cuts, abrasions, and first degree burns. To construct the sample, we chose every family where the mother was known to be the abuser and a random sample of the remaining families.

Child Neglect Sample

The sample of 164 child-neglecting mothers was selected from a sampling frame of 381 female-headed AFDC families who were receiving child protective services for neglecting one or more children. To be screened into the sampling frame the family had to (1) meet the four general study criteria; (2) have one or more children who were neglected in at least one of the following eight areas—physical health, mental health, nutrition/diet, personal hygiene, household sanitation, physical safety in the home, supervision of activities, and/or arrangements for substitute child care; and (3) not have any children who were known to have been abused. Neglect was considered to have occurred if the caseworker gave the family a rating of 4 on the Magura-Moses nutrition/diet scale or a rating of 3 on any of the remaining seven Magura-Moses scales (Magura and Moses, 1986). A minimum rating (4 for nutritional and 3 for the other types of neglect) indicated that the child was at significant risk for physical, emotional, and/or developmental harm as a result of the omission in care. To construct the sample, we chose every white family and a random sample of the Afro-American families.

Nonmaltreating Sample

The sample of 376 nonmaltreating mothers represents all mothers from a 2.1 percent systematic sample (n = 788) of the 37,158 families receiving AFDC but not child protective services during January 1984 who met the general study criteria and had never been a recipient of any of the child welfare services provided by BCDSS, including child protective services, foster care, services to families with children, and/or single parent services. While purging the sample of families with a history of child welfare services from BCDSS does not guarantee that the sample will be free of maltreators, it considerably reduces the probability. However, to the extent that the nonmaltreating sample includes families with serious child care problems that have not come to the attention of BCDSS, study findings will underestimate differences between groups.

Sample Recruitment

The 692 members of the three samples were approached by letter and then by an interviewer if they did not respond to the letter. Of the 692, 518 (74.9 percent) agreed to participate: 119 (72.3 percent) of the neglect sample, 118 (75.6 percent) of the abuse sample, and 281 (74.7 percent) of the nonmaltreating sample. Mothers were interviewed in their homes some time during the period 9/1/84–6/31/85 by trained interviewers who were unaware of the child maltreatment status of their assigned respondents. Participants were compensated $15.00.

Measures

Each of the four categories of characteristics was defined in terms of multiple variables. Variables were selected on the basis of their ability to (1) allow comparison of our findings with those of earlier efforts and (2) extend knowledge about the particular category.

Growing-up experiences were operationalized by ten variables plus educational achievement (operationalized as last grade completed). First, we were interested in determining if experiences with maltreatment—being sexually abused, physically abused, or physically neglected—discriminated between the mothers. A mother was considered sexually abused if she responded positively to either of the following questions: "Prior to your eighteenth birthday,

1. did anybody touch your breasts, genitals, or other private parts or force you to touch their's or somebody else's private parts against your wishes?
2. did anyone ever force you to have any kind of sexual intercourse with them or someone else against your wishes?"

A mother was considered physically abused if she had been beaten severely, very often, or often by any of the various adults living in the same household(s) in which she had lived prior to her eighteenth birthday. A mother was considered physically neglected if she responded "very frequently" or "frequently" to any of the following statements:

1. I went hungry because there was not enough to eat.
2. I didn't have decent clothes to wear.
3. I was really sick but no one took me to the doctor.

Second, we were interested in determining if the extent of psychological nourishment and the status of attachments during the growing-up years discriminated between the mothers. Attachment to parents/primary caretakers was operationalized by an index of six items from the Michigan Screening Profile of Parenting (Schneider, Helfer, and Pollock, 1972). Data developed on the profile show that this particular set of items successfully discriminates between maltreating and nonmaltreating mothers. A high score on the index indicates stronger attachment to parent figures and lower abuse likelihood. To determine if the mother had a close confidante during the growing-up years we asked, "Was there anybody who you really felt close to—somebody you could turn to for help and support when you had a problem or were really feeling bad about something?" As an overall assessment of the mother's perception of the adversity of her living conditions, we asked, "Did you ever run away from home prior to your seventeenth birthday?"

Third, we were interested in determining if a variety of other experiences not tapped by the above variables discriminated between the mothers. We examined Giovannoni and Billingsley's (1970) variable of family structure (whether the mother grew up in an intact family), and also continuity of care (how many different persons the mother lived with), whether the mother had ever lived in a foster home, and extreme poverty during childhood (if the mother had ever lived in a household that received Aid to Families of Dependent Children).

Childbearing patterns were operationalized by four variables—number of live births, number of unplanned live births, spacing in years between the first and second child, and age at first live birth. Since the aim of examining this construct was to determine the need for family planning interventions, number of live births is a better indicator of a mother's childbearing patterns than is the more commonly assessed number of children living at home at the time she became known to protective services. Many mothers do not have all of their children living with them—some may be with relatives, others may be placed in foster or group care, and still others may be grown and living on their own. A live birth was identified as unplanned according to the following formula: when a respondent answered "no" to the question, "At the time you became pregnant, did you yourself want to have another baby at some time?" or "sooner than I wanted" to the question, "Did you become pregnant sooner than you wanted, later than you wanted, at about the right time, or didn't you care?"

Social functioning was operationalized by ten variables. To obtain an idea of whether frequency of contacts with relatives is an important correlate—the Wolock and Horowitz (1977) findings suggested "yes"— we separately examined frequency of contacts with four categories of relatives—mother, father, siblings, and grandparents. Mothers who responded that they lived with the relative or saw the relative once or twice per week were categorized as "in frequent contact." To determine if being psychologically attached to others, particularly relatives, was an important discriminating characteristic—the Giovannoni and Billingsley (1970) findings suggest it is—we asked a series of questions. This began with, "If you had a very personal and serious problem, are there any people, including those in your household, with whom you could discuss it?" To determine if the attachment was more likely to be with a relative than a neighbor or friend—the Giovannoni and Billingsley (1970) findings suggest it is—we asked mothers to indicate their relationship to their confidante (i.e., friend, relative, boyfriend, etc.). To obtain an idea of how much support they might be getting from this confidante, we asked how frequently they saw this person. To gain further information about possibly significant attachment relationships, we asked the mothers if they had a boyfriend (someone they had been steadily dating for at least three months and had intercourse with at least once). To obtain information about the degree of comfort and security provided by this relationship we asked two more questions:

1. "How often do you worry or feel concerned about the problems that exist in your relationship with your boyfriend?"
2. "How much would you like to change your relationship with men?"

Finally, to obtain some idea of whether having persons to help with the care of their children is an important discriminating variable, we asked, "Do you have any relatives, friends, or neighbors who regularly help you take care of your children?"

To determine the mother's level of *emotional well-being* we explored three of its indicators—depression, alcohol problems, and drug problems. Depression was operationalized in several ways. The Beck Depression Inventory (Beck, 1970), a widely used twenty-one-item scale, was used to assess severity of depression on the day of the interview. A score of 13 on this scale is considered indicative of a clinically significant level of depression. Next, the lead question from the depression section of the Diagnostic Interview Schedule (DIS) (Robins et al., 1981) was used to determine if the mother had ever had two weeks or more of being depressed. To assess severity of depression over the mother's lifetime, she was asked (1) if she ever talked to a mental health professional (social worker, counselor, psychologist, or psychiatrist) about depression or nervous kinds of problems and (2) if she had ever been admitted to a hospital or other treatment kind of program where she stayed overnight because of emotional problems or problems with nerves.

To determine if the mother had ever had any kind of problem with alcohol or drugs we asked two questions from the DIS (Robins et al., 1981). With respect to alcohol, we asked, "Have you ever had periods of time when you kept drinking for a couple of days or more without sobering up?" With respect to drugs, we asked, "Have you ever had periods of time, say two weeks or more, when you were using heroin, cocaine, LSD, or PCP?"

Data Analyses

Data analyses were carried out by type of maltreatment—physical abuse or physical neglect—and, within each type of maltreatment, by ethnicity (e.g., Afro-American neglectors were compared with Afro-American nonmaltreating (control) mothers, white abusers were compared with white control mothers, etc.). All analyses were bivariate, carried out via chi-square or t-test, whichever was appropriate. The significance level for all tests was set at p > .05. While carrying out so many tests increases the probability of finding statistical differences when there are none, given the embryonic current state of knowledge about discriminating characteristics, such an exploratory approach is indicated. However, as a result of this problem, findings must be interpreted with great caution, being construed as suggestive rather than definitely supportive of differences.

Obtaining a statistically significant finding with the chi-square test, the analytic technique used for the majority of our analyses, is dependent on sample size (the larger the sample the greater the likelihood of a significant finding) (Hanushek and Jackson, 1977). Because our black samples were so much larger than our white samples (see table 3–1), to

Table 3–1
Ethnic Distribution for the Three Samples

Ethnicity	Nonmaltreating in percent (n = 281)	Abuse in percent (n = 118)	Neglect in percent (n = 119)
Afro-American	86.5 (243)	77.1 (90)	67.2 (80)
White	13.5 (38)	22.9 (28)	32.8 (38)

assure that sample size did not influence findings, we took the precaution of reducing the size of the black maltreating and control samples making them identical to the white maltreating and control samples. We did this by generating random samples of Afro-American control, neglectful, and abusive mothers. Analyses for neglect by *both* Afro-American and white mothers were performed on samples of 76 mothers (38 controls and 38 neglectors). Analyses for abuse by white mothers were performed on a sample of 66 (38 controls and 28 abusers) while analyses for neglect by black mothers were performed on a sample of 76 (38 controls and 38 neglectors).

Description of Samples

As might be expected given the ethnic demographics of Baltimore, the sample is predominantly black. Table 3–2 contains information about the proportion of white and Afro-American mothers in each of the three samples. It is important to remember when examining the distributions that only the nonmaltreating sample represents a true random sample. The two maltreating samples were selected from their respective sampling frames by oversampling certain groups. As noted, for the neglect sample we selected every white neglector and a random sample of the black neglectors, and for the abuse sample, we selected every situation in which the mother was the abuser and a random sample of the remaining situations. The purpose of this sample selection process was to assure enough white respondents and enough mother abusers to allow for valid comparisons. However, as a result of the sampling method, the distributions for abuse and neglect do not represent the true distribution by race for the respective populations.

Examination of four demographic characteristics (see tables 3–2

Table 3–2
Demographic Characteristics: Neglectful Mothers

	Black		White	
Characteristics	*NM* (*n* = 38)	*Neglect* (*n* = 38)	*NM* (*n* = 38)	*Neglect* (*n* = 38)
Age in years	25.6 (5.1)	27.9 (5.4)	27.0 (6.3)	28.0 (6.0)
AFDC (years receiving)	4.5 (4.0)	6.4* (4.6)	4.1 (5.3)	7.8** (6.3)
Ever married (percent)	18.4	34.2	60.5	73.7
Ever employed (percent)	68.4	52.6	60.5	44.7

Note: NM means nonmaltreating mothers.
 * $p < .05$
 ** $p < .01$

Table 3-3
Demographic Characteristics: Mothers with Abused Children

	Black		White	
	NM	Abuse	NM	Abuse
Characteristics	(n = 38)	(n = 38)	(n = 38)	(n = 28)
Age in years	25.6	27.1	27.0	29.6
	(5.1)	(5.1)	(6.3)	(4.9)
AFDC (years receiving)	4.5	6.4*	4.1	7.2*
	(4.0)	(3.6)	(5.3)	(5.5)
Ever married	18.4	25.0	60.5	57.1
Ever employed	68.4	50.0	60.5	46.4

Note: NM means nonmaltreating mothers.
* p < .05

and 3-3) indicates that only one of the four discriminates between the mothers. Findings reveal that ethnicity has no effect on amount of time receiving AFDC but maltreatment status does. Abusers and neglectors of both races had been receiving AFDC longer than their comparable controls.

Findings and Discussion

This study focused on determining if the psychosocial characteristics of Afro-American maltreating mothers differ from those of comparable white mothers. Findings are presented by category of characteristic with the results for neglect presented first and the results for abuse second.

In examining our findings, we conclude that a characteristic discriminates between the two racial groups when the maltreating sample from one racial group significantly differs from their controls while the maltreating sample from the other racial group fails to differ from theirs. When *both* ethnic groups are either similar to or significantly different from their nonmaltreating counterparts we conclude that the characteristic does *not* discriminate between the two ethnic groups for the particular type of maltreatment. When a characteristic fails to discriminate, we go on to examine whether the mothers of the two racial groups (regardless of maltreatment status) differ from each other with regard to the characteristic. When they do, we conclude that the characteristic is likely to be typical of the ethnic group as a whole rather than the maltreators of that ethnic group. In addition, we count the number of characteristics within a category that are significantly associated with each type of maltreatment for each race. Even though these characteristics are likely to be correlated, this will give us some sense of whether a category is potentially a better predictor of abuse or neglect by one of the two ethnic groups and help us to interpret the findings with respect to discrimination.

Growing-Up Experiences

Child Neglect

Findings reveal that as a category, growing-up experiences do discriminate between black and white neglectors. The two groups of maltreators differed with respect to four of the eleven experiences (see table 3–4). Three of the differences are due to black mothers significantly differing from their nonmaltreating controls while only one derives from the white neglectful mothers differing from theirs. Neglectful black mothers compared with their nonmaltreating counterparts were:

1. *more* likely to have spent part of their growing-up years in foster care.
2. *less* likely to have had someone they could turn to for help and support when they had a problem or were feeling bad about something.
3. *less* attached to their parents/primary caretakers.

Table 3–4
Growing-Up Experiences: Neglectful Mothers

Growing-Up Experiences	Afro-American		White	
	NM (n = 38)	NEG (n = 38)	NM (n = 38)	NEG (n = 38)
Highest grade completed	11.2 (1.5)	10.4 (1.7)	9.8 (1.8)	9.1 (1.7)
Sexually abused	7.9	31.6**	13.2	31.6*
Physically abused	5.4	10.5	21.1	26.3
Physically neglected	7.9	23.7	18.4	23.7
No confidante	5.3	23.7*	15.8	29.0
Schneider-Helfer Index Score of attachment to parents	19.8 (3.3)	17.4** (4.3)	17.4 (4.2)	18.0 (4.0)
Grew up in intact family	39.5	29.0	47.4	29.0
Spent time in foster home	0	18.4**	7.9	15.8
Discontinuity in care	31.6	44.7	34.2	60.5*
AFDC recipient	34.2	40.0	22.2	27.0
Ran away from home	5.3	34.2**	13.1	42.1**

Note: NM means nonmaltreating mothers.
* p < .05
** p < .01

White neglectful mothers *did not* differ from their controls with respect to the above three characteristics *but* they did differ with respect to discontinuity in care. They were *more* likely than their nonmaltreating peers to have lived with at least one caretaker other than the one who raised them for the most number of years. Interestingly, the discontinuity of care indicators, being in foster care and living with someone other than the person who reared the mother, and the attachment indicators, the Helfer-Schneider Index of Attachment to Primary Caretaker and having someone to confide personal problems to, figured more prominently in predicting neglect in African-American mothers than did the maltreatment during childhood indicators.

Examination of the number of significant differences between each racial group and their controls suggests that growing-up experiences may be a *somewhat better predictor of neglect for black mothers than white mothers*. Five of the ten characteristics were significantly associated with neglect by black mothers while three of eleven were associated with neglect by white mothers.

On the basis of the above findings *alone* one might be tempted to conclude that the African-American neglectful mothers might have had more adverse growing-up experiences than the white neglectful mothers. However, such a conclusion is unwarranted without examining why the white neglectful mothers did not differ from their controls with respect to as many characteristics as the black neglecting mothers. Examination of findings with respect to all eleven characteristics suggests that white mothers failed to differ with respect to four of the variables *not* because fewer white neglectors had adverse experiences but because more white nonneglecting mothers *did have* adverse experiences.

Both white neglectors and white controls were almost equally as likely to have been neglected as the black neglectors—23.7 percent of white neglectors, 18.4 percent of the white controls, and 23.7 percent of the black neglectors reported being physically neglected compared with 7.9 percent of the black nonmaltreating mothers.

Both white neglectors and white controls were almost equally as likely as black neglectors to have had depressed scores on the Schneider-Helfer Index of Attachment to Primary Caretaker—the score for white neglectors was 17.4, for the white controls 18.1, and for the black neglectors, 17.4 compared with 19.8 for the black nonmaltreators.

White mothers as a group (i.e., regardless of their maltreatment status) were significantly more likely to have been physically abused than black mothers as a group ($x^2 = 8.74$, df $= 1$, p $> .01$).

White mothers as a group were significantly less likely to have completed as many grades as the black mothers as a group (F $= 25.58$, df = 1, p < .0001). *Thus while it is possible to say that growing up experiences may be a better predictor of neglect by black mothers, it is not warranted to conclude at this point that white neglectful mothers were less likely to have had adverse experiences.*

Generally, our findings are consistent with those of earlier efforts (Giovannoni and Billingsley, 1970; Wolock and Horowitz, 1977). Like the Giovannoni and Billingsley study, we did not find family structure (living in an intact family) and education to be significant discriminators between the two ethnic groups. Similar to Wolock and Horowitz, we did find growing-up experiences to be a somewhat better overall predictor of neglect by black mothers.

Physical Abuse

Similar to the findings with respect to neglect, results pertaining to abuse reveal that as a category, growing-up experiences do discriminate between black and white abusers. The two groups of maltreators differed with respect to five of the eleven growing-up experiences (see table 3–5). Three of the differences are due to black mothers significantly differing from their nonmaltreating controls, and two derive from the white abusive mothers differing from theirs. Abusive black mothers compared with their nonmaltreating counterparts were:

Table 3–5
Growing-Up Experiences: Mothers with Abused Children

	Afro-American		White	
Growing-Up Experiences	NM (n = 38)	NEG (n = 38)	NM (n = 38)	NEG (n = 28)
Highest grade completed	11.2 (1.5)	10.4* (1.5)	9.8 (1.8)	9.7 (1.8)
Sexually abused	7.9	7.1	13.2	37.0*
Physically abused	5.4	7.1	21.1	25.0
Physically neglected	7.9	14.3	18.4	25.0
No confidante	5.3	25.0*	15.8	10.7
Schneider-Helfer Index Score of attachment to parents	19.8 (3.3)	17.1* (5.6)	17.4 (4.2)	14.9* (5.4)
Grew up in intact family	39.4	32.1	47.4	35.7
Spent time in foster home	0	7.1	7.9	10.7
Discontinuity in care	31.6	39.3	34.2	60.7*
AFDC recipient	34.2	59.3*	22.2	37.0
Ran away from home	5.3	13.9	13.1	21.4

Note: NM means nonmaltreating mothers.
* p < .05

1. *more* likely to complete *fewer* grades in school.
2. *less* likely to have had someone they could turn to for help and support when they had a problem or were feeling bad about something.
3. *more* likely to have been recipients of AFDC.

White abusive mothers compared with their nonmaltreating counterparts were:

1. *more* likely to have been sexually abused.
2. *more* likely to have lived with at least one caretaker other than the one who raised them for the most number of years.

Examination of the number of significant differences between each racial group and their controls does *not* suggest that growing-up experiences are a better predictor of abuse by either racial group. Four of the eleven characteristics were significantly associated with abuse by black mothers while three of eleven were associated with abuse by white mothers.

Even though growing-up experiences do not appear to be a significantly better predictor of having an abused child by either white or black mothers, it is not warranted to conclude that white and black abusive mothers are comparable with respect to the adversity of their experiences. Examination of the findings for all eleven characteristics suggests that white mothers may be more likely to have had adverse experiences than black mothers with respect to at least four of the characteristics.

Even though physical abuse as a child is not a predictor of abuse for either white or black mothers, white maltreating and control mothers were almost equally as likely to have been physically abused and, as a group, were significantly more likely than black mothers as a group to have been abused (x^2 = 7.25, df-1, p < .01).

With respect to attachment to primary caretaker(s), even though both black and white abusers significantly differed from their controls, comparison of the scores of white control mothers and black abusive mothers shows that they differ by only 0.3 of a point. Furthermore, comparison of white mothers as a group to black mothers as a group shows that white mothers were significantly less attached to their caretakers (F = 4.35, df = 1, p < .04).

With respect to education, white mothers as a group were found to have completed significantly fewer years of school (F = 16.95, df = 1, p < .001).

Even though white control mothers were significantly less apt than white abusive mothers to have experienced discontinuity of care, comparison of the proportion that did with the proportion of black abusive mothers who did shows little difference; 39.5 percent of black abusive mothers versus 34.2 percent of white nonmaltreating mothers lived for a time with someone other than the person who raised them. *Thus, even though the construct of deficiencies in growing up experiences does not appear to be a better predictor of propensity to abuse by one race over the other, close examination of the findings suggests that white mothers with and without abused children may have been more likely to have had adverse experiences than their comparable black counterparts.*

Comparison of all these findings with those of the Hampton study (1987) reveals that both studies agree with respect to sexual abuse—white mothers as a group were more likely to have been sexually abused while they were growing up—and disagree with respect to education. Conceivably, the discrepancy with respect to education reflects the failure of the Hampton study to control for socioeconomic status; the black mothers in his analysis were quite a bit poorer than white mothers.

Childbearing Patterns

Child Neglect

Findings with respect to the category, childbearing patterns, reveal that it is *not* an important discriminator between Afro-American and white neglectful mothers (see table 3–6). Not a single variable discriminated between the two racial groups. Despite this, however, the category is a *very good* predictor of neglect. With respect to three of the four variables, *both* groups of neglectors significantly differed from their non-maltreating peers. They were:

1. *more* likely to begin bearing their children at an earlier age.
2. *more* likely to have more live births.
3. *more* likely to have more unplanned live births.

The presence of similar patterns of results for black and white neglecting mothers does not mean that they have similar childbearing patterns. Examination of results with respect to all four patterns suggests that the two ethnic groups differ with respect to two patterns. As a group, white mothers are significantly older at first birth than black mothers (F = 4.15, df = 1, p < .04) *and* black mothers have more unplanned live births than white mothers (F = 4.34, df = 1, p < .04).

Comparison of our findings and those of earlier efforts (Giovan-

Table 3–6
Childbearing Patterns: Neglectful Mothers

	Afro-American		White	
	NM	AB	NM	AB
Childbearing Patterns	(n = 38)	(n = 38)	(n = 38)	(n = 38)
Livebirths	1.9	3.7***	2.1	3.5***
	(1.2)	(2.2)	(1.2)	(1.6)
Age at 1st livebirth	19.4	18.2*	20.1	18.6*
	(2.7)	(2.8)	(3.4)	(2.2)
Space in years between	3.6	2.8	2.4	2.6
1st and 2nd child	(2.8)	(1.9)	(1.5)	(1.1)
Unplanned livebirths	1.3	2.1*	1.1	1.8**
	(1.1)	(1.9)	(.78)	(1.3)

Note: NM means nonmaltreating mothers. All analyses for both black and white mothers were performed on the size indicated above except for "space in years," in which case the analysis was performed on a sample of 52.

* p < .05
** p < .01
*** p < .001

noni and Billingsley, 1970; Wolock and Horowitz, 1977) reveals that they are consistent. Neither number of live births nor the earlier studies' number of children living at home when the mothers were interviewed discriminates between ethnic groups; however, the variables are significant predictors of neglect by both ethnic groups.

Child Abuse

Similar to neglect, findings (see table 3–7) with respect to abuse suggest that the category, childbearing patterns, is *not* a good discriminator between black and white mothers. Only one of the four variables, number of unplanned live births, is associated with race. White abusive mothers have significantly *more* such births than their controls, while black mothers do not. Unlike the neglect findings, however, the abuse findings do not suggest that the category is a particularly good predictor for either racial group. For the black abusers only one of the four characteristics (number of live births) was a predictor, while for the white abusers only two were predictors. Even though this construct does not appear to be a good predictor of abuse by either ethnic group, it is unwarranted to conclude that the two racial groups of mothers are characterized by similar childbearing patterns. Closer examination of the findings suggests one difference. As a group, white mothers begin bearing their children at an older age than black mothers (F = 6.43, df = 1, p < .01).

Comparison of our findings with respect to number of live births

Table 3–7
Childbearing Patterns: Mothers with Abused Children

| | Afro-American | | White | |
| | NM | AB | NM | AB |
Childbearing Patterns	(n = 38)	(n = 38)	(n = 38)	(n = 38)
Livebirths	1.9	2.8**	2.1	3.5**
	(1.2)	(2.8)	(1.2)	(1.8)
Age at 1st livebirth	19.4	18.2	20.1	19.6
	(2.7)	(3.1)	(3.4)	(3.1)
Space in years between 1st	3.6	2.6	2.4	2.5
and 2nd child	(2.8)	(2.1)	(1.5)	(1.5)
Unplanned livebirths	1.3	1.8	1.1	1.9*
	(1.1)	(1.2)	(.78)	(1.3)

Note: NM means nonmaltreating mothers. All analyses for both black and white mothers were performed on the sample sizes indicated above except for "space in years," in which case the analysis was performed on a sample of 43.
 * p < .01
 ** p < .001

and Hampton's (1987) findings with respect to number of children reveals that they are discrepant. Hampton demonstrated that, as a group, black mothers had more children than white mothers. Like his findings with respect to education, it is possible that the excess number of children characteristic of black mothers is a reflection of their lower socioeconomic status in his sample.

Social Functioning

Physical neglect. The construct, social functioning, appears to be a *relatively good discriminator* between the two racial groups (see table 3–8). Afro-American and white mothers differed with respect to seven of the eleven social functioning characteristics. Again, black mothers were much more likely to differ from their nonmaltreating counterparts than white mothers. Six of the differences are due to black mothers significantly differing from their nonmaltreating controls while only one derives from the white neglectful mothers differing from theirs. Neglectful black mothers compared to their nonmaltreating counterparts were:

1. *less* likely to have frequent contact with their mothers.
2. *less* likely to have frequent contact with their fathers.
3. *more* likely to worry a lot about the problems in the relationships with their boyfriends.
4. *more* likely to want to change their relationships with men a lot.

Table 3–8
Current Social Functioning: Neglectful Mothers

	Afro-American		White	
	NM	AB	NM	AB
Current Social Functioning	(n = 38)	(n = 38)	(n = 38)	(n = 38)
Frequency contact with:				
mother	73.7	46.0**	57.9	52.6
father	39.5	10.8**	23.7	15.8
siblings	79.0	68.4	79.0	48.7**
grandparents	21.1	24.3	13.2	5.3
Has a boyfriend	73.7	73.0	44.4	52.8
[1]Degree of worry about problems with boyfriend				
none	44.4	53.6**	50.0	52.4
some	51.9	17.9	22.2	14.3
a lot	3.7	28.6	27.8	33.3
Degree of change mother wants in way she relates to men				
none	65.8	55.3***	68.4	57.9
some	34.0	13.2	18.4	10.5
a lot	0	31.6	13.2	31.6
Doesn't have confidante	5.3	31.6**	5.3	15.8
[2]Identity of confidante				
boyfriend	0	7.7	13.9	12.0
relative	83.3	73.1	61.1	46.9
nonrelative	16.7	19.2	25.0	40.6
[2]Frequency of contact with confidante				
less than once/week	5.6	23.1*	13.9	12.5
Others to help with children				
none	68.4	71.1	52.6	57.9

Note: NM means nonmaltreating mothers. All analyses for both black and white mothers were performed on the sample sizes indicated above except for those marked with a [1] and a [2]. In the case of the variable marked with a [1] the analysis for black mothers was performed on a sample size of 55 (all mothers with a boyfriend) and for white mothers a sample size of 39. For variables marked with a [2], those pertaining to a confidante, analyses for black mothers were performed on a sample size of 62 and for white mothers a sample size of 68.

* $p < .05$
** $p < .01$
*** $p < .001$

5. *more* likely to *not* have a confidante—someone with whom they could share their most serious and personal problems.

6. *more* likely to see their confidante less than one time per week.

While white neglectful mothers *did not* differ from their controls with respect to the above six characteristics, they did differ with respect to how frequently they visited their siblings. Compared with their nonmaltreating peers, they were *less* likely to visit frequently with their sisters and brothers.

Examination of the number of significant differences between each racial group and their controls suggests that social functioning may be a *better predictor of neglect among black mothers than white mothers.* Six of the eleven characteristics were significantly associated with neglect by black mothers while only one was associated with neglect by white mothers.

On the basis of the above findings *alone* one might be tempted to conclude that the African-American neglectful mothers function less well socially than white neglectful mothers. However, as mentioned above, with respect to growing-up experiences, such a conclusion would be premature without looking more closely at why the white mothers failed to differ from their controls. Examination of results with respect to all eleven patterns identifies three differences that suggest that the failure of at least these characteristics to predict neglect by white mothers is *not due to better social functioning on the part of the neglectful mothers but rather poorer functioning on the part of the nonmaltreating mothers compared with the African-American non-maltreating mothers.*

Both white neglectful and control mothers are less likely to have a boyfriend than their black counterparts and as a group tend toward being less likely to have a boyfriend than black mothers as a group ($x^2 = 7.75$, df $= 1$, p $< .10$).

Despite the fact that fewer white mothers have a boyfriend, those that do tend to worry more about the problems in their relationship with this boyfriend than black mothers; the proportion of white control mothers worrying about these problems was just about as high as the proportion of black neglectful mothers who worried (27.8 versus 28.6) and eight times as great as the proportion of black nonneglecting mothers who worried (27.8 percent to 3.7 percent).

Both white neglectful and control mothers are less likely to visit frequently their grandparents than their black peers and, as a group, are significantly less likely to visit than black mothers ($x^2 = 5.11$, df $= 1$, p $< .05$).

Also of interest are the findings with respect to the identity of the confidante for black and white mothers. White mothers, as a group, differ significantly from black mothers relative to the identity of the confidante ($x^2 = 9.09$, p $< .01$). Black mothers were more likely to choose a relative than white mothers.

Comparison of our findings with those of earlier efforts is difficult because of differences in operational definitions and methods of analysis. However, generally speaking our findings are discrepant from those of the earlier efforts. Wolock and Horowitz's (1977) study found that social isolation was an important predictor of neglect among white mothers but not black mothers, whereas our findings reveal the opposite. Giovannoni and Billingsley's (1970) results show that frequency of contact with kin is not a predictor of neglect by either black or white mothers, whereas our findings reveal the opposite. The one possible consistency between our findings and those of Giovannoni and Billingsley (1970) pertains to degree of attachment to relatives. Both of us found that black mothers as a group were significantly more likely to be attached to relatives than white mothers.

Table 3–9
Current Social Functioning: Mothers with Abused Children

	Afro-American		White	
Current Social Functioning	NM (n = 38)	AB (n = 38)	NM (n = 38)	AB (n = 28)
Frequency of contact				
mother	73.7	35.7**	57.9	28.6*
father	39.5	7.1**	23.7	14.3
siblings	79.0	46.4**	79.0	35.7***
grandparents	21.1	21.4	13.2	7.1
Has a boyfriend	73.7	63.0	44.4	65.4
[1]Degree of worry about problems with boyfriend				
none	44.4	50.0*	50.0	57.9
some	51.9	27.8	22.2	15.8
a lot	3.7	22.2	27.8	26.3
Degree of change mother wants in way she relates to men				
none	65.8	57.1**	68.4	53.6*
some	34.2	21.4	18.4	7.1
a lot	0	21.4	13.2	39.3
Doesn't have confidante	5.3	25.0*	5.3	14.3
Identity of confidante				
boyfriend	0	14.3	13.9	20.8
relative	83.3	71.4	61.1	50.0
nonrelatives	16.7	14.3	25.0	29.2
[2]Frequency of contact with confidante				
less than once/week	5.6	19.1	13.9	12.5
No one to help with children	59.9	50.9	52.9	70.4

Note: NM means nonmaltreating mothers. All analyses for both black and white mothers were performed on the sample size indicated above except for those marked with a [1] and a [2]. In the case of the variable marked with a [1], the analysis for black mothers was performed on a sample size of 45 (all mothers with a boyfriend), and for white mothers a sample size of 37. For variables marked with a [2], those pertaining to a confidante, analyses for black mothers were performed on a sample size of 57, and for white mothers a sample size of 60.

  * $p < .05$
 ** $p < .01$
*** $p < .001$

Physical Abuse

While social functioning does discriminate between white and black mothers, the differences are not particularly impressive, particularly compared with neglect (see table 3–9). Afro-American and white mothers differed with respect to three of the eleven characteristics. All three were due to black mothers significantly differing from their non-maltreating controls. Abusive black mothers compared with their non-maltreating counterparts were:

1. *less* likely to have a confidante.
2. *more* likely to worry about the problems characteristic of their relationships with their boyfriends.
3. *less* likely to see their fathers frequently.

As might be expected given the above findings, examination of the number of significant differences between each racial group and their controls suggests that social functioning may be a *better predictor of having an abused child by black mothers than white mothers.* Six of the nine significant analyses were associated with black mothers having an abused child while three were associated with white mothers having an abused child.

Examination of the findings to determine why social functioning is a poorer predictor of having an abused child by white mothers does not reveal any significant differences between white and black mothers as a group, suggesting that the social functioning of black abusive mothers *may* indeed be poorer than that of white mothers. Our findings must be considered suggestive of the presence of racial differences as no extant research on abusive families has examined social functioning in an appropriate manner.

Emotional Well-Being

Child Neglect

Findings with respect to this construct suggest that it is a relatively powerful discriminator between black and white neglectors. The two groups of mothers differed with respect to five of the six emotional well-being indicators (see table 3–10). All five of the differences are due to neglectful black mothers significantly differing from their non-maltreating counterparts. Neglectful black mothers compared with their controls were:

Table 3–10
Emotional Well-Being: Neglectful Mothers

| | Afro-American | | White | |
Emotional Well-Being	NM (n = 38)	AB (n = 38)	NM (n = 38)	AB (n = 38)
Beck Depression Score	9.1 (7.3)	16.6** (11.8)	13.1 (10.1)	17.2 (13.6)
Two weeks of depression ever	42.1	65.8*	52.6	79.0*
[1]Treatment for depression	12.5	52.0**	65.0	73.3
[1]Hospitalization	0	24.0*	10.0	30.0
Alcohol binges	5.3	26.3**	13.2	18.4
Two weeks of hard drug use	0	10.5*	7.9	5.3

Note: NM means nonmaltreating mothers. All analyses for both black and white mothers were performed on a sample of 76 except for those variables marked with a [1], in which case the analyses were performed on only those control and maltreating mothers who scored 14 or greater on the Beck Depression Inventory (n = 41 for the analyses involving black mothers and n = 50 for those involving white mothers).

* $p < .05$
** $p < .01$

1. *more* depressed on the day of the interview. Their average Beck Depression Inventory score indicates a degree of depression that is clinically significant (a score of 14 or greater is considered significant by Beck [1970]).

2. *more* likely to have received treatment from a mental health professional for their depression.

3. *more* likely to have been hospitalized for at least one night because of personal or emotional problems.

4. *more* likely to have binged on alcohol.

5. *more* likely to have used hard drugs (heroin, cocaine, PCP, etc.) for two weeks.

Examination of the number of significant differences between each racial group and their controls suggests that emotional well-being may be a *better predictor of neglect among black mothers than white mothers*. All six of the characteristics were significantly associated with neglect by black mothers while only one of the six, ever having been depressed for at least two weeks, was associated with neglect by white mothers. Comparison of these findings with those of Wolock and Horowitz (1977) reveals important discrepancies. The earlier study found that emotional well-being was not a predictor of neglect for either black or white mothers; however, as mentioned earlier, this finding may be a function of Wolock and Horowitz's measures and/or method of analysis.

While emotional problems appear to be better predictors of neglect by black mothers than white mothers, it is unwarranted to conclude from these findings that neglectful black mothers are more likely to have serious mental health problems than neglectful white mothers. Close examination of all six characteristics reveals that white mothers failed to differ from their controls with respect to at least one indicator, *not* because fewer white neglectors had mental health problems but because more white nonneglecting mothers *did have* such problems. White neglectors and their controls were more likely to have been treated for depression than their counterparts in the black sample, *and*, as a group, were significantly more likely to have obtained such help than black mothers ($x^2 = 10.16$, df $= 1$, p $< .01$).

Child Abuse

Findings with respect to emotional well-being reveal that it does discriminate between black and white abusers but not as substantially as it does for neglect. The two groups of mothers differed with respect to three of the six emotional well-being indicators (see table 3–11). All three of the differences are due to black abusive mothers significantly differing from their nonmaltreating counterparts. Abusive black mothers compared with their controls were:

1. *more* likely to have received treatment from a mental health professional for their depression.

Table 3–11
Emotional Well-Being: Mothers with Abused Children

| | Afro-American | | White | |
| | NM | AB | NM | AB |
Emotional Well-Being	(n = 38)	(n = 38)	(n = 38)	(n = 28)
Beck Depression Score	9.1	11.6	13.1	16.8
	(7.3)	(9.8)	(10.1)	(11.6)
Two weeks of depression ever	42.1	46.4	52.6	71.4
¹Treatment for depression	12.5	46.2*	65.0	85.0
¹Hospitalization	0	23.1*	10.0	25.0
Alcohol binges	5.3	21.4*	13.2	17.9
Two weeks of hard drug use	0	0	7.9	10.7

Note: NM means nonmaltreating mothers. All analyses for both black and white mothers were performed on the sample size indicated above except for those marked with a ¹, in which case analyses were performed on only those control and maltreating mothers who scored 14 or greater on the Beck Depression Inventory (n = 29 for the black abusers and n = 40 for the white abusers).
* p < .05

2. *more* likely to have been hospitalized for at least one night because of personal or emotional problems.

3. *more* likely to have binged on alcohol.

Like the results with respect to neglect, findings suggest that emotional well-being may be a better predictor of abuse for black mothers than white mothers. However, and also similar to the results of the neglect analyses, this is *not* entirely because white abusive mothers are characterized by a higher degree of emotional well-being but rather because the white controls are characterized by a lower degree of well-being. A larger proportion of the white control mothers had ever had two weeks of depression than the black abusive mothers, and, as a group, more white mothers had ever been depressed for two weeks than black mothers (x^2 = 8.63, df = 1, p < .05). And, as might be expected given the above differences, white control mothers were more likely to have received treatment for their depression than the black abusive mothers, and as a group were significantly more likely than black mothers as a group to have obtained help from a mental health professional (x^2 = 15.27, df = 1, p < .01).

Comparison of these findings with those of Hampton's (1987) reanalysis of NIS-1 data reveals that the results of the two studies are discrepant. Hampton found that alcohol problems were somewhat more characteristic of white abusive mothers and that emotional problems were more characteristic of black abusive mothers. Generally, we found just the opposite.

Conclusions and Implications

This study, like earlier efforts, reveals differences among the psychosocial characteristics of Afro-American and white child-neglecting mothers as well as child-abusing mothers.

For both neglect and abuse, three of the four categories of characteristics—growing-up experiences, social functioning, and emotional well-being—include a number of attributes and experiences that discriminate between the two ethnic groups. With respect to many of the variables that define each category, Afro-American and white maltreating mothers differ. Overall, 50 percent (16 of 32) of the characteristics discriminated between neglectful mothers of the two ethnic groups and 38 percent (12 of 32) discriminated between the two for abuse. For all three of the categories, these differences are significantly more likely to be a result of the black maltreating mothers, rather than the white maltreating mothers, differing from their nonmaltreating counterparts. For example, of the eight social functioning characteristics that discriminated between black and white neglectors, seven were due to differences between the black neglectors and their nonmaltreating peers. Unlike white maltreating mothers, black maltreating mothers compared with black control mothers reported more isolation during their growing-up years, negative perceptions of attachment to parent(s), more foster care placements, greater isolation from immediate family members and others during adulthood, more worry about relationship problems with men, severe depression, and a greater likelihood of substance abuse.

Very relevant to the implications of these findings for theory, research, and clinical practice is the reason black maltreating mothers, but not white maltreating mothers, differed from their nonmaltreating peers with respect to so many attributes and experiences. Our analyses suggest that the ability of these characteristics to discriminate were due, at least in some instances, *not* to better functioning on the part of white maltreating mothers vis-à-vis black maltreating mothers but rather to the superior functioning and less adverse growing-up experiences characteristics of the black nonmaltreating mothers compared with their white counterparts. For example, with respect to some characteristics—that is, negative perceptions of attachments to parents during the growing-up years—white maltreators and their controls differed little from the black maltreators. For other characteristics—that is, worry about relationship problems with men, severe depression, and so on—white mothers (regardless of maltreatment status) actually showed a significantly higher incidence than black mothers.

The characteristics that discriminate between the two ethnic groups for abuse are not identical to those that discriminate between the two groups for neglect. Of the twenty characteristics that functioned as discriminators, only eight were discriminators between the two races for both abuse and neglect. This group of eight included disruptions in care during childhood (living with someone other than the parent/primary caretaker for a period of time), infrequent contact with natural father during adulthood, worry about relationship problems with boyfriend, lack of a confidante, out-patient as well as in-patient treatment for depression/personal problems, and problems with alcohol use.

However, because some of the attributes and experiences that define each category were designed to measure the same construct, or the intensity of a particular problem, or the scope of a specific difficulty, it is important to obtain some idea of whether the twelve differences among specific discriminators for the two types of maltreatment are truly meaningful ones. Comparison of the characteristics that discriminated between the two racial groups for each type of maltreatment identified both similarities and differences. Overall, however, there tended to be more similarities than differences. The few possible meaningful differences included isolation from family members and use of hard drugs by neglectful mothers and an increased incidence of childhood sexual abuse and more unplanned children for abusive mothers. There are two possible interpretations of this similarity among discriminators: (1) when race is held constant at least some of the differences in the correlates of physical abuse and neglect disappear, or (2) the characteristics that we examined are not among the group of important discriminators. If we had examined stresses and strains during the period prior to maltreatment we might have found more discriminators.

Implications for Research

Conclusions regarding the implications of this study for future research and clinical practice must be drawn cautiously. In the absence of other similarly conducted, *recent* studies we are in the dark with respect to both replicability and generalizability. Our results, particularly those with respect to the white mothers, may not be generalizable. Baltimore's low-income white and black populations may differ in systematic ways from the populations of other large cities. Following are four recommendations. The first two pertain to future research on the effect of ethnicity on the correlates of child abuse and neglect. The latter two pertain to future research on child maltreatment in general.

1. *Researchers should attempt to replicate findings from existing studies as well as test characteristics that have not yet been examined.* To establish a body of knowledge about the effect of ethnicity on the correlates of child abuse and neglect it is extremely important that future studies examine the same characteristics using the same measures and the same study design as this effort and that of Giovannoni and Billingsley (1970). Such efforts will help to consolidate existing results by determining if they are replicable, and will be particularly helpful in determining if the findings of this study as well as the others are generalizable to populations other than the ones studied.

Since our findings suggest that the particular characteristics we examined are less likely to be associated with abuse and neglect by white than Afro-American mothers, it is important to expand the search for correlates to characteristics that have not yet been examined. Given the current state of knowledge it is impossible to determine whether the correlates of abuse and neglect by white mothers are fewer in number or just different than the correlates of abuse and neglect by black mothers. *However,* at this point, our best hunch is that the causes of maltreatment by white mothers may be fewer in number than those for black mothers. If white mothers as a group do demonstrate poorer social functioning and more mental health problems than black mothers as a group, it makes sense that the causes/correlates of maltreatment by these mothers may be fewer in number than those for comparable black mothers. Any added stress—such as that posed by excess numbers of children, unplanned children, eviction, and so forth—will tend to overwhelm their limited coping abilities and possibly lead to maltreatment.

2. *Researchers should move toward the use of multivariate analysis of data.* Currently, all of the studies (with the exception of that conducted by Wolock and Horowitz [1977]) have used bivariate examinations of their data. While these are helpful in identifying which of several characteristics included within a particular category (i.e., growing-up experiences, social functioning, etc.) are associated with maltreatment, they convey nothing about (1) which of the characteristics within a particular category are the best predictors of maltreatment and (2) the relationship between characteristics within and between categories. Yet, both types of information are important for developing theory and identifying possible effective prevention and treatment approaches.

3. *Researchers should seriously consider separately analyzing their data by race even if the focus of their study is not the effect of ethnicity on the correlates and consequences of maltreatment.* Many major studies (e.g., Altemeier et al., 1979; Egeland and Vaugh, 1981; Herrenkohl, Herrenkohl, and Egolf, 1983; Starr, 1982) that have included both white and Afro-American families in their samples have *not* taken race into consideration when analyzing their data. The results of the present investigation as well as the earlier studies suggest that failure to include race as a factor in maltreatment research may well increase error variance leading to a decrease in our ability to accurately determine the cause and correlates of maltreatment.

4. *Research should be conducted with samples experiencing a particular form of maltreatment rather than with a mixture of different forms regardless of the intent of the study.* Even though this study did not find many meaningful differences among the correlates of abuse and neglect once race was held constant, there were some. This finding in tandem with those of other efforts (e.g., Dietrich, Starr, and Weisfeld, 1983) suggests that the common practice of combining samples containing different types and/or mixtures of maltreatment without conducting separate analyses on the different types may well work against increasing knowledge about child maltreatment.

Implications for Prevention and Intervention Strategies

Current strategies for treating maltreating families, particularly neglectful ones, are notoriously unsuccessful (Daro, 1985). In fact, in a recent article entitled, "Is Treatment Too Late? What Ten Years of Evaluative

Research Tell Us," Cohen and Daro (1987) conclude that "putting all resources into intervention after the fact does not make much sense . . . intervention much earlier with families would produce better results" (p. 440).

Consequently, one of our most important mandates for the future is the identification of effective prevention strategies and the target populations at which they should be aimed. This does not mean, however, that the search for effective treatments is unimportant. With the seemingly ever-increasing numbers of families that are coming to the attention of child protective services, we also need to continue our search for strategies that will reduce recidivism. While this study does not warrant *any* conclusions about the causes of maltreatment by families of the two different races, findings are not totally without implications for primary, secondary, and tertiary prevention.

Targeting Prevention Efforts

This study's results suggest that the target populations for prevention efforts may need to differ by race. As a group, the population of very low-income white mothers (at least, in Baltimore) appears to be functioning quite a bit poorer than the population of comparable black mothers, suggesting that they may be at much higher risk for maltreatment than black mothers. Supportive of this possibility are findings from the First National Study of the Incidence and Severity of Child Abuse and Neglect (NIS-1) (Burgdorf, 1981), which showed that low-income white families have significantly higher rates of child maltreatment than comparable poor black families.

On the basis of our findings and those from NIS-1, we think that the most cost-effective use of resources would be to target the entire population of low-income white mothers but only a subgroup of the low-income black population. Perhaps the best subgroup of black mothers to target, at least according to our findings, is teenagers, particularly those who bore their first child prior to eighteen, have a history of adverse growing up experiences, are poorly attached to their primary caretaker, lack close personal relationships, and are not in very frequent contact with their families.

Family Planning—Prevention Potential

All of the maltreating mothers had more live births than their non-maltreating counterparts, and neglectful mothers of both races as well as white abusive mothers had more unplanned live births than their nonmaltreating peers. With respect to primary prevention, widespread family planning outreach, education, and special forms of assistance aimed at the target groups may well help to prevent the birth of unplanned children and, as a result, the excess numbers of children who are so likely to overwhelm the coping abilities of women whose ability to care for children is already compromised by their own adverse growing-up experiences and poor social functioning.

With respect to secondary prevention, special efforts need to be made to identify high-risk teenage black mothers, ones who have the characteristics identified above, at the birth of their first child. Provision of a special package of services, including psychosocial support and family planning assistance, may well decrease the probability that these mothers will eventually maltreat.

With respect to tertiary prevention, it is crucial that child protective service caseworkers assess the family planning adequacy of all clients regardless of race. Mothers who continue to bear children are increasing their own risk for maltreatment recidivism. A fairly recent study (Johnson and L'Esperance, 1984) of factors associated with recurrences of abuse and neglect revealed that one of the best predictors was large numbers of children. Unpublished findings from the data set that supported this study show that mothers who bear children *after* the first instance of child maltreatment are at greatly increased risk for recidivism and chronic neglect.

Attention to Maternal Depression—
Potential Prevention

The psychiatric literature (e.g., Longfellow, Zelkowitz, and Saunders, 1981; Weissman, Paykel, and Klerman, 1972) has consistently documented that depressed mothers are more likely than nondepressed ones to be hostile, rejecting, and indifferent to their children and to be neglectful especially with respect to feeding and supervision. A recent report by Zuravin (1990) showed that mothers who score as moderately depressed on the Beck Depression Scale are at risk for physical violence to their children while mothers who score as severely depressed are at very high risk of verbal abuse of their children, but not physical violence. Given these findings, the serious depression that is common to a large majority of white mothers provides clinicians in primary care pediatric and general medicine clinics as well as community mental health centers with an excellent means for identifying mothers who may be at high risk for child maltreatment. When depressed mothers have many children, are socially isolated, have conflictual relationships with their boyfriends, a history of adverse growing-up experiences, and no one to help with child care, clinicians should be particularly concerned about maltreatment and make an expressed effort to (1) explore with the mother how she is feeling about the stress associated with caring for her children, (2) watch her and her children very carefully for signs of child maltreatment, and (3) provide extra services, particularly ones designed to provide help with child care.

With respect to tertiary prevention, child protective service case-workers need to be very alert to the level of depression characteristics of each of their maltreating mothers regardless of race. It is conceivable that maternal depression may help to explain, at least in part, the very notable lack of success associated with child protective service interventions. If no one realizes the extent of the mother's depression and/or helps her to get appropriate treatment, maltreatment is not likely to abate until the problem abates, and may recur when and if the depressive symptoms return. Consequently, it is particularly important that child protective service programs routinely incorporate into their intake procedure mental health assessments for maltreating mothers and assure that psychiatric/psychological consultation is routinely available to caseworkers and their supervisors.

Appendix 3–1

The Schneider-Helfer Index included the following six items:

1. My father and I have always gotten along well.
2. My mother and I have always gotten along well.
3. Although my mother tried to make helpful hints to me, it always ended up sounding like criticism.
4. The main thing that I remember from my childhood is the love and warm feelings my parents showed me.
5. I have always been very close to my mother.
6. As a child I often felt that no one paid much attention to what I wanted and needed.

Response alternatives to these items were strongly agree (given a numerical rating of strongly agree (5), agree (4), neither agree nor disagree (3), disagree (2), and strongly disagree (1). To create the index score all items stated in the negative were reversed and then the numerical values attached to each mother's statements were added. Thus the higher the index score the stronger the attachment.

Part III
Interspousal Violence

4
Victimization of Mothers of Abused Children: A Controlled Study

Linda McKibben
Edward De Vos
Eli H. Newberger

W ith the publication twenty-seven years ago by Kempe and colleagues (1962) of the influential paper, "The Battered Child Syndrome," a diagnostic concept was coined that stipulated a causal connection between the aggressive actions of a perpetrator (a parent or foster parent) and the symptoms of a child victim. In the intervening years, the notion has been formalized in laws obliging physicans and others to report child abuse, and the concept has been expanded in clinical studies and legal definitions of child abuse (Newberger and Bourne, 1978).

An important conceptual advance was made in 1980 with the publication of the Straus, Gelles, and Steinmetz (1980) national survey of family violence, in which parent to child violence was perceived as one among many modes of physical aggression within families. Violence between parents was estimated to be as frequent as, or more frequent than, violence toward children. Violence between parents and toward children was estimated from interviews to be related. Women who were victims of severe violence, for example, were 150 percent more likely to use severe violence in resolving conflicts with their children than women who were not.

A recent review of data from studies concerning the posited intergenerational transmission of violence suggests that minimally 30 percent of children will express toward their own offspring physical or sexual abuse or extreme neglect similar to that which they had suffered (Kaufman and Zigler, 1980).

Reprinted with permission from *Pediatrics* 84 (3), 531–35.

This work was supported, in part, by grants from the National Center on Child Abuse and Neglect (90-CA-1184) and the National Institute of Mental Health (5 T32 MH 18265).

We thank Robert M. Reece, M.D., for helpful support in the formulation and conduct of the research.

Although a literature is developing regarding the psychological impact of violence between adults on children, there are few reports of physical victimization of both children and mothers (Pascoe et al., 1981; Elbow, 1982; Nelson, 1984; Jaffe et al., 1985; 1986; Hershorn and Rosenbaum, 1985; Stark and Flitcraft, 1988). With a view to exploring the extent of overlap of maternal and child abuse, a retrospective case-control study was designed.

Methods

Case Selection

Cases were selected through a multitiered review of all child abuse reports filed at Boston City Hospital during the six-month period, January 1, 1986, through July 6, 1986. Given the purpose of this study, only those reports filed by emergency room staff were retained for further review; there were ninety-five such filings (59 percent of the total).

These reports were evaluated by the following inclusion criteria: (1) physical examination findings positive for signs of physical abuse except where sexual abuse was the chief complaint; (2) presence of biologic mother at the time of the child protective report; and (3) injuries that were not self-inflicted. Reasons for exclusion included injury known to be inflicted by day-care worker or a case that was deemed "unsubstantiated" after investigation by the Massachusetts Department of Social Services.

On the basis of these inclusion and exclusion criteria, sixty-three case reports were retained for further review. The mothers' charts were then obtained through the following process. First, the mother's name and address, as listed on the child abuse report, were compared with those of the insurance guarantor (usually the mother) on the child's computerized demographic record. The mother's social security number was often available from this source. Subsequently, the mother's name was entered into the hospital's computerized data base. These records were reviewed and the mother's identity was verified through a comparison of social security number, address, and consistency of information in the medical chart itself (e.g., birth records of the child).

Following a definite match, the medical record number was retrieved and the medical chart requested. Sixteen mothers had no medical record numbers at Boston City Hospital and presumably had not received medical care there. Forty-seven charts were requested; five of these were not available after two requests from the medical records department. The remaining forty-two charts were reviewed. Ten of these medical records were excluded because of insufficient information.

Control Selection

Control mothers were also selected based on initial review of children's records. The emergency room daily logs were scanned for records of children with nontraumatic complaints who had sought medical attention within the same month as the index case. In addition to time of emergency room visit, the children were also matched for age, sex, race, and socioeconomic status (dependency on Medicaid was used as a proxy for low socioeconomic status). The same process used to locate a case mother's chart was used to retrieve the control mother's medical chart.

Chart Review

Thirty-two cases and thirty-two control mothers' charts were evaluated and assigned to one of four categories of maternal victimization: (1) diagnostic, (2) suggestive, (3) notable for relationship problems and psychosomatic complaints, and (4) nonsuggestive. These categories were operationalized using the following criteria: (1) diagnostic—a chart with explicit data both confirming intentional physical trauma and identifying the perpetrator as an intimate man; (2) suggestive—a chart with documented intentional physical abuse but with no specification of the perpetrator's identity, either as man or woman, acquaintance or stranger; (3) relationship problem—a chart without specific indication of physical abuse but rather of significant marital relationship problems with such associated psychosomatic complaints as hyperventilation syndrome, depression, and tension headaches; and (4) nonsuggestive—a chart with no evidence of physical abuse and/or relationship problems. (It should be recalled that charts with insufficient information for evaluation were excluded before this review.) The following additional information was extracted from the medical record: mother's date of birth, race, employment status, type of health insurance coverage, and number of other children.

The data were gathered from the medical records by one of us, who was unaware of the hypothesis and the classification status of case and control mothers. Because the first eligible control mother was used, however, there was little opportunity for bias in the selection of the comparison group. The possible intrusion of bias in the coding of data from the records was addressed in meetings among the coauthors as the study proceeded.

The study design was reviewed and approved by the chief of the

Boston City Hospital's Child Protection Program, the chairman of the Department of Pediatrics, and the Institutional Review Board before the initiation of the research.

Statistical Methods

Data analysis was done with statistical methods appropriate to the level of measurement of the variables and to the sampling design of the study. The appropriate unit of analysis for the central questions in this retrospective study was the matched pairs that constituted the sample rather than individual subjects. Thus, for example, the major question regarding differences in the presence or absence of violence against mothers of case children and control children was addressed using McNemar's test with a continuity correction (Fleiss, 1981). Where the variable being considered was at least interval level, as in the comparison between cases and controls regarding maternal age, a paired t-test was used.

Results

The child's record served as the basis for selection of control children's records. They were matched for sex, age, race, socioeconomic status, and time of emergency room visit. The matching variables are compared in table 4–1.

Table 4–1
Case and Control Children Variables That Served as the Basis for Matching

	Cases Children	Cases Children
Sex (No.[%])		
Male	15 (46.9)	15 (46.9)
Female	17 (53.1)	17 (53.1)
Age		
Mean	7.04 y	6.89 y
Range	6 mo–17 y	3 mo–16 y
Race/ethnicity (No.[%])		
Black	23 (71.9)	
Hispanic	7 (21.9)	
White	2 (6.3)	
Health coverage (No.[%])		
Medicaid	25 (78.1)	25 (80.6)
Blue Cross/Blue Shield	2 (6.3)	4 (12.9)
Private	3 (9.4)	1 (3.2)
Health maintenance organization	2 (6.3)	1 (3.2)

All control children were seen in the pediatric emergency room within one month of their target case child's visit. The criteria for matching were adequately met. Characteristics of case mothers and control mothers are compared in table 4–2.

Although case mothers were somewhat younger than control mothers, the difference was not statistically significant (paired t = −1.83, P = .08). Similarly, although case mothers were twice as likely to be employed than control mothers, the difference again was not significant (McNemar's test, x^2 = 3.125). Case and control mothers did differ significantly, however, on marital status and parity. Fewer than one of five case mothers were married (19.4 percent) in comparison to nearly half of the control mothers (45.2 percent) (McNemar's test, x^2 = 4.083, P < .05). Similarly, case mothers had more children (1.28 versus 0.56 children); the difference was significant (paired t = 2.70, P = .011).

The central focus of this study was the relationship between child abuse and violence against mothers in mother-child pairs in which a protective report was filed on behalf of the child at emergency room visit. The cross-tabulation of maternal victimization categories for case and control pairs is given in table 4–3. The marginal totals indicate that case pairs were far more likely to be classified in the suggestive and diagnostic categories (37.5 percent and 21.8 percent, respectively) than were the control pairs (9.4 percent and 3.1 percent, respectively).

The scale of violence against mothers, however, is not really ordinal. The amount of violence within the suggestive category may have been greater than within the diagnostic category; the difference was that a perpetrator was identified in the latter and not in the former.

Table 4–2
Case and Control Mother Variables

	Case Mothers	Control Mothers
Employment status (No. [%])		
Unemployed	22 (68.7)	28 (87.5)
Employed	10 (31.3)	4 (12.5)
Age (y)		
Mean	28.81	31.25
Range	17–49	17–51
Marital status (No.[%])		
Married	6 (19.4)	14 (45.2)
Single	25 (80.6)	17 (54.8)
Other children (No.)		
Mean	1.28	0.56
Range	0–4	0–3

Table 4–3
Cross-Tabulation of Victimization Categories for Case and Control Mothers (Full Categorization)

Case Category	Control Category				Total No. (%)
	Non-suggestive	Relationship Problems	Suggestive	Diagnostic	
Nonsuggestive	6	1	0	1	8 (25.0)
Relationship problems	5	0	0	0	0 (15.6)
Suggestive	9	1	2	0	12 (37.5)
Diagnostic	5	1	1	0	7 (21.8)

Thus, there were alternative methods for collapsing the table, depending on emphasis.

A cross-tabulation of dichotomized maternal victimization categories that identify the mother as victim, disregarding the identity of the perpetrator and his relationship to the mother, is presented in table 4–4. Thus, the diagnostic and suggestive categories were pooled, and relationship problems and nonsuggestive categories were pooled.

The case pairs were far more likely to be victims of violence than were the control pairs (59.4 percent versus 12.0 percent, respectively). One of eight control mothers was a victim of violence, an impressive prevalence, and nearly three of five case mothers were victimized. The difference was highly significant (McNemar's test, $x^2 = 11.53$, $P < .001$).

The difference between case and control pairs with respect to the victim of violence dichotomy as shown in table 4–4 was striking. The result requires no elaboration with respect to the child-focused variables that served as the basis for case and control selection. Nevertheless, given the differences between case and control pairs on mother-level variables (vis-à-vis number of other children, maternal age, and marital status), the difference needs to be examined in more detail.

A significant difference was noted earlier between case mothers and control mothers with respect to the number of other children. A one-

Table 4–4
Cross-Tabulation of Victimization Categories for Case and Control Mothers (Mother as Victim Dichotomy)

Case Category	Control Category		Total No. (%)
	Victim	Nonvictim	
Victim	3	16	19 (59.4)
Nonvictim	1	12	13 (40.6)

way analysis of variance was performed on the case data to evaluate the relationship between this variable and maternal victimization. The analysis revealed no overall significance when using the full four-category victimization scale. However, case mothers categorized as suggestive and diagnostic victims of violence had more children than did mothers in the other two categories. The dichotomized violence scheme was employed and a t-test was used to compare victims of violence (mean = 1.47 children) with nonvictims (mean = 1.00 children); the difference was not significant (t = 1.158).

A significant difference was also noted earlier in the ages of case and control mothers as analysis was conducted of case data to determine whether within that group any relationship existed between maternal victimization and maternal age. Again, the overall differences using all four violence categories were not statistically significant. However, victimized case mothers appeared somewhat older than nonvictimized mothers. A t-test on the dichotomized grouping indicated that victimized case mothers (mean age 30.84 years) were significantly older than nonvictimized case mothers (mean age 25.85 years) (t = 2.213, P = .034). For control mothers, no differences in age were found.

Marital status, as well, demonstrated a significant relationship to case-control status. The case data were analyzed to test whether or not a relationship existed between victimization and marital status. The results appear in table 4–5. Whereas 16.7 percent of married case mothers were victims of violence, 68.0 percent of single case mothers were victims, more than four times the rate (x^2 = 5.236, P = .022).

A similar analysis was conducted for control mothers. Although the number of control mothers who were victims of violence was small, the results were consistent with the case data. Fewer than one in four single mothers was a victim of violence, although all four victims were single; none of the married control mothers were victims (Fisher's exact test [one-tail], P = .076).

Given the original focus of this study and the relationship between marital status and victimization, an analysis was performed limited to case-control pairs of the same marital status. In this subsample, case pairs were again far more likely to be victims of violence than were

Table 4–5
Victimization and Marital Status of Mothers of Abused Children

Child	Mother's Marital Status	
	Married	Single
Victim (No. [%])	1 (16.7)	17 (68)
Nonvictim (No. [%])	5 (83.3)	8 (32)

control pairs (66.7 percent versus 22.2 percent, respectively). Six of nine mothers of case children were victimized, in comparison with two of nine mothers of control children. The difference was again significant (McNemar's test, $x^2 = 4.90$, P < .05).

Discussion

The 59.4 percent concurrence of maternal victimization and child abuse in this study is impressive and worrisome. The findings exceed previous estimates in the literature.

Stark and Flitcraft (1988) reviewed the medical records of mothers of children referred to a child protective team at Yale–New Haven Hospital during one year without restriction to emergency room visits. Their "positive" and "probable" groups were defined similarly to our categories of diagnostic and suggestive, respectively. In their study, these two groups accounted for 41 percent of the cases of victimization. Their positive group, in a manner similar to our own diagnostic group, accounted for approximately 25 percent of the cases; in our own, the result was 23 percent. However, our suggestive group was more than double their probable group (40 percent versus 16 percent, respectively). Our finding of three times the amount of violent marital conflict may signify greater risk for the Boston mothers, assuming that health care providers in both locations are similarly documenting these issues. This comparison suggests that traumatized children visiting inner-city emergency rooms are at high risk for exposure to violence against their mothers.

Pascoe et al. (1981) reviewed records of children who were referred during a two-year period to a child-protection team in North Carolina, where a majority of families were rural. Their results revealed a higher prevalence of wife abuse in women with multiple pregnancies and in alcoholic families. Overall, they found a 40 percent prevalence of wife abuse when the child's records were supplemented with information from social workers involved with the cases. The authors suggested that this rate was high partly on the basis that the social workers were attuned to family violence issues.

As a corollary, Stark and Flitcraft's (1988) probable and our suggestive groups may also be composed of women abused by male partners; but their medical records may not document the abuse sufficiently. Many health care providers have insufficient knowledge and understanding of family violence (Snyder and Newberger, 1986) and many victims seek medical care with nontraumatic complaints (Goldberg and Tomlanovich, 1984).

The finding of an association between maternal victimization and single marital status corroborates the findings of Goldberg and Tomlanovich (1984). They demonstrated an increased risk of spouse abuse in unmarried women.

More research concerning the convergence of child abuse and spouse abuse would appear urgently to be needed. From so few published data, nearly all composed principally of families in poverty, little can be confidently generalized. Nor are any of the reports able sufficiently to probe the kinds of information about family life that would be most useful to practitioners: information concerning the child: medical and developmental history and present status, handicapping conditions, quality of relationships to caregivers; information concerning the mother: medical and psychologic history and present status, family and social history including victimization, perceptions of people and institutions who may have tried to help her, history of the spousal relationship, and the priority and meaning of the abused child; information concerning the abuser(s): medical and psychologic history and present status, family and social history including victimization, history of previous relationships with women and children, educational and employment status, use and abuse of psychoactive substances.

To address the problem of child and spouse abuse in clinical practice, we recommend the wider use of domestic violence protocols in adult and pediatric medical care. The systematic collection of data and engagement of protective interventions should include both children and their mothers.

Emergency room staff should be equipped with basic knowledge of the legal rights of domestic violence victims and their roles as legally mandated reporters of child abuse and neglect. In addition, they should be advised to document their professional interactions fully.

Conclusion

The striking overlap in this study between the victimization of children and their mothers suggests a need for a serious redefinition of both problems focusing on violence in the family. Such a family-level conceptualization may be difficult to bring about in today's environment of specialized services and smaller human service budgets. But we believe that certain steps can be taken. Just as the staff of pediatric emergency rooms can take the time, pursue the training, and advocate for increased access to services to contend with the realities of mothers' lives, so may the professionals who hear mothers' complaints, from physicians and nurses, to battered women's shelter workers, begin systematically to consider the safety and welfare of their offspring.

5

Spousal Violence:
A Cross-Racial Perspective

Lettie L. Lockhart

Woman battering, also known as wife abuse, spousal violence, and domestic violence, is a well-established tradition in our society (Greenblat, 1983). Throughout most of our history, violence among intimates was considered rare, harmless, and/or necessary. In fact, only in the past one hundred years have American men lost the legal right to use physical violence to control their wives.

Data that contradict this tradition underlie contemporary efforts to change historical attitudes. For example, countless newspaper and magazine articles have presented horrifying case studies that parade dramatically before the public the high rates and devastating consequences of spousal violence. Various studies have confirmed that abuse is far from exceptional: Walker (1979) estimated that one woman in two will be abused during the course of her marriage. In 1980 Straus, Gelles, and Steinmetz reported that approximately 1.8 million wives are abused each year by their husbands. According to the U.S. Department of Justice (1986), more than one thousand women were victims of spousal homicides. From the replication of their 1975 national study, Straus and Gelles (1986) reported that rates of spousal violence are still high, but that they declined between 1975 and 1985. Straus and Gelles asserted further, "If any other crime or risk to physical well-being involved almost two million wives and husbands, plus much larger numbers at some point in their marriages, a national emergency would be declared" (1986, p. 50).

It is increasingly clear that spousal violence, once thought to be relatively rare (Gelles, 1980), actually may be a social problem of major proportions in all segments of our society, regardless of racial and/or social class background. Although spousal violence is considered a universal problem, previous investigators suggested that it is primarily a lower-class phenomenon and that minority women, especially African-American women, are abused at a disproportionately higher rate than European-American women (Straus, Gelles, and Steinmetz, 1980). Moreover, several researchers have suggested that differences in spousal violence between racial groups may be the result not of racial background but of social class or indicators of social class, such as education, income, and/or occupational status (Dobson, 1981; Lockhart, 1985; Staples, 1976a). Many of these assertions are grounded only in assumptions because very few empirical studies have been conducted on the extent and nature of spousal violence in the African-American community; nor have comparisons been made between racial groups, especially with social class differences controlled (Allen, 1979; Lockhart, 1985; 1987; Lockhart and White, 1989). The few empirical studies of spousal violence in the African-American community or across racial groups have suffered from poor problem conceptualization, faulty data collection procedures, inappropriate data analyses, and ideologically biased interpretations of findings (Straus, Gelles, and Steinmetz, 1980). The literature reveals that these and other research deficiencies combine to hamper and obscure our understanding of racial differences and of the manifestations of spousal violence in our society.

Marital Violence and Race

A comprehensive assessment of the effects of race on spousal violence must be based on a careful examination of previous research on case reports, on the reporting process, and on the interpretation of these reports. Because no laws mandate the reporting of spousal violence, researchers often have relied on indirect measures such as the number of abuse allegations and calls handled by divorce courts, the police department, mental health and medical clinics, battered women's shelters, and other public social service agencies (Bard and Zacker, 1976; Boundouris, 1971; Dobash and Dobash, 1981; Gelles, 1980). Estimates of rates and conclusions regarding the extent and nature of spousal violence based on official police statistics and clinical populations do not provide an adequate basis for between-race comparisons because African-Americans and/or lower-class individuals are overrepresented in these official populations (Lockhart, 1985). Staples (1976) argues that such individuals may be overrepresented in official statistics regarding spousal violence because of their socioeconomic and colonized status rather than their race. Many researchers, using such biased data and failing to consider or control for social class differences, concluded hastily that African-American couples are more violent than European-American couples. Such conclusions prevent a more comprehensive understanding of differences and similarities between races.

The first large-scale investigation of family violence was conducted in 1976 by Straus, Gelles, and Steinmetz (1980). Their purpose was to examine the magnitude of spousal violence among Americans. Their estimates and extrapolations were based on the self-reports of 2,143 American couples (147 African-American and 1,996 non–African-American), who responded to Straus's (1979) Conflict Tactics Scales (CTS). Straus and his colleagues (1980) reported that 11 percent of the African-American women, as compared with 3 percent of the European-American women, were victims of wife abuse; they concluded that wife abuse was 400 percent more frequent among African-Americans than among European-Americans. Straus, Gelles, and Steinmetz also reported that husband abuse occurred twice as frequently among African-Americans. They suggested that the "black males could be using acts of violence on their wives to compensate for cultural deprivation of resources such as income or prestige, or else that black males' violence might be a reflection of the macho image of men that condones and encourages acts of physical aggression" (Straus, Gelles, and Steinmetz, 1980, p. 136). These researchers raised the question about culturally accepted machismo by asking, "If we argue minority males are violent because they are attempting to live up to a culturally prescribed model of aggressive and dominant male, then how do we explain the fact that black men are twice as likely as white men to be abused by their wives?" (p. 136).

It has been suggested that batterers and victims often are the product of traditional sex-role socialization (Roy, 1977). Although the present literature on spousal violence does not include African-Americans in sufficient numbers to assess the cross-cultural validity of the assertion by Straus, Gelles, and Steinmetz (1980), researchers have investigated the nature of sex-role socialization in African-American families. Lewis (1975) proposed that the male-female duality that dominates sex-role socialization in European-American families is not the same in African-American families. She suggested further that the "African-American child does distinguish between males and females, but, unlike the European-American child, he is not inculcated with standards which polarize behavioral expectations according to sex" (Lewis, 1975, p. 228).

Straus and his colleagues (1980) cautioned that "simply presenting rates of violence by race could be misleading" (p. 133). They suggested that apparent racial differences actually may be due to differences in income, education, employment status, and cultural expectations and values concerning violence. These researchers, however, failing to heed their own warning, drew conclusions about racial groups without explicitly considering possible class differences that allowed stereotypical assertions about racial differences to go unchallenged.

Cazenave and Straus (1979), using the data collected by Straus, Gelles, and Steinmetz (1980), sought to determine whether levels of spousal violence differed across racial groups and social classes. Their results showed that 8 percent more African-American husbands than European-American husbands had inflicted severe violence on their wives. When they controlled for family income, they found that African-American husbands were less likely than European-American husbands to have slapped their wives; this finding held true in all income groups except in the $6,000–11,999 range, the lowest income group. A control for the husband's occupational class also suggested that among African-American husbands whose income fell below this range, the rate of severe husband-to-wife violence and wife slapping was higher than among their European-American counterparts.

Fagen, Stewart, and Hansen (1983) collected data from 270 victims of domestic violence in order to determine which situational and background characteristics differentiated those who battered only their marital partners from those who also engaged in extradomestic violence. The results of their racial comparisons of spouse abuse revealed that European-Americans were more violent both inside and outside the home. Fagen and his colleagues (1983) cautioned that the issue of race remains enigmatic and warrants further investigation.

The African-American community, like the European-American community, is highly diverse in regard to economic status, family structure, occupational pursuits, life-style, and the extent and nature of spousal violence (White, 1981). Sweeping statements about racial groups on any of these dimensions are bound to be damaging oversimplifications. The present investigation is designed to enrich our understanding of these issues and thus to lay the foundation for more rigorous research on spousal violence between racial groups and across social class backgrounds. This comparative study explores social class differences in rates and patterns of spousal violence across two racial groups. Specifically, I sought to answer the following questions:

1. Are there any significant race and race-by-class differences in the extent and nature of spousal violence?

2. Are there any significant race and race-by-class differences in the sources of conflict that lead to spousal violence?

3. What are the effects of race, social class, violence in family of origin, and level of marital satisfaction on the extent and nature of spousal violence?

Methodology

The Sample

The author used a survey designed to compare the incidence of marital violence among 307 African-American women and European-American women from a range of social classes.[1] The sampling procedure deliberately sought heterogeneity in order to elucidate theory on this topic (Cook and Campbell, 1979). Rather than using a strictly proportionate sample, the procedure was designed to achieve as much variation as possible in social class characteristics and in other background variables.[2] The author sought approximately equal numbers of African-American and European-American women across the three social class positions (upper, middle, and lower) who did not constitute a clinical population. She desired heterogeneity in the background variables as well as in the principal explanatory variable of social class, so that if these variables had a significant association with the incidence of marital violence, the sample would contain enough variability to reflect their actual explanatory power in statistical analyses.

During the winter of 1982, the author made personal contact with groups to collect the data in a major southeastern metropolitan city. She collected data from seventy different community groups ranging in size from four to forty-six participants. All groups were contacted in advance, were informed of the nature of the study, and were invited to participate. The return rate was approximately 88 percent.

The respondents were African-American and European-American women who were legally married to or cohabiting with their marital partners.[3] They represented a cross section of ages, educational levels, occupations, and social class positions. Of the 155 African-American respondents, 35.5 percent (n = 55) were upper class, 36.8 percent (n = 57) were middle class, 27.7 percent (n = 43) were lower class. Of the European-American respondents, 30.9 percent (n = 47) were upper class, 38.8 percent (n = 59) were middle class, and 30.3 percent (n = 46) were lower class. Social class was measured by Hollingshead and Redlich's (1958) two-factor index of social position.

Sixty-eight percent (n = 105) of the African-American respondents and 52.9 percent (n = 82) of their marital partners had more than a high school education, as did 76 percent (n = 116) of the European-American respondents and 73.7 percent (n = 112) of their marital partners. The difference between African-American and European-American respondents was not significant, but there was a significant difference between their marital partners' education levels. Sixty-three percent (n = 97) of the African-American respondents and their marital partners were in clerical/sales or lower occupational categories on the Hollingshead occupational index. Seventy-one percent (n = 108) of the European-American respondents and 54 percent (n = 82) of their marital partners were in such positions. Significant occupational differences existed between African-American and European-American respondents as well as between their marital partners. The average age was 36.1 (sd = 10.2) for African-American respondents and 37.5 (sd = 13.5) for European-American respondents; the age differences between the two groups was not significant. The average length of the relationship was 11.8 years among African-American respondents and 13.5 years among European-American respondents; this difference, however, was not significant.

Dependent and Independent Variables

The first section of the questionnaire asked for demographic information. The second section sought data on violence in the family of origin (VFO), which was used as an independent variable. Previous research has suggested that an individual may learn marital violence as a child in a violent home and may repeat it as an adult (Gelles, 1974; Petersen, 1980). Petersen (1980) used a sample of 602 married or formerly married women in Maryland to determine whether violence is learned from the family of origin and transmitted across generations, and to ascertain the relationship between wife abuse and social class. He concluded that women who grew up in violent homes reported more abuse than did women from nonabusive families of origin. Petersen concluded further that women of lower-class background who were raised in violent homes were far more likely to report that they were victims of wife abuse than were middle- and upper-class women who did not come from violent families of origin. In this study, violence in the family of origin was defined as violence between the respondents' parents or between the respondents' partners' parents during the time when the respondents or their partners lived in their respective parents' homes. This investigation used only data pertaining to violence in the respondents' partners' family of origin. The author used violence in the partners' family of origin in order to understand more clearly how witnessing marital violence by males affects current intimate relationships, and to learn whether racial and race-by-class differences exist.

The third section of the questionnaire requested information on sources of conflict and on level of marital satisfaction. Marital satisfaction was measured by the Index of Marital Satisfaction (IMS) (Hudson, 1982), which has an alpha reliability coefficient of .94 and good construct validity. For the purpose of this investigation, IMS findings were grouped into two categories: respondents who scored below 35 were defined as not having a clinically significant marital satisfaction problem, whereas those whose score was above 35 were classified as having such a problem. The fourth section of the questionnaire requested information on the nature and the extent of husband-to-wife (CTS-HWV) and severe husband-to-wife (CTS-SHWV) violence, using Straus's CTS (Straus, 1979). These measures were the principal dependent variables in this investigation (Straus, Gelles, and Steinmetz, 1980).

Findings

Incidence of Husband-to-Wife Violence

As shown by the data presented in table 5–1, 35.5 percent of the respondents reported that they were victims of one or more of the types of physical attacks that fall under the operational definition of husband-to-wife violence. Among the respondents who reported violence in their marital relationship, husband-to-wife violence was not an isolated incident; the median occurrence was four times during the year before the investigation.

There was no significant difference between the proportion of African-American (35.4 percent) and of European-American (35.5 percent) women who reported that they had been victims of husband-to-wife violence during the previous year (X^2 = .001; df = 1; p > .05). Additional comparisons between the two racial groups show that among the abused respondents, there was no statistically significant difference between the median number of times when African-Americans (median = 3.6) and European-Americans (median = 4.3) were victims of husband-to-wife violence (X^2 =.73; df = 1; p > .05).

Table 5–2 presents the racial comparison of incidence of husband-to-wife violence, with controls for social class. Although a smaller proportion of upper-class African-American women (18.2 percent) than of upper-class European-American women (29.8 percent) reported that they were victims of husband-to-wife violence, the 11.6 percent difference was not statistically significant (X^2 = 1.90; df = 1; p > .05). In addition, there was no significant difference between the median number of times when abused upper-class African-American women (median = 5.8) and abused upper-class European-American women (median = 3.5) reported that they were victims of husband-to-wife violence (X^2 =.44; df = 1; p > .05).

A significantly larger proportion of middle-class African-American women (45.6 percent) than of middle-class European-American women (27.1 percent) reported that they were victims of husband-to-wife violence (X^2 = 4.29; df = 1; p > .05), but the median difference between the two groups was not significant (X^2 =.04; df = 1; p > .05). Fifty-two percent of the lower-class European-American women, as compared with 44.2 percent of the lower-class African-American women, reported that they were victims of husband-to-wife violence; this difference was not significant (X^2 =.57; df = 1; p > .05). The median difference between the number of times when lower-class African-American (median = 3.8) and European-American (median = 6.2) women reported that they were victims of husband-to-wife violence also was not significant (X^2 = 3.5; df = 1; p > .05).

Table 5-1
Respondents' Reports of Husband-to-Wife Violence by Respondents' Race and Median Number of Incidents

	Respondents							Incidents		
	African-American		European-American					African-American	European-American	Total Sample
Husband-to-Wife Violence Index	n	%	n	%	No. of Women	% of Total Sample		Median	Median	Median
Total with experiences	55	35.48	54	35.53	109	35.5		3.6	4.3	4.8
Threw something at wife	26	16.80	23	15.10	49	16.0		2.7	3.4	3.4
Pushed, grabbed, or shoved wife	48	31.00	49	32.20	97	31.6		2.3	2.8	2.6
Slapped wife	26	16.80	28	18.40	54	17.6		2.1	2.4	2.2
Kicked, bit, or hit with fist	15	9.70	20	23.20	35	11.4		2.1	2.7	2.5
Hit or tried to hit with something	10	6.50	19	12.50	29*	9.5		2.5	3.3	3.2
Beat up wife	11	7.10	11	7.20	22	7.2		2.3	2.3	2.3
Threatened wife with a knife or gun	4	2.60	8	5.30	12	3.2		2.0	2.5	2.5
Used a knife or gun	—	—	4	2.60	4**	1.3		—	1.5	1.5
Total with no experiences	100	64.52	98	64.47	198	64.5				
Total sample	155	100.00	152	100.00	307	100.0		.27	.28	.28

Note: The chi-square test was used to test differences between the racial groups.

*p ≤ .10
**p ≤ .05

Table 5-2
Respondents' Reports of Husband-to-Wife Violence by Race and Social Class

Husband-to-Wife Violence Index	African-American Respondents' Social Class						European-American Respondents' Social Class						Total Number of Women	Percentage Total Women
	Upper		Middle		Lower		Upper		Middle		Lower			
	n	%	n	%	n	%	n	%	n	%	n	%		
Had experiences	10	18.2	26	45.6	19	44.2	14	29.8	16	27.1	24	52.2	109	35.5
(Median number of incidents)		(5.8)		(2.5)		(3.8)		(3.5)		(3.5)		(6.2)		(4.8)
No experiences	45	81.8	31	54.4	24	55.8	33	70.2	43	72.9	22	47.8	198	64.5
Total	55	100.0	57	100.0	43	100.0	47	100.00	59	100.0	46	100.0	307	100.0

Note: The chi-square statistic was used to test significant differences; p ≤ .05.

Source of Conflict by Race, with Controls for Class

Were there any significant associations between sources of conflicts and respondents' race or across race, while social class position was controlled? The data presented (all percentages sum to 100 percent for each class position) are only for those sources of conflicts where the author found significant associations (p ≤ .05) between the racial groups.

As shown by Kendall's Tau-b, racial identification had low positive associations with sources of conflict. The Tau-b for each of the significant associations between the African-American and the European-American respondents were the man's job (Tau-b = .14, p = .008), decision making (Tau-b =.10, p = .03), friends (Tau-b = .14, p = .007), and relatives (Tau-b = .11, p = .02). Marital conflicts around the man's employment and friends and the man's job had the strongest associations with race, whereas conflicts around decision making and relatives produced the weakest significant associations. In addition, the positive direction of these associations showed that European-American respondents tended to report more conflicts in these areas than did African-American respondents. When respondents were asked how often these disagreements resulted in violence, no significant difference was found between the two racial groups (Tau-b = .10, p < .05).

Among upper-class respondents, more European-American than African-American respondents reported more conflict around housekeeping responsibilities (Tau-b = .20, p < .02) and decision making (Tau-b = .16, p < .05). Middle-class African-American respondents reported more conflict around the man's jealousy (Tau-b = .15, p < .05) than did middle-class European-American respondents. Middle-class European-American respondents, however, reported more conflicts around the children (Tau-b = .16, p < .04) than did their middle-class African-American counterparts. More lower-class European-American than African-American respondents reported conflicts regarding the man's job (Tau-b = .21, p < .03), friends (Tau-b = .26, p < .007), and relatives (Tau-b = .23, p < .02). There was no significant race-by-class difference in the frequency with which respondents reported that these conflicts resulted in violence.

Effects of Race, Class, Marital Satisfaction, and Violence in the Marital Partner's Family of Origin

To identify the distinctive contributions of each of the independent variables on current levels of husband-to-wife violence (HWV) and severe husband-to-wife violence (SHWV), the author conducted hierarchical analyses of variance (ANOVA). The model presented in table 5–3 was significant (F = 5.35; df = 20; p ≤ .0001) and explained 53 percent of the variance in husband-to-wife violence among the respondents in this investigation. The simple main effect of race was not related significantly to husband-to-wife violence. The main effects, however, of social class, marital satisfaction, and one category of violence in the family of origin (VFO)—partner's father abused partner's mother (PFAPM)—were related significantly to the incidence of such violence. Lower-class respondents' mean score for husband-to-wife violence (X = 13.2; sd = 8.6) was significantly higher than that for upper-class respondents (X = 9.0; sd = 2.6). In addition, respondents who re-

Table 5–3
Analysis of Variance Summary Table: Husband's Use of Violence by Race, Social Class, Marital Satisfaction, and Violence in the Family of Origin (Partner's Parents)

Sources of Variation	Sum of Squares	df	Mean Squares	F-Ratio
Main Effects	1378.22	6	229.70	11.26**
Race	30.85	1	30.85	1.51
Social class	362.59	2	181.30	8.88**
Marital satisfaction (MS)	694.00	1	694.00	34.00**
Partner's father abused partner's mother (PFAPM)	281.89	1	281.89	13.81**
Partner's mother abused partner's father (PMAPF)	8.89	1	8.89	.44
Two-Way Interactions	825.05	14	58.93	2.89**
Race by class	40.25	2	20.13	.99
Race by marital satisfaction	55.66	1	55.66	2.73
Race by partner's father abused partner's mother (PFAPM)	.50	1	.50	.02
Race by partner's mother abused partner's father (PMAPF)	68.21	1	68.21	3.34
Class by marital satisfaction	242.56	2	121.28	5.94*
Class by partner's father abused partner's mother	97.53	2	48.76	2.39
Class by partner's mother abused partner's father	80.28	2	40.14	1.79
Marital satisfaction by partner's father abused partner's mother (PFAPM)	1.10	1	1.10	.05
Marital satisfaction by partner's mother abused partner's father (PMAPF)	49.65	1	49.65	2.43
Partner's father abused partner's mother (PFAPM) by partner's mother abused partner's mother	189.31	1	189.31	9.30*
Explained	2203.27	20	110.16	5.40*
Residual	1980.13	97	20.41	
Total	4183.48	117	35.76	

R = .73
R^2 = .52
* $p < .01$
** $p < .001$

ported more marital discord (X = 14.9; sd = 3.4) had higher husband-to-wife violence scores than respondents who reported lower levels of marital discord (X= 8.7; sd = 2.6). As for the main effect of violence in the family of origin, respondents who stated that their mothers-in-law were victims of spousal violence reported higher levels of husband-to-wife violence in their current marital relationships (X = 15.5; sd = 9.8) than did respondents who did not make such a statement (X = 9.0; sd = 3.5).

Three significant two-way interactions were presented in the model. The interactional effect of social class and levels of marital satisfaction on incidence of husband-to-wife violence show that lower-class respondents who reported higher levels of marital discord reported higher levels of husband-to-wife violence (X = 19.2; sd = 10.9) than did their middle-class (X = 12.2; sd = 8.5) and upper-class (X = 11.2; sd = 4.7) counterparts who reported marital discord. Respondents who reported abuse of both mother-in-law and father-in-law (X = 14.6; sd = 9.8) reported higher levels of husband-to-wife violence in their relationship than did respondents who reported no marital violence in their partner's family of origin (X = 8.6; sd = 2.1).

The Effect of Race, Social Class, Marital
Satisfaction, and Violence in the Family of Origin

Severe husband-to-wife violence, also known as wife beating, consists of the last five items of Straus's Conflict Tactics Scale (kicking, hitting, or hitting wife with a fist; hitting or trying to hit with something; beating; threatening with a knife or gun; using a knife or gun) (Straus, 1979). The model presented in table 5–4 examines the effects of race, class, marital satisfaction, and violence in the family of origin on the incidence of several forms of husband-to-wife violence. The model was significant (F = 5.31; df = 20; p ≤ .0001) and explained 52 percent of the variance in these forms of violence. The main effect of race was not significant, but the mean effects of social class, marital satisfaction, and violence in the family of origin (VFO)—partner's mother abused by partner's father—were related significantly to incidence of severe husband-to-wife violence. An examination of the raw means reveals that lower-class respondents (X = 6.7; sd = 4.2) reported higher levels of wife beating than did their middle-class (X = 5.6; sd = 2.8) and upper-class (X = 5.2; sd = 1.5) counterparts. Respondents who reported higher levels of marital discord also reported higher levels of wife beating. Further, respondents who reported that their mothers-in-law were victims of violence reported higher levels of wife beating (X = 8.2; sd = 4.9) than did respondents who reported that their mothers-in-law were not victims of violence (X = 5.1; sd = 1.8).

Five significant two-way interactions were reflected in this model.

Table 5–4
Analysis of Variance Summary Table: Husband's Use of Violence by Race, Social Class, Marital Satisfaction, and Violence in the Family of Origin (Partner's Parents)

Sources of Variation	Sum of Squares	df	Mean Squares	F-Ratio
Main Effect	263.80	6	43.97	8.67***
Race	11.16	1	11.16	2.20
Social class	37.58	2	18.79	3.71*
Marital Satisfaction (MS)	128.16	1	128.16	25.29***
Partner's father abused partner's mother (PFAPM)	78.29	1	78.29	15.45***
Partner's mother abused partner's father (PMAPF)	8.61	1	8.61	1.70
Two-Way Interactions	274.43	14	19.60	3.87***
Race by class	21.30	2	10.65	2.10
Race by marital satisfaction (MS)	13.13	1	13.13	2.59
Race by partner's father abused partner's mother (PFAPM)	26.89	1	26.89	5.18*
Race by partner's mother abused partner's father (PMAPF)	.11	1	.11	.02
Class by marital satisfaction	33.75	2	16.87	3.33*
Class by partner's father abused partner's mother (PFAPM)	65.14	2	32.57	6.43**
Class by partner's mother abused partner's father (PMAPF)	26.24	2	13.12	2.59
Marital satisfaction by partner's father abused partner's mother (PFAPM)	27.12	1	27.12	5.35*
Marital satisfaction by partner's mother abused partner's father (PMAPF)	7.49	1	7.49	1.48
Partner's father abused partner's mother (PFAPM) by partner's mother abused partner's father	53.87	1	53.87	10.63**
Explained	538.23	20	26.91	5.31***
Residual	491.64	97	5.07	
Total	1029.87	117	80	

R = .73
R² = .52
 * p < .05
 ** p < .01
 *** p < .001

Although the main effect of race was not significant, a significant interactional effect existed between race and partner's mother abused by partner's father. That is, European-American respondents who reported that their mothers-in-law were abused (X = 9.2; sd = 5.7) reported more wife beating in their marital relationships than did African-American respondents who made such a report (X = 7.0; sd = 3.6). Lower-class respondents who reported marital discord in their marital relationships reported higher levels (X = 9.1; sd = 5.6) of wife beating than did the other respondents. Respondents who reported higher levels of marital discord (X = 9.3; sd = 5.3) and also reported that their mothers-in-law were abused reported higher levels of wife beating than did their counterparts. Finally, respondents who reported that both mothers-in-law and fathers-in-law were abused reported higher levels of wife beating (X = 10.7; sd = 8.1) than did respondents who did not report violence in partner's family or origin.

Discussion

The family life of African-Americans has shown strength and resilience in the face of almost constant external threats. Although we can celebrate these strengths, which have made survival of the African-American family possible, some issues must be addressed as we seek to improve the quality of life in the African-American community. One such issue is violence between marital partners. Little has been written and few empirical studies have been conducted on the comparative extent and nature of marital violence among African-Americans and European-Americans. All too frequently this social problem is portrayed as endemic among African-Americans (Straus, Gelles, and Steinmetz, 1980).

This study used a purposive sample designed to enhance comparability by drawing on groups that were balanced according to race and social class. Consequently the conclusions cannot be generalized safely to broader populations or geographic regions. Nevertheless, investigations that are designed to examine racial differences, as opposed to making post hoc racial inferences, can provide more powerful comparative and theoretically relevant evidence when key variables such as social class are controlled explicitly. In this investigation the author accounted for social class effects by means of sampling procedures and through appropriate statistical manipulations.

Marital relationships that are characterized by shared decision-making patterns and household responsibilities tend to be the least violent (Gelles and Cornell, 1985). Several authors have described the African-American family as egalitarian in its decision-making patterns (Lewis, 1975; Staples, 1976a); others have portrayed African-American families as matriarchal in structure (Moynihan, 1965). The results of this study support the former viewpoint: More European-American respondents than African-American reported more conflicts around decision making and household responsibilities. As Lewis (1975) states, many African-American families attach greater importance to getting the job done than to the gender of the person performing the task. Middle-class African-American respondents in this investigation reported more marital conflicts over jealousy. Staples (1976a) reported that jealousy is most likely to be the primary cause of spousal violence among African-American couples. He suggested further that an African-American man who is living with a woman but is not married to her tends to be more prone to violence motivated by jealousy than is a married African-American man. The results of these analyses point to the need to develop theoretical and methodological frameworks that allow researchers to examine both process and outcomes of marital conflicts around such issues as decision making and household responsibilities. The reports by either partner or about one partner's role may be limited without some actual observational data in both conflictual and nonconflictual situations.

Overall the author found no significant differences between the proportions of African-American and European-American women who reported that they were victims of husband-to-wife violence during the year before this investigation. Researchers of previous studies had suggested that African-American couples are more violent than European-American couples (Cazenave and Straus, 1979; Straus, Gelles, and Steinmetz, 1980). The present analyses revealed one significant class-linked racial difference: a larger proportion of middle-class African-American women than of middle-class European-American women reported that they were victims of violence by their marital partners.

The results of this investigation may support Staples's (1976a) conclusion that African-American couples are not inherently more violent in their marriages than European-American couples. Staples suggests further that higher levels of marital violence, when they do exist, may be due to the particular social predicament of African-Americans in American society. Along this line, many African-Americans have achieved middle-class positions only recently as a result of relatively recent changes in the social, economic, and political structures of our society. Middle-class African-Americans who acquired their status recently retain the norms, values, and role expectations of their lower-SES developmental experiences as well as acquiring those associated with their new status. Consequently, aggressive and violent methods of problem solving between marital partners may be part and parcel of their subcultural norms and developmental experiences. Many middle-class African-Americans also are subject to great stress because of the uncertainty and tenuousness of their newly acquired position; this situation may influence their use of violence (McAdoo, 1981).

Although research cannot resolve this issue definitively, the results highlight a need for greater theoretical elaboration of the complex interactive process among violent behaviors, attitudes, and socioeconomic realities that attends racial differences than has been acknowledged generally. The author used hierarchical analyses of variance procedures in an attempt to obtain additional theoretical explanations of the effects of race, class, violence in the family of origin, and marital satisfaction. The main effect of race was not significant, but wife beating was more prevalent among white couples than among black couples who reported that their mothers-in-law were abused by their fathers-in-law.

Regardless of race, the environment in which marital partners were raised seems to be an important contributor to husband-to-wife violence and wife beating (Roy, 1982; Walker, 1979). Violence in the partner's family of origin and its interactional effects with social class and with levels of marital discord explain further how this variable affects violence in marital relationships. Previous studies demonstrated that sex-role socialization in the home environment of both partners is also a significant contributor to violence against women. A question that stems from this finding is whether violence in the wife's family of origin is as strong in explaining current levels of violence toward women as is violence in the partner's family of origin. Further research must examine the differential nature of sex-role socialization more closely in general, and between as well as within racial groups.

Future research on family violence, especially studies assessing racial differences, should be conducted with careful consideration of social class as a confounding variable. Socioeconomic backgrounds vary in all racial groups; members of each have experienced a variety of socialization influences. Both partners also must be studied in future investigations of the extent and nature of spousal violence in general, but especially among African-American couples, so that we can further our theoretical knowledge and our approaches to practice with the community. We need especially an expansion of theory to encompass the wide variety of characteristics among black families in the United States. Thus the richness of all families' patterns of interaction may be examined more validly and compared from a culturally relative and relevant perspective with families of other races and cultures across this society (Allen, 1979; Turner, 1972).

Notes

1. The author obtained social class positions by adapting the Hollingshead two-factor index of social position. To reflect the recent trend toward dual-employed families, she modified the Hollingshead index to obtain a joint family social class position. Separate social class scores for each marital partner were calculated on the basis of each partner's educational level and occupation; then the two social class scores were summed and divided by two. The author also collapsed Hollingshead's five social class positions into three: I–II = upper, III

= middle, and IV–V = lower. For a detailed discussion of the Hollingshead two-factor index of social position, see Hollingshead and Redlich (1958).

2. Unfortunately, geographic variation was not included. The sample was drawn from one geographic area.

3. Sixteen (10.3 percent) of the black women were cohabitating with their marital partners as husband and wife; the remaining 89.7 percent were legally married to their partners. Thus the term *marital partner* is used here to refer both to legally married persons and to those who were cohabitating as husband and wife.

6

Racial Differences among Shelter Residents: A Comparison of Anglo, Black, and Hispanic Battered Women

Edward W. Gondolf
Ellen Fisher
J. Richard McFerron

Introduction

Shelters for battered women have, in recent years, begun to face the racial questions that other human services have characteristically encountered (Schechter, 1982). In particular, how should shelters modify their services to accommodate racial differences? In order to respond meaningfully to this issue, we need to have a better appreciation of the racial differences among shelter women.

Some of the basic questions to consider in this regard are: Do shelter women of one race have more income and education than others as one might assume? Does one group or another suffer more severe abuse and warrant specialized treatment for their injuries? Is there any group that is particularly reluctant to seek or obtain services?

This exploratory study analyzes data from Texas shelter intake interviews with Anglo (white), black, and Hispanic women in order to answer these questions. Selected background, abuse, and help-seeking variables were cross-tabulated by race and subsequently entered into a stepwise discriminant function to determine the most differentiating factors.

In general, the Anglo shelter women appear to be of higher socio-

Reprinted with permission from *Journal of Family Violence 3* (1), 39–51.

The author wishes to thank the Texas Council on Family Violence and the Texas Department of Human Services for their cooperation in collecting and sharing the data. I am particularly grateful to the shelter staff and battered women who completed the intake interviews at a time of crisis. This research was supported by an NIMH fellowship in Clinical Services Research (NIMH T32 MH17184) and by a faculty research grant from the IUP Graduate School.

economic status than the Hispanics, but are comparable to the black women in this regard. However, the three racial groupings appear to have experienced similar severity of abuse and levels of help seeking. These tendencies counter some of the research on racial grounds and help-seeking behavior in the field of mental health. Moreover, they imply that programmatic and policy initiatives must address the lack of mobility, especially of the Hispanic women.

A Review of Racial Differences

There has been very little empirical study of the racial differences among shelter residents, even though there has been much discussion of the matter among clinicians and activitists (White, 1985). The extensive research on differences among racial groups seeking assistance from human services in general provides, however, some generalizations that may be applicable to shelter women (Block, 1981; Fischer, 1969; Cannon and Locke, 1977; Kravits and Schneider, 1975).

According to the mental health research, black women in shelters would tend to draw less comprehensive service (Evans et al., 1986; Wood and Sherrets, 1984), and rely more on friends and family for support (McKinlay, 1975; McAdoo, 1978; Neighbors, 1984; Warren, 1981). The research on Hispanics implies that Hispanic women in shelters would tend to be the most disadvantaged economically, and be married longer and fewer times (Frisbie, 1986). The Hispanic women are also more likely to tolerate more abuse, which would be reflected in seeking less help. When they did seek help, they would characteristically be more likely to call on police.

A few studies on race and abuse suggest further that blacks and Hispanics are more likely to tolerate their abuse and receive more severe abuse than whites. The most notable of these studies is a race and class analysis of the National Family Violence Survey (N = 2143) conducted by Cazenave and Straus (1979). The authors conclude: "The persistence of higher rates of spousal violence for the large income group containing the black working class, and for blacks in both occupational groups, suggests that even aside from income differentials black spousal violence is notably high" (Cazenave and Straus, 1979, p. 295).

A study of Mexican-American and Anglo women in a Texas shelter (n = 50) found that both groups appeared to have experienced equivalent amounts of abuse. The Hispanic women, however, were more tolerant of the abuse and identified fewer types of behaviors as abuse (Torres, in press). They were also more likely to recommend contacting the police than the Anglo women.

The generalizations about racial influence, however, must be weighted with caution, according to other studies on intraracial differences. For instance, the current studies on black social networks demonstrate the complexity of racial differentiation influenced by a variety of family variables (Neighbors and Jackson, 1984; Taylor, 1986). Intraracial differences are apparent among Hispanics, as well. Marital stability is influenced by whether one is foreign or native born, the degree of acculturation, generation since immigration, religiosity, and available social supports (Keefe, 1982). Moreover, it is argued that ethnicity is an emergent process influenced by one's social environment as well as by cultural attributes (Gelfand and Fandetti, 1986).

Method

This study attempts to substantiate further the racial differences among shelter residents using a secondary data base of Texas shelters interviews. The interview questionnaires are standardized reporting forms developed jointly by the Texas Council on Family Violence and the Texas Department of Human Services and administered at each client's intake by the staff of the fifty Texas shelters. A total of 5,708 out of 9,064 interviews from an eighteen-month period (1983 to 1985) were found acceptable for the analysis.[1] Fifty-seven percent are Anglo women, 15 percent are black, and 29 percent are Hispanic in this final sample.

Variables

Variables that relate to the background, abuse, and help-seeking differences identified in the previous research were selected from the questionnaire. The background questions included variables such as "personal income," "combined income," "number of children," and "education level" with ordinal responses.[2] Also, the batterer's substance abuse, general violence, and arrests were assessed as totals of the different kinds of each item mentioned.

The abuse items (physical abuse, verbal abuse, child abuse, injury, and previous abuse) allowed for multiple responses to a series of ranked categories. The highest ranked (or most severe) response for the abuse items, reported by each woman, was used to indicate the "most severe" of each abuse item (as in Bowker, 1983) (see appendix 6–1). Each separate response category was also analyzed as a "dummy" variable in the initial cross-tabulations.

The principal help-seeking variable is "previous help seeking," which is the total number of different informal and formal help sources (eleven possible) contacted prior to coming to the shelter. (The listing patterns that were used by Bowler (1983).) Other help-seeking variables included the total number of different "services obtained" while in the shelter (eight possible), and "services to be continued" after leaving shelter and "care sought" for injury, which were calculated in a similar fashion. The categories for each of these variables were also treated as dummy variables in the cross-tabulations. The woman's "planned living arrangements" on leaving the shelter was registered in one of three categories: return to batterer, live separately, or undetermined.

Analysis

The analysis of the data consists of bivariate cross-tabulations and discriminant analyses of partitioned race groupings. The bivariate analysis served as a data reduction procedure and a means for generating descriptive statistics of the groupings. Each of the variables (including the response categories used as dummy variables) was cross-tabulated with race (Anglo, black, Hispanic).

Chi-square (χ^2) statistics were computed for each cross-tabulated variable with the full sample. Those cross-tabulated variables with a significance level of $p < 0.00001$ were used to develop a description of the racial groupings of women (see table 6–1 for a representative portion of those variables). The designation of this high significance level attempts to compensate for inflation of chi square by the large sample size.

Discriminant analyses were then computed to determine the combination of variables that most differentiate five possible racial combinations, or "partitions" of race groupings, that is, Anglo-

Table 6–1
Cross-Tabulations of Variables by Race

Total (column)	Anglo (57%)	Black (15%)	Hispanic (29%)	Row Total (100%)
Background variables				
Combined income				
$10 or less	33	36	54	39
$10,001 to $20,000	35	39	32	35
$20,001 or more	32	25	15	26
$x^2 = 201.76(4)$; $p < 0.00001$				
Personal income				
None	56	48	61	57
$5,000 or less	19	25	23	21
$5,002 to $10,000	14	15	12	13
$10,001 or more	10	12	4	9
$x^2 = 81.92(6)$; $p < 0.00001$				
Education				
Less than 12 yrs.	41	29	63	45
High school diploma	39	44	26	36

Table 6–1 continued

Total (column)	Anglo (57%)	Black (15%)	Hispanic (29%)	Row Total (100%)
Some post–h.s./college	21	27	10	19
$x^2 = 339.39(4)$; p < 0.00001				
Times married				
Never married	10	22	15	16
One time	52	64	66	61
Two times	28	11	14	17
Three or more	10	3	5	6
$x^2 = 55.13(6)$; p < 0.00001				
Length of Relationship				
Less than 1 year	17	15	10	15
1 to 5 years	49	49	41	46
More than 5 years	34	37	49	39
$x^2 = 115.19(4)$; p < 0.00001				
Number of Children				
0	14	11	7	11
1	27	24	21	25
2	31	30	27	30
3 or more	28	35	45	34
$x^2 = 154.76(6)$; p < 0.00001				
Abuse variables				
Physical abuse (most severe)				
Grab, push, slapped	17	11	15	16
Punched	15	17	14	15
Kicked	28	24	31	28
Weapons used	39	48	40	41
$x^2 = 44.71(6)$; p < 0.00001				
Duration of abuse				
1 to 12 months	35	35	28	33
1 to 5 years	44	42	39	43
5 years or more	22	23	33	24
$x^2 = 78.67(4)$; p < 0.00001				
Help-seeking variables				
Previous help seeking				
0 to 2 sources	48	44	45	47
3 to 4 sources	33	36	35	35
5 to 10 sources	19	21	20	19
$x^2 = 7.39(4)$; not. sig.				
Care sought (for injuries)				
None	21	18	22	21
1 source	59	16	25	16
2 sources	16	17	14	16
3 to 6 sources	21	23	14	19
$x^2 = 63.97(6)$; p < 0.00001				
Services to be continued				
None	36	34	37	35
1 to 2 services	40	35	35	38
3 to 8 services	25	31	29	27
$x^2 = 25.34(4)$; p < 0.00001				

n = 5708

versus-black-versus-Hispanic; Anglo-versus-black-and-Hispanic, and so on (see table 6–2). Thirty variables, which were shown to be influential in the bivariate analysis and were determined to be relatively independent from each other ($r < 0.4$), were entered into a stepwise analysis. (The variable for "duration of abuse" was deleted from the discriminant analysis because it was highly correlated with length of relationship.) A random sample of five hundred was initially drawn for each discriminant function and cross-validated on a subsequent sample of the same size.

A subsequent discriminant analysis was conducted controlling for

Table 6–2
Discriminant Analysis of Partitioned Race Groups[1]

	Partition[2]				
	A/B/H	A/BH	A/B	AB/H	A/H
Variable					
Combined income	0.65	0.55		0.70	0.70
Times married	0.60	0.65	0.55	0.40	0.42
No personal income*	0.41	0.37		0.42	0.41
Relationship length	−0.35	−.029		−0.46	−0.40
General violence	0.31	0.37	0.37		0.24
Abuse frequency	−0.29	−0.23		−0.37	−0.35
Previous abuse	−0.21	−0.27			−0.19
Threatened killing*	0.15			0.21	0.25
Previous help seeking	0.05		−0.29	0.18	
Batterer arrested*	0.04	0.18	0.25		
Child abuse*	0.04		−0.22	0.22	0.17
Batterer in counseling*	0.01		−0.34		
Education	−0.01		−0.34		
Emergency room care*			−0.26		
Weapons used*			−0.19	0.19	
Age of woman				0.20	0.21
Severe injury			0.29		
Function statistics					
Eigenvalue	0.22	0.21	0.21	0.21	0.26
Canonical correlation	0.43	0.41	0.42	0.42	0.45
Wilks lambda	0.72	0.83	0.82	0.83	0.79
Chi square	88.96	52.12	39.49	52.07	53.10
Degrees of freedom	26	8	12	11	10
Significance (0.00001 across)					
Correct classification	58%	62%	77%	73%	69%

1. Thirty variables on background, abuse, and help seeking were entered into a stepwise analysis for each partition. Fourteen variables were deleted as insignificant in all of stepwise analyses; woman's occupation, number of children, marital status, abused in previous relationship, severity of batter's substance abuse, severity of physical abuse, severity of verbal abuse, threatened to harm children, duration of the abuse, total kinds of care sought, total kinds of injuries, total number of shelter services obtained, planned living arrangements, and the batterer's response to the abuse. Those variables with asterisks (*) are dummy variables (n = 500).

2. A, Anglo; B, black; H, Hispanic.

income. That is, a discriminant function was calculated for the Anglo-versus-black-versus-Hispanic comparison in four combined income categories (Low = 0–$10,000; Medium = $10–20,000; High = $20–30,000; and Very High = $30,000 or more).

Qualifications

As with much of the research in this field, several qualifications must be drawn. First, the measures of abuse remain highly problematic. One compensation in our analysis is the inclusion of multiple indicators for abuse and its impacts. A second qualification related to the first is that the variables in this study measure only the more objective factors, and do not account for the differences in subjective experience. It is highly likely that the abuse or service response may be interpreted differently through different cultural norms and experience.

Third, the data are drawn from battered women receiving shelter in one particular state. Without a comparable control group, it is difficult to generalize our findings to women in other states or, more importantly, to battered women in general. The size and racial proportions of the sample, however, allow for a more sophisticated analysis of some fundamental questions in shelter service.

There are several additional qualifications with regard to race. One is that there is increasing diffentiation within the racial groups themselves. The Hispanic women, in particular, are subject to different levels of acculturation (Cuellar, Harries, and Jasso 1980; Gelfand and Fandetti, 1986).

Second, the level of reporting bias is likely to differ among the groups, and therefore distort the findings on abuse. As mentioned, Torres (in press) found that Hispanics reported a smaller range of abusive behaviors and were in general more tolerant of the abuse. Third, socioeconomic status also substantially confounds the racial differences, as the findings suggest, and raises problematic issues with regard to the relationship of race and class (Petersen, 1980).

Results

Bivariate Analysis

The racial groupings appear to differ, as expected, in terms of the background variables for income and marital status (see table 6–1). The differences in terms of abuse, however, were minimal overall. Also, the help-seeking behavior of the women, both before and during shelter, was relatively similar.

In terms of combined income, 32 percent of the whites, 35 percent of blacks, and 52 percent of the Hispanics were below the poverty line. The black women tended, however, to have educational, occupation, and personal income levels comparable to the Anglos; these levels for both the Anglos and blacks were substantially higher than for the Hispanics.

The Hispanics characteristically were married the longest, had much lower education, employment, and job status. The Anglo women, on the whole, were slightly older and had the fewest children.

The different racial groups of women reported receiving comparable kinds of physical, verbal, sexual, and child abuse. The outstanding exception was that black women more often (48 percent) reported having a weapon used against them, versus the Anglo and Hispanic women (39 percent). The frequency of abuse was also relatively the same for all the groups (42 percent once a week). The Hispanic women, however, tended to report the longest duration of abuse (32 percent more than 5 years versus 21 percent for the Anglos and blacks).

In terms of help seeking, the women from different racial groups sought about the same amount of different kinds of assistance prior to entering the shelter ("previous help seeking"). Hispanic women, however, were the least likely to contact a friend, minister, or social service, suggesting their relative social isolation. A greater percentage of Anglos visited or phoned a social service, and more black women contacted a minister or police, as the mental research suggests. An equal percentage of women previously contacted the shelter, left home, or obtained legal service.

The women obtained about the same number of different kinds of shelter services. (Anglo women obtained on average a total 3.0 of a possible 7.0 services, as opposed to 3.3 services for the Hispanic and black women.) Nevertheless, the Anglo women had fewer children to service and more of their own cars. Sixty-two percent had their own cars, whereas only 40 percent of the non-Anglo women had cars.

The Anglos, furthermore, did expect to continue using fewer services after leaving the shelter, perhaps reflecting their greater resources. However, fewer Anglo women planned to live separate from the batterer despite their greater mobility (66 percent versus 71 percent and 73 percent). This may be a reflection of the proportion of Anglo batterers in counseling (see Gondolf, in press).

Multivariate Analysis

A stepwise discriminant analysis verifies the combined influence of these variables in differentiating the racial grouping of battered women (table 6–2). Personal income, marital norms, and general violence remain relatively influential across different partitioning of the groups, except for the "Anglos versus blacks" partition. In this case, the income variables and length of relationship are not significant, while variables related to arrest, child abuse, and education are. Moreover, the discriminant results suggest that the most pronounced differences are between the Anglos and blacks, on the one hand, and the Hispanics, on the other, rather than between white and nonwhites.

More specifically, the highest discriminant coefficients in the function for "Anglos versus blacks and Hispanics" (or whites versus nonwhites), with times married (0.65) being the most influential instead of combined income (0.55). Nevertheless, the influence of income (0.70) is the greatest for the partitions of "Anglos and blacks versus Hispanics" and "Anglos versus Hispanics."

The function statistics indicate that the power of the respective discriminant analyses is at best moderately strong. The "Anglo versus Hispanics" partition, however, is the strongest (eigenvalue = 0.26) accounting for 0.31 percent of the variance (Wilks Lambda = 0.79). It is interesting that despite a great range and number of variables used in the analysis, there is still a substantial portion of the variance unexplained. Some of this may, no doubt, be accounted for by the cultural differences within racial groups and the general shortcomings of the abuse measures mentioned in the discussion of qualifications.

The discriminant functions that control for income show comparable results both in terms of explanatory power and coefficient strength. Low, medium, and high income levels show "times married" to be equally as influential in differentiating the racial groups (0.43, 0.64, 0.56), but "length of relationship" is not as influential (−0.15, −0.06, 0.12). The difference in "general violence" (−0.35, −0.52, 0.53, −0.65) and "severity of injury" (−0.27, 0.43, −49, 0.38) among the racial groups, on the other hand, appears to have increased when income level is controlled. Additional cross-tabulations, however, show that the most violent and most injurious group varies from income level to income level. In sum, combined income or "class status" does not appear to appreciably alter the pattern of differences among the racial groups.

Discussion

As might be expected, the racial groups differed most of all in terms of income related variables. However, they differ very little in terms of abuse and help seeking, as Bowker (1983) and Walker (1984) found in their studies of battered women. One interesting finding with regard to income is that the black shelter women were on a par with the Anglos in terms of personal income, and a greater proportion of them were employed. (Also, their batterers were less generally violent and had fewer previous arrests than the Anglos.) One possible inference is that lower income blacks are not as likely to seek shelter and are underrepresented in this study. They may be more likely to rely on informal networks for support, as other research on human service utilization suggests.

A second and probably more important finding is the difference in marital norms that appear to be related to socioeconomic status and duration of abuse. Specifically, Hispanic women appear to be bound by a norm of "loyal motherhood." They tend to be married younger, have larger families, and stay in relationships longer. They are similarly poorer, less educated, and longer abused than their counterparts.

These findings point particularly to the difficult position of the Hispanic women in shelters. These women appear to be burdened not only by language differences and discrimination but also by limited mobility due to larger families, less personal income, and more binding marital norms. In sum, the Anglo and black women appear to have more in common, suggesting that the significant differentiation does not necessarily fall along color lines alone.

The Hispanic women especially need more economic and educational supports to help them in their crisis, as well as in general. They need to be given priority in terms of housing, social welfare benefits, child care, and transportation. This need is compounded by the fact that a substantial portion of Hispanic women in Texas shelters are undocumented citizens and are not eligible for public assistance. Much of their aid must therefore come from church or private groups devoted to assisting "undocumented" worker families.

In this light, shelters need to act as service centers for economic disadvantage, as well as abuse. This is apparent in the fact that nearly half of all the Texas shelter women have no personal income and at least a third come from families living below the poverty line. Other statewide studies have shown the disproportionate amount of abuse among lower income groups (Petersen, 1980).

How shelters can more effectively respond to these economic needs remains problematic, especially given their limited resources and their crisis-oriented service. Shelters must expand to provide more extensive programs of economic assistance, as many have done, and other community agencies must give higher priority to aiding battered women. This ideal is unlikely, however, unless some substantial economic changes are made. Ultimately, social policies must be implemented that reduce the economic burdens of shelter women and women in general.

Notes

1. Those women who were under sixteen years of age and not physically abused (i.e., not battered women) were deleted from the final sample (6 percent), along with duplicate and incomplete questionnaires. The incomplete questionnaires (part two or part three not finished) were from women who were referred elsewhere, or who were from two shelters that did not comply with the instructions. The distribution on the general background and abuse questions of part one of these questionnaires was comparable to the remaining sample. This suggests that the deleted incomplete questionnaires did not particularly bias the results. Also, the small number of Asian women (211) was considered too small for significant analysis and deleted.

2. For example, the question for number of children designated the following response categories: (1) none, (2) 1, (3) 2, (4) 4, (5) 5 or more. The question about highest education level included response categories for less than twelfth grade, high school diploma or equivalent, some college or post–high school vocational training, and college degree.

Appendix 6–1

The researchers established ranked orderings (least to most severe) of the responses for abuse and help-seeking items based on prevailing conceptualizations in the field and submitted them to a team of shelter staff and clients for modification or confirmation. For example, the item for physical abuse was: "If you were physically abused which of the following happened? The batterer: (1) threw things, (2) held you against your will, (3) pushed you around, (4) slapped you, (5) pulled your hair, (6) choked you, (7) burned you, (8) punched you, (9) kicked you, (10) used a weapon or object against you." This ranking reflects the ranking of the widely used Conflict Tactics Scale. There are a few exceptions to this formulation. For instance "frequency of abuse" during the past six months is indicated by either (1) only once, (2) two to five times (3) once or twice a month, (4) once a week or more. "Duration of abuse" uses a similar set of responses ranging from "one month or less" to "more than five years." "Previous abuse" refers to the number of different kinds of abuse experienced as a child.

Part IV
Violence toward the Elderly

7
Elder Abuse in the Black Family

Oliver J. Williams
Linner Griffin

Introduction

The social impact of the baby boom and the projected increase in the number of elderly persons in the United States in the twenty-first century have been well documented (Allan and Brotman, 1981; Covey, 1983; Mayer et al., 1977). In addition, life expectancy among older people is increasing (Boyer, 1974; Covey, 1983). This fact suggests that today's aged and middle-aged people will live longer; today the life span is seventy-plus years, longer than ever in our nation's history. Longer life expectancy and increased numbers of older people make the circumstances of aging highly important to the helping professions. Social service and health professionals must learn as much as possible about older people in our society to ensure a proper fit between helping programs and the individuals they are to serve.

Medical advances and protective legislation for the aging have changed greatly the length and character of life among America's older citizens. Economic concerns and increased mobility have changed the appearance of helping networks. The advent of the nuclear family means that responsibility for dependent older persons must be shared by smaller and smaller numbers of people. This situation has resulted in a strain on the traditional family support system.

Thus, stress, in combination with ageism toward vulnerable family members, may predispose some persons to be abusive toward older men and women. Issues of aging and abuse will be viewed with increasing interest because by the year 2000 one-half of the United States population will be over fifty years of age (Butler and Lewis, 1983).

Abuse has different meanings to different groups of people. Psychologists, physicians, social workers, and other helping professionals have difficulty in defining it. The term "is confusing because it covers many types of abuse [and] there is no consensus . . . about its parameters" (Straus and Gelles, 1986). Abuse, as used in this chapter, is modified from a definition proposed by Straus and Gelles. It is defined as the intention or the perceived intention of causing pain, harm, or injury to another person. This is a broad definition, which permits consideration of physical, social, and emotional issues.

Giordano and Giordano (1984) noted that one out of ten older persons living with family members may be subject to abuse; this proportion translates to 2.5 million elderly persons a year. In a Massachusetts study of older people living in noninstitutional settings, 86 percent of the abusers were relatives, 80 percent of the victims were women, and 40 percent of the victims had visible injuries (Martin and Beezely, 1977). Elderly victims are less likely to report abuse because of concern for themselves as well as for the perpetrator (Edye and Rich, 1983). Only one in six cases of elder abuse is ever reported to legal authorities or social agencies (U.S. Select Committee on Aging, 1980).

The great influx of immigrants to the United States from eastern and western Europe and other parts of the world during the nineteenth and twentieth centuries caused this country to be called the melting pot of the world. The term *melting pot* describes the amalgam of cultures that together form the culture of the United States. The national motto, *E Pluribus Unum* (from many one), suggests that this mixture is viewed as admirable. Growth and order have been achieved through democratic principles, which make the will of the majority paramount in decision making. This fascination with majority rule has proved problematic for minorities, those groups of persons socially and culturally different from the majority population.

Black Americans represent the largest minority group in the United States. Similarly, the black elderly represent the largest minority group among the aged population. Conservative estimates place the population of black elderly persons at more than 2.6 million persons (U.S. Census Bureau, 1981). Yet little information is available about the unique circumstances of the black elderly in this country.

United States Census Bureau data reveal, for example, that among blacks as among whites, females have a longer life span than do males (Dancy, 1977; Jackson, 1980). Unique among blacks, however, is the historical existence of the strong matriarch, who has received much credit for preserving the black family, often while employed outside the home. The resulting familial configuration differs from that which often appears in the literature on the vulnerable older female.

Because information concerning the black elderly is scarce, we lack information about abuse among this large segment of the population (Cazenave, 1981). (Indeed, any information about black people in research studies has been limited.) Cazenave (1979) noted that little information about elder abuse in minority populations was available. He encouraged researchers to explore elder abuse among black people.

Concerns of the black elderly are often called politically inexpedient or irrelevant to the larger, national picture. Researchers frequently perceive older blacks as part of the larger older adult population. Indeed, they are, but they are also unique, for they are survivors of a past that socially and politically bears little resemblance to the present.

The remainder of this chapter will examine issues that should be considered in conducting research about elder abuse in the black population. We will describe similarities and discrepancies between information about the Caucasian population in the United States and the population of black elders.

Current Research

Much of the existing data identifies characteristics of elder abuse in the majority population group and offers the surmise that the same conditions exist among black elders. Yet there is no direct evidence to support or refute this "grouping" practice. Research is needed to determine the incidence of elder abuse among black Americans, the characteristics or circumstances of abuse toward black elders, and whether or how abuse toward the black elderly differs from the traditional criteria cited in the literature.

Researchers such as Straus and Gelles (1986) observe that there is an intergenerational cycle to violence. In support of these authors, Myers and Shelton (1987) note that "some cases of elder abuse occur in homes where there are lifelong patterns of abuse and violent relationships" (p. 377). Steinmetz (1978) found that only one out of 400 children raised in nonviolent homes was abusive to an elder parent when he or she became an adult. In contrast, she found that one of every two adults who were abused as children abused an elder parent when they became adults. Unresolved conflicts may result in the victimization of the older person when he or she becomes vulnerable in later years. Through intergenerational social learning, the abusers may find sanctions or justification for the abuse. Therefore it is important to break this intergenerational cycle of violence in order to end it.

Other researchers have proposed that familial stress increases the probability of elder abuse. The stress can emanate from several areas: (1) the physical and emotional difficulties of caring for low-functioning elders, (2) lack of "regular" assistance for caregivers from community programs, and (3) the sacrifice of caregivers' pleasure or relaxation time to elders' needs. At a national Adult Protective Services Conference held in San Antonio in 1987, the typical victim of abuse was described as

1. a white female who resides with the perpetrator.
2. middle class.
3. having a severe mental or physical impairment.
4. seventy-five years of age or older.

The typical perpetrator was described as

1. a relative of the victim.
2. an adult child.
3. female.
4. middle-aged.
5. sharing a residence with the aged person.
6. having other internal or external stresses in her life.

What about the profiles of the typical black victim and perpetrator? Are they the same as those described above? To what extent does the unique social and cultural experience of the black family in America influence research findings? Are there methodological concerns regarding research on elder abuse among blacks? Does sample size influence findings? How culturally sensitive are studies that deal with elder abuse? Researchers must be concerned with these issues and ethnocultural differences when conducting studies in this area.

The Need to Include Black-Centered Variables in Studies on Elder Abuse

During the 1980s the literature on elder abuse received increased attention. Yet the literature on elder abuse in the minority populations is still quite sparse. Although some similarities may exist between majority and minority families with regard to abuse, some differences may exist as well. To what extent are differences present? Sokolovsky (1985) notes that it is important to consider "the difference that differences make" (p. 6). The various explanations of elder abuse, for example, rarely consider the influence of culture. In studies that investigate elder abuse, the nonuse of specific variables that define the minority experience may reduce the accuracy and generalizability of information concerning the black aged.

In one of the few empirical studies that include blacks, Cazenave and Straus (1979) found that elderly black persons were much less likely to be abused by relatives than were elderly white persons. This difference, they suggest, may be due to the extended family networks that may serve as a buffer to abuse. In contrast, Hwalek and Sengstock (1986) found no statistical difference between whites and blacks in their study on elder abuse. Therefore there is no clear picture on the issue.

Cazenave (1981) noted "that studies about elder abuse, which included blacks as a part of the samples, have not had sufficient numbers of black aged or have not explored details of black life or the black elderly . . . and the inclusion of any information about black people has been limited and received very little attention." In one respect or another, Cazenave's remarks could apply even to the studies by Cazenave (1979) and by Hwalek and Sengstock (1986).

Sokolovsky (1985) notes that this issue is present in any investigation involving research on the ethnic minority aged. Blacks may not fit the typical profile of the victim or perpetrator cited earlier. Elder abuse among blacks may be a result of familial exposure to violence, male socialization to violence, long-standing familial conflicts, or stress on the primary caretaker due to the needs of the frail elder family member. Although it is believed that many of these concepts and characteristics have universal application, the extent of the differences is unknown. To increase the accuracy of information about elder abuse among minority groups, it is important not only to include sufficient numbers of minority-group members in the sample but also to consider those characteristics that influence minority experiences.

Societal influences, for example, direct the patterns of behavior among blacks and shape the black experience in this country. Black elders share a unique heritage that differs from that of other aged persons in the United States. This heritage has given them an identity as a people with common attitudes and shared values. The situation of blacks has been affected by historical events such as slavery, the search for uniform civil rights, poverty, and the biased political interpretation of laws. This background has influenced how and why blacks' lives and family configurations are different from those of whites. Accordingly, history may have influenced not only issues seen as contributing to abuse among blacks, but also society's response to violence in the black community.

Societal influences may predispose some blacks to behave violently. Historically, blacks have been treated violently through racism, either interpersonally or institutionally. Could these experiences prove to be a form of social learning for some blacks who abuse? Directly or collectively, blacks experience emotional and systematic racism in many forms including verbal or physical attacks, lack of access to equal education or equal employment, lack of access to equal housing, lack of economic opportunities, and poor health services. They are also subject to sociological and psychological attacks (Thomas and Sillen, 1976).

Although these experiences do not justify violent behavior, Cazenave (1981), Hare (1979), and Asbury (1987) note that violence may be a way of reacting to the limited options available to meet definitions of success generated by the majority. This comment suggests that the degree to which young or aged blacks have been able to achieve economic or developmental success, as defined by the larger society, may affect directly how these individuals interact within the black family. Failure to meet the majority criteria may increase the potential for violent expression.

Accordingly, societal abuse begets abuse that may take the following forms:

—Attacks against oneself: suicide or substance abuse

—Attacks against one's family: sibling abuse, child abuse, parent abuse, spouse abuse, elder abuse (neglect, physical violence, emotional trauma, exploitation, sexual violation, homicide)

—Attacks against one's community: violence toward friends or neighbors.

Hawkins (1987) notes that society has responded to violence in black families through the use of stereotypical and historical patterns of racism that have devalued the lives of black people. Violence within the black family is viewed as "normal"; it is acceptable when confined within the black community. Indeed, blacks in this country have a distinctive experience that provides insight into their perceptions, their behaviors, and their interpersonal and intrafamilial experiences in relation to domestic violence. To what extent would these issues affect research findings?

The following example also highlights the importance of considering differences. Although abuse occurs in households at varying income levels, most victims of elder abuse are reported to be white and living in middle-class families. Many of the perpetrators of abuse are reported to be white, middle-class women whose children are ready to leave home. The middle-class perpetrator is ready to rediscover her relationship with her spouse, to find a new career, or to return to school. At this time, when she is eagerly anticipating a change in her life, she may be forced to take on the responsibility for an elder parent or in-law who comes into her home.

This description of victims and perpetrators may differ in several ways from the usual situation in the black community. Hill (1971) states that older black people very often live in multigenerational families and their children are more likely to come to live with them in their homes. In contrast, an elderly white person is more likely to move in with his or her children in the children's home.

Historical traditions and societal influences may predispose blacks to arrange their familial interactions differently from whites. Researchers such as Herskovits (1958) have linked the extended family pattern of blacks, which is common in the southern United States, to western Africa. Hill and Shackleford (1975) and Billingsley (1968) conducted research that confirmed the existence of the black multigenerational family proposed by Hill (1971). They, too, considered it more likely that aged black persons would have family members live with them in their residences than that they would move in with relatives. When ranked by frequency, relatives who moved in with elders included the following: (1) daughters who are divorced, widowed, or separated, and their children; (2) the aged person's children and their spouses; (3) grandchildren or other relatives such as nephews, nieces, cousins, and younger siblings; and (4) other family members.

Other familial configurations have been commonplace among black communities in the southeastern United States since the days of slavery. Both kin and nonkin families existed; elderly relatives, or in many cases nonrelatives, raised many children of slave parents. Such families were seen as a major source of cohesiveness among blacks during that destructive period of history (Hill and Shackleford, 1975). The same pattern existed in more recent times. In 1975, half of the black families headed by women age sixty-five and over included children who lived with them but were not born of the elder women (Hill and Shackleford, 1975).

The tendency for different generations of black family members to live together was and is a strategy for pooling limited resources. Extended family patterns always have been a stabilizing force in the black community. Some researchers regard this strategy as a buffer against certain forms of abuse, such as child abuse or elder abuse (Straus, 1979). Billingsley (1969) states that rates of certain types of abuse are lower among blacks than among whites. In contrast, Staples (1976), Straus (1979), and Gil (1970) noted that blacks may have higher rates of certain forms of violence than whites and other minorities. Research, however, has not revealed enough information about abuse toward the black elderly to confirm what does or does not happen.

The various familial configurations of black families raise an interesting issue, however, in identifying the abusers. Is the abuser the elder's biological child? An eighteen- to thirty-year-old relative who is not a biological child? A grandchild? A nonrelative? Is there more exploitation of resources than physical abuse of the black elderly? Is the older black person more likely to name the perpetrator through formal or informal networks? Is the abuse more deeply hidden within the family (kin or nonkin) network than in white families? Is the extended family truly a buffer against elder abuse? If so, in what way?

Another difference between the perpetrators and victims described earlier and the reality of the black experience is economic. Blacks are disproportionately poor and are underrepresented in the middle class (AARP Minority Affairs Initiatives, 1987). The Center on Budget and Policy Priorities (1988) noted the following about poverty among blacks:

The poverty rate for black Americans rose significantly in 1987, de-spite continued growth in the United States economy and a decline in the poverty rate for white Americans. Poverty rates are now higher for blacks than they were in most years in the 1970's. The black poverty rate rose from 31.1 percent in 1986 to 33.1 percent in 1987, as the number of blacks who are poor climbed by 700,000. One of every three blacks lived in poverty in 1987.

By contrast, the white poverty rate fell from 11 percent to 10.5 percent. Poverty rates increased for many groups of blacks: children, elders, young families, married couple families, and female-headed families (p. iv).

Regarding poverty, specifically among the elderly, the report states:

The gap between the poverty rate for the black and the white elderly has widened. In 1978, a black elderly person was 2.8 times more likely to be poor than a white elderly person. By 1987, a black elderly person was 3.4 times as likely to live in poverty than his or her white counterpart. The poverty rate for black Americans aged 65 and over was 33.9 percent in 1987. A third of all black elderly people are poor. In contrast, the poverty rate for white elderly is 10.1 percent (p. 2).

If the character of black families has been affected by changes in our society, such as the erosion of traditional social support networks in families and neighborhoods, one of the results may be increased elder abuse. Staples (1976) suggests that blacks are not inherently violent and that rates of violence among blacks in other countries are lower than those among both black and white Americans. He suggests that the explanation for higher rates of violence among black Americans may be due to their predicament in American society.

Barriers to Research on the Black Aged

Sokolovsky (1985) suggests that because ethnicity is associated with the use of informal social support networks, this association may justify, for some people, ignoring certain problems or reducing service to the ethnic minority aged. He adds that the literature on ethnicity as a resource for the ethnic minority aged is excessively optimistic, especially in regard to informal social supports and family networks of exchange.

Some researchers may view the need to explore elder abuse among the black aged as unwarranted because of the existence of informal social support networks and strong family traditions. Both may be regarded as buffers to prevent the potential for abuse. For example, the extended family, traditional attitudes, and religious affiliations are viewed as preventing abuse. Although it is true that these qualities are strengths among black Americans, it is likewise true that elder abuse occurs among blacks, as in every other group of Americans.

Although minorities such as blacks look to networks of family and friends for support, the ability of these networks to respond effectively is variable. Informal networks may be effective in dealing with specific problems, but they may not have adequate resources or knowledge to respond to certain other problems faced by the aged family member (such as physical abuse, psychological abuse, exploitation, and neglect). Accordingly, unmet needs may exist in various aspects of the minority aged person's life.

Many researchers note that an important ingredient in remedying the problem of elder abuse is increasing the services for primary caregivers (Myers and Shelton, 1987). Social and health programs provide numerous services aimed at relieving caregivers of some of the responsibilities of providing continuous care to their older relatives, thereby relieving the caregivers' stress.

When one thinks of increasing services to white, middle-class caregivers, certain types of support come to mind, such as home health care and medications. If elder abuse is aggravated by the lack of social services, which causes caregivers (perpetrators) to be overwhelmed by providing services to a dependent relative, the minority aged are more vulnerable to abuse than other groups because they suffer from a lack of services and inferior treatment (Jackson, 1980). To a population that is already underserved, such as the black community, one questions where to begin. Multiple needs exist—financial, medical, and residential. What services are most appropriate? The task of providing services should not discourage scholars and planners from attempting to address the needs. "Benign neglect" is a common form of abuse, which is cited by professionals who simply do not know where to begin. Researchers who explore elder abuse specifically among blacks may not only highlight the issues but also may provide direction regarding solutions.

Another concern is that many blacks are uneasy about support offered by the traditional public or private agencies; they may feel more comfortable in using informal black support networks or a combination of informal and formal support by blacks (Neighbors and Jackson, 1984; Taylor and Chatter, 1986). What are the implications of this issue as it relates to elder abuse and service delivery?

Cazenave (1981) and Hwalek and Sengstock (1986) suggest that future studies explore abuse among populations that typically are not regarded as victims of abuse. The issues of traditional support networks, gaps in research, typical profiles of black victims and abusers, and poverty in the black community, particularly among the black aged, should be reasons enough to encourage studies about abuse of black elders.

Conclusions

We recommend that future research explore the character and the nature of elder abuse in the black community. Acquiring empirical information is a necessary first step in improving services to this underserved population. A second step is to address strategies for program implementation.

It is important that the helping professions respond to the problem of elder abuse in the black community. On the basis of the information presented, we offer the following recommendations.

First, education about the problem of elder abuse should be provided to the informal and formal networks within the black community. Such efforts should include kin and nonkin relationships, churches, senior citizen centers, mental health centers, and health care centers.

In addition, educational efforts should attempt to promote a nonjudgmental attitude among the helpers of both the victims and the perpetrators of domestic violence. It is important to accept the person, not the client's negative behaviors. This step is important not only to encourage trust in the community, but also to encourage both victims and abusers to involve themselves in recovery.

Finally, even though it is recognized that education may be one form of primary prevention, other forms of prevention and treatment should be available in the black community for clients in need of services. Many private and public service agencies are available to the community at large, but research has shown that blacks do not make adequate use of such agencies. Public agency access points must be placed within the black community to encourage use by blacks. To facilitate this recommendation, we make three suggestions:

1. The availability of the local access points of service agencies should be highly publicized.

2. Administrators, planners, and practitioners of all public service providers should become familiar with the issues, the concerns, and the nature of the black experience in general, and of black elder abuse in particular.

3. Traditional black community services and the access points of public agencies should attempt to bridge gaps of difference and to reduce competition among themselves. There is more than enough need for their services.

Part V
Family Homicides

8

Black Women Who Kill Their Loved Ones

Coramae Richey Mann

In the mid-1980s, the National Institute of Health determined that homicide was a leading cause of deaths among blacks in the United States, and as such constituted a public health crisis for the African-American subpopulation.[1] This report came as no surprise to black Americans, who live daily with the potential of fatal violence, or to a very small group of social scientists, who investigate homicide. In the case of black American women who commit homicide, the scarcity of available data is even more lamentable because studies of homicide that explore gender and race have revealed consistently that black women rank second in frequency of arrests for murder and nonnegligent homicide (Riedel and Lockhart-Riedel, 1984; Sutherland and Cressey, 1978; Wolfgang, 1958).

The increasing number of deaths among black males, indicated by a criminal homicide victimization rate of over 58.5 per 100,000 (Riedel and Lockhart-Reidel, 1984) defines the epidemic proportions of this phenomenon. Because homicide is primarily intersexual and intraracial, the typical victim of a black female who kills is a black male who is close to her. Other homicide victims—children and other relatives—also occupy significant places in the lives of black women. This chapter describes homicide circumstances and events in the lives of black women who were arrested for killing the ones they loved.[2]

Previous Studies of Black Female Killers of Loved Ones

Empirical studies of homicide[3] typically draw on a variety of data sources; the most commonly used are The FBI's *Uniform Crime Reports* (UCR), which concern the offender, data from the National Center for Health Statistics (NCHS), which generally focus on the victim, prison records of incarcerated murderers, and the homicide arrest records of city police. Most of these studies take a macro-level approach that restricts gender and race considerations. The few studies that include the racial status of women who kill are limited by their exclusion of the victim/offender relationship; therefore, in the studies described below that identify black female homicide offenders, many of the black offenders' relationships with their victims can be extrapolated only on the basis of the victim/offender relationships reported for the female group as a whole.

The first empirical study to include details on black female homicide offenders was made in 1958 by Wolfgang, who examined violent crime in Philadelphia through the use of arrest records. During the period studied (1948–1952), black women constituted 85.2 percent of the women arrested for a homicide. Wolfgang found that 46.7 percent of the black women had killed family members. Moreover, a woman was more likely than a man to kill her partner; the husband was the victim in 45 percent of the cases among blacks where victim/offender relationship was identified (Wolfgang, 1958). Similarly, in a California prison study by Cole, Fisher, and Cole (1968), 43.2 percent of the sample were black women incarcerated for homicide; these women also were found to have killed their children (12 percent) or someone with whom they had had an interpersonal relationship (56 percent).

The Florida prison data reported by Gibbs, Silverman, and Vega (1977) also shows that on the average, more than one-half (55.9 percent) of the incarcerated black women had killed a family member. These women represented 60.5 percent of the homicide offenders studied. A comparable figure for family slayings (57.3 percent) is reported by McClain (1982–83), whose six-city study population was entirely black.

Since these studies were reported, it appears that the proportions of black women who kill have risen, as have the proportions of victims who are close family members. Wilbanks's (1983) study of homicide in Dade County, Florida (Miami), found that the 59.6 percent of black women arrested for homicide had killed family members disproportionately (70.2 percent). Formby (1985) examined a decade of homicides in Tuscaloosa County, Alabama (1970–1979), and reported that 64 percent were black female homicide offenders whose victims were family members. Over an even longer period (1960–1984), Hewitt and Rivers (1986) found that 64 percent of the women arrested for homicide in Delaware County, Indiana (Muncie), were black, and that 75 percent of the people they killed were family members. All of the victims of black female homicide offenders in Detroit from 1982 to 1983 were family members, according to Goetting (1987), who also reports that 96.4 percent of the female killers were black.

Finally, Weisheit (1984), who examined the prison records of 460 female homicide offenders between 1940 and 1966 and between 1981 and 1983 "to determine changes in the character of the offender and the criminal event itself," reveals that 73 percent of the sample were black (p. 471). Within the total group, the victim/offender relationship was predominantly interpersonal: 45 percent of the victims were lovers or spouses, 9 percent were children, and 3 percent were other relatives (Weisheit, 1984). Except for the finding that knives were reported as the preferred weapon in earlier studies (e.g., Cole, Fisher, and Cole, 1968; Wolfgang, 1958), Weisheit's (1984) results generally reflect a summary of the findings in the aforementioned studies of women killers: "Most homicides by females take place in the home, involve the use of a gun, and are acts where the offender has no accomplices or companions present. . . . (M)ost victims are spouses, lovers, or friends, and a small number were children of the offender" (p. 486).

For the most part, the findings reported in this chapter corroborate those of the earlier studies; as we shall see, however, some differences exist that appear to reflect today's times.

The Research Data

A sample of 296 women arrested for murder in 1979 and 1983 provided the demographic data on 150 black women who killed someone with whom they had a primary relationship and gave the circumstances of the homicides. Most of the sample cases (77.7 percent; N=230) were black; they were drawn from Atlanta, Baltimore, Chicago, Houston, Los Angeles, and New York City, cities in which the homicide rate was higher than the national average in those years. Because of the exploratory nature of the larger study from which this sample was drawn, descriptive data and case analyses are the primary reporting methods.

Of the 230 black women who had taken another person's life, the victim/offender relationship was ascertained in 227 cases: 122 of the homicides (81.3 percent) concerned victims who were, or once had been, in intimate sexual relationships with the offenders, and who will be identified hereafter referred to as *significant others*.[4,5] Children of the offenders were the victims in seventeen cases (11.3 percent), and the remaining eleven cases involved other relatives (7.3 percent).[6]

The data on the 150 women who killed someone they loved (the *study group*) were analyzed from two perspectives on a number of characteristics concerning the offender, the victim, the homicide, and the criminal justice history and processing of the offender. First, I compared the study group through cross-tabulations[7] with those black women who had killed someone who was not a primary person to them—the *contrast group*—to determine whether there were any significant differences between the two groups. Second, I investigated the subgroups within the study group of those who killed their loved ones to see whether they differed: for example, is a woman who kills her partner similar to one who kills her child? The small numbers in the child-victim and other relative-victim categories preclude any generalizations about the latter comparisons, but are offered primarily as a guide for future researchers.

Comparison by Victim Group

In describing black women who killed loved ones with other black women who committed crimes, I found generally that the two groups have distinctive demographic profiles. Members of the study group, who range in age from thirteen to sixty-one years, tend to be about five years older than women in the contrast group, have attained higher levels of education, have slightly more children, and are more likely to be employed. As seen in table 8–1, only two of these social characteristics—age and motherhood—are statistically significant. Nonetheless, the proportions suggest that black women who kill their loved ones tend to be more representative of our familial society than are those who kill others.

Differences also exist between the victims of women in the study group and of those in the contrast group. Although the mean ages of their victims are similar (table 8–1), significantly more of the victims of the study group are over age twenty-five, whereas the contrast group killers more frequently took the lives of those under twenty-five. More important, these victims are not their children, because all the cases of parents who kill their children are found in the study group. Therefore these young black women, half of whom are under age twenty-five, killed other young people in their age group (39 percent), most of whom were also black (84.4 percent). They are also significantly more likely to have killed whites (10.4 percent) and Hispanics (5.2 percent) than are the women in the study group. As is typical of a racially segregated society, and in agreement with previous research findings, black women kill those closest to them who happen to be of the same race and of the opposite gender. On the other hand, although males were the primary victims in both groups, black women in the contrast group were three times more likely to kill other women.

Homicide Characteristics

The reasons given for the homicides differentiate the two groups further. Most of the seventy-seven women in the contrast group killed

Table 8–1
Selected Offender/Victim Characteristics by Victim Group (in percentages)*

| | Victim Group | | |
| | Study Group: Loved One (n = 150) | Contrast Group: All Other (n = 77) | |
Characteristic of:			Significance**
Offender			
Age (mean years)	(32.7)	(27.6)	.005[1]
Under 25	32.7	51.9	
Over 25	67.3	48.1	
Education (mean years)	(11.0)	(10.8)	NS
Elementary	2.0	5.2	
Some high school	29.3	39.0	
Beyond high school	68.7	55.8	
Employed			
Yes	31.3	20.0	NS
No	68.8	80.0	
Mother			
Yes	80.6	41.9	.000[2]
No	19.4	58.1	
Children (mean number)	(1.9)	(1.3)	NS
Victim			
Age (mean years)	(34.2)	(33.1)	.01[3]
Under 25	24.0	39.0	
Over 25	76.0	61.0	
Race			
Black	98.7	84.4	.0000[4]
White	1.3	10.4	
Hispanic	—	5.2	
Gender			
Male	89.3	67.5	.0000[5]
Female	10.7	32.5	

* Does not include missing cases.
** Chi-square, degrees of freedom
1. 7.94, 1 df
2. 21.74, 1 df
3. 5.52, 1 df
4. 17.86, 1 df
5. 16.34, 1 df

acquaintances, friends, and strangers.[8] In 59 percent of the cases the offender absolved herself of responsibility for the crime by claiming self-defense (28.8 percent), innocence (15.1 percent), or accidental homicide (15.1 percent). Identical motives were expressed by most of the women who killed loved ones (68.7 percent), but substantially more of these women claimed self-defense (51 percent). In an effort to understand more clearly whether the two groups differed significantly in the reasons they gave for killing, I dichotomized motive into "emotional" and "other."[9] I expected that black women who killed their loved ones would be more likely to cite emotional reasons than those who did not kill someone with whom they were involved in a primary relationship. As seen in table 8–2, the study group was significantly

Table 8–2
Homicide Characteristics by Victim Group (in percentages)*

| | Victim Group | | |
| | Study Group: Loved One (n = 150) | Contrast Group: All Other (n = 77) | |
Characteristic of:			Significance**
Homicide			
Offender alcohol use			
Yes	29.2	46.3	.02[1]
No	70.8	53.7	
Offender narcotic use			
Yes	7.3	16.1	NS
No	92.7	83.9	
Victim alcohol use			
Yes	51.3	50.9	NS
No	48.7	49.1	
Victim narcotic use			
Yes	9.5	10.7	NS
No	90.5	89.3	
Victim precipitation			
Yes	75.5	61.6	.03[2]
No	24.5	38.4	
Premeditated			
Yes	57.7	61.1	NS
No	42.3	38.9	
Offender role			
Alone	97.3	68.4	.000[3]
With others	2.7	31.6	
Motive			
Emotional	75.5	54.9	.0003[4]
Other	24.5	45.1	
Method			
Gun or knife	88.0	89.6	NS
Other	12.0	10.4	
Number of wounds			
Single	61.1	52.0	NS
Multiple	38.9	48.0	

* Does not include missing cases.
** Chi-square, degrees of freedom
1. 4.84, 1 df
2. 4.51, 1 df
3. 38.85, 1 df
4. 12.95, 1 df

more likely to kill in an emotional situation (75.5 percent) than was the contrast group (54.9 percent). Furthermore, only one case in the study group had an economic motive, but more than 8 percent of the slayings by the contrast group were committed for economic reasons; many involved a robbery or a drug deal that resulted in a felony killing.

Whereas women in the two groups did not differ substantially in the choice of weapon, the number of wounds inflicted, or whether the homicide was premeditated, the percentages in table 8–2 reveal that the less emotionally charged killings by members of the contrast group were more likely to be premeditated and to involve multiple wounds. In addition, members of the contrast group were more than eleven times more likely to kill with an accomplice (31.6 percent) than were women who killed loved ones (2.7 percent). On the other hand, although the victims tended to precipitate their own deaths in primary relationship cases (75.5 percent) more than in other cases (61.6 percent), alcohol or narcotics used by the victim before the homicide did not differ significantly between the groups. Alcohol use distinguished the groups, however: 46.3 percent of the women in the contrast group had used alcohol, compared with only 29.2 percent of the women who killed loved ones. Women in the contrast group also were twice as likely to have used narcotics (16.1 percent versus 7.3 percent of the study group), but this difference was not statistically significant.

In sum, the circumstances involved in the homicides by the study group reinforce the picture of an emotionally charged slaying of a loved one who tended to precipitate his or her death at the hands of a lone offender. The offender is someone close to them. This homicide scenario differs sharply from the profile of the typical woman in the contrast group, who premeditates her killing and perpetrates it with the help of another person.

Criminal Justice Characteristics

The findings on criminal histories and the response of the criminal justice system confirm the differences between these two groups of offenders. Not unexpectedly, the women who did not kill someone close to them were found to have prior arrest records (66.7 percent) and prior arrests for violent crimes (45.5 percent) in significantly more instances than their study group counterparts. Table 8–3 shows that fewer than half of the killers of loved ones (48.1 percent) had been arrested previously and that fewer than one-third had histories of arrest for violent offenses (30.7 percent). Although the study and the contrast groups differ on these traits, the percentages reflecting the extent of their involvement in the criminal justice system suggest that black

Table 8–3
Criminal Justice Characteristics by Victim Group (in percentages)*

	Victim Group		
Characteristic of:	Study Group: Loved One (n = 150)	Contrast Group: All Other (n = 77)	Significance**
Offender violent history			
Yes	30.7	45.5	.04[1]
No	69.3	54.5	
Offender prior record			
Yes	48.1	66.7	.01[2]
No	51.9	33.3	
Final disposition			
Prison	37.9	50.0	NS
No prison	62.1	50.0	
Prison time			
(mean years)	(6.9)	(10.0)	NS
5 years or less	52.8	45.7	
More than 5 years	47.2	54.3	

* Does not include missing cases.
** Chi-square, degrees of freedom
1. 4.11, 1 df
2. 6.30, 1 df

women who kill are involved disproportionately in that system, whoever their victims may be. This finding supports the conclusions of previous research, which shows the uneven distribution of black women in the criminal justice system as the result of violent crimes.

Also of note is the finding that black women who kill someone with whom they have an interpersonal relationship are less likely to receive a prison sentence; when sent to prison, they are sentenced to less time than those whose homicides involve persons more distant from them. The difference is not significant, however. No more than one-half of these offenders were sentenced to prison; the maximum sentence for the contrast group was a mean of ten years. It is possible that these outcomes give modest support to the theory of devaluation of a black life,[10] although this theory has not been tested.

Comparison by Victim/Offender Relationship

The preceding section of this chapter compared the aggregated group of black women who killed their loved ones with the remaining persons in the sample. This segment delves further into the relationship between the offender and her victim, using the same characteristics as those examined previously. As noted, the victim/offender relationships were categorized as significant others, child, or other relative. The first category, *significant others*, includes the majority of the victims, who had the following interpersonal relationships with their killers: married, common-law married, lovers, divorced, or separated (N = 122). The second category includes the seventeen children slain by their mothers. In the *other relative* group the eleven victims were mother (2), father (1), stepfather (2), brother (2), sister (1), cousin (1), and in-law (2).

The Offenders

Black women who killed their children were younger than those whose victims were other loved ones. As shown in table 8–4, more than one-half of those who committed filicide (homicide in which the murderer is a parent of the victim) were under twenty-five years of age. This finding is in contrast to those for members of the other two groups, who were predominantly over age twenty-five and also were about seven years older on the average than the women who killed their children. This finding is not unexpected because (with the exception of two cases in which the offenders' offsprings were twenty-four and twenty-six years of age) fifteen of the seventeen victims killed by their mothers were age nine or under; six of the children were less than one year old. The significant difference in victims' ages, reflected in table 8–4, also indicates the youthfulness of the filicide offenders, whose victims had a mean age of five years. This finding is in contrast to the other two groups, who primarily killed adults over age twenty-five and most frequently in their late thirties.

Educational level also distinguishes the black mothers who killed their children from those who killed other loved ones. Not only were these young mothers more likely to have had some college experience; they also averaged 12.3 years of education, compared with 11 years for the "significant others" group and only 9.6 years for those who killed other relatives. Because all three groups were similarly overrepresented in unemployment status, the higher educational level of the mothers who killed apparently was not reflected in employment.

The Victims

The significant age differences among the victims of the three groups of offenders can be attributed to the child killers, because the victims who were significant others or who were relatives were of about the same age (mean = 37.8 and 38.8 years respectively); those who were relatives tended to be slightly older. Furthermore, with the exception of

Table 8–4
Selected Offender/Victim Characteristics by Victim/Offender Relationship (in percentages)*

	Victim/Offender Relationship			
Characteristic of:	Significant Other (n=122)	Child (n=17)	Other Relative (n=11)	Significance**
Offender				
Age (mean years)	(33.4)	(26.2)	(34.8)	NS
Under 25	31.1	52.9	18.2	
Over 25	68.9	47.1	81.8	
Ed. (mean years)	(11.0)	(12.3)	(9.6)	.002[1]
Elementary	0.8	—	18.2	
Some high school	31.1	17.6	27.3	
Beyond high school	68.0	82.4	54.5	
Employed				
Yes	35.0	18.8	11.1	NS
No	65.0	81.3	88.9	
Mother				
Yes	78.6	100.0	57 1	.03[2]
No	21.4	—	42.9	
Children (mean number)	(1.8)	(2.1)	(2.0)	NS
None	6.1	—	—	
1 to 3	86.4	88.2	36.4	
More than 3	7.6	11.8	63.6	
Victim				
Age (mean years)	(37.8)	(5.0)	(38.8)	.0000[3]
Under 25	15.6	94.1	9.1	
Over 25	84.4	5.9	90.9	
Race				
Black	98.4	100.0	100.0	
White	1.6	—	—	
Gender				
Male	97.5	35.3	81.8	.0000[4]
Female	2.5	64.7	18.2	

* Does not include missing cases.
** Chi-square, degrees of freedom
1. 17.33, 4 df
2. 6.76, 2 df
3. 57.91, 2 df
4. 61.38, 2 df

one interracial, significant-other relationship, all of the victims were black, like their killers.

Analyses of the victim's gender, however, produced an extremely interesting finding. As noted by Mann (in press),

> throughout time (and in some cultures today), boys have been valued higher than girls, generally because family lines and inheritances were

traced through males (Empey, 1978: 63). Several studies of child killings suggest that devaluation of female children still exists. As a result
of her 17 year Chicago homicide study, Block (1985: 46) states, "For
the youngest age group, race/ethnicity is not as important as gender in
homicide victimizations. The proportion of murdered females who
were killed at young ages was consistently higher than the proportion
of murdered males who were killed at young ages." In Totman's study
(1978: 70) girl victims slightly exceed boy victims and Hawkins
(1986: 33) reports higher 1983 U.S. homicide rates for both black and
white females under age one than for males in that age group. Even a
Canadian study by Silverman and Kennedy (1988: 117) reveals that
57 percent of the infanticide victims whose deaths were caused by
their mothers were females.

The results of the present study tend to support the idea that a female
child has less worth than a male child: Significantly more mothers
killed females (64.7 percent) than killed males. In contrast, men were
more often the victims of the remaining black female homicide offenders in the study. Females were understandably more frequent victims in
the "other relative" category than in the "significant others" subgroup.
Only three cases of female victims were found in the latter category;
they were homosexual lovers.

Homicide Characteristics

The circumstances and events surrounding the homicide are similar in
many ways for all three groups, but table 8–5 shows that the women
who killed their progeny differed significantly on some homicide characteristics from those who killed other loved ones.

Previous homicide research shows that either the victim or the
offender usually had been under the influence of alcohol (Goetting,
1987; McClain, 1982–83; Suval and Brisson, 1974; Wilbanks, 1983;
Wolfgang, 1958). Among the killers of significant others and of other
relatives, about one-third of the offenders in this study had been drinking before the homicide. Conversely, none of the women who killed
their offspring had been drinking. Although the difference is not significant, and although only three cases were involved, these mothers were
proportionately more likely than the other two groups studied to have
used some drug other than alcohol (18.8 percent). This finding could
be explained by their youth. In one case the twenty-five-year-old
mother was drugged so heavily that when she and her two-month-old
daughter were found, it was discovered that the baby, who had been
dead for more than a day, also suffered dehydration and malnutrition.
The mother, who was still under the influence of an unidentified con-

Table 8–5
Homicide Characteristics by Victim/Offender Relationship (in percentages)*

	Victim/Offender Relationship			
Characteristic of:	*Significant Other (n=122)*	*Child (n=17)*	*Other Relative (n=11)*	*Significance***
Offender alcohol use				
Yes	33.7	—	33.3	.02[1]
No	66.3	100.0	66.7	
Offender narcotic use				
Yes	5.1	18.1	11.1	NS
No	94.9	81.3	88.9	
Victim alcohol use				
Yes	5.61	11.1	40.0	.03[2]
No	43.9	88.9	60.0	
Victim narcotic use				
Yes	9.3	—	20.0	NS
No	90.7	100.0	80.0	
Premeditated				
Yes	59.0	57.1	45.5	NS
No	41.0	42.9	54.4	
Offender role				
Alone	99.2	82.4	100.0	.0003[3]
With others	0.8	17.6	—	
Motive				
Emotional	82.9	41.2	90.9	.0003[4]
Other	17.1	58.8	9.1	
Victim precipitation				
Yes	84.3	11.8	81.2	.0000[5]
No	15.7	88.2	18.2	
Weapon				
Gun or knife	96.7	17.6	100.0	.0000[6]
Other	3.3	82.4	—	
Number of Wounds				
Single	60.3	64.7	63.6	NS
Multiple	39.7	35.3	36.4	

* Does not include missing cases.
** Chi-square, degrees of freedom
1. 7.60, 2 df
2. 7.24, 2 df
3. 16.60, 2 df
4. 16.45, 2 df
5. 42.47, 2 df
6. 89.97, 2 df

trolled substance, told the police that she did not know what had happened. A twenty-eight-year-old housewife and mother of four, when queried about the homicide of her five-year-old son, stated, "I never wanted any of my children." Allegedly she was under the influence of PCP when she beat the boy to death with an ax handle. Her common-law husband said that the offender once had thrown boiling water on him while he was asleep and that she often had "flashbacks" from her heavy PCP use.

Determining premeditated murder is highly speculative unless the perpetrator admits that he or she preplanned the killing, because a charge of premeditation requires both intent to kill and motive. Although the homicide files of these women tend to imply that premeditation was involved in more than half of the filicide cases (57.1 percent), close examination of the records challenges the notion that they had any prior schemes to kill their children. An examination of the motives given by mothers in these cases suggests either an accident (29.4 percent) or innocence (17.6 percent) as the most frequent reason for the child's death. These explanations, in addition to blaming others (5.9 percent) and economic considerations (5.9 percent), account for 58.8 percent of these cases.

In contrast, emotional reasons were given frequently by women who killed significant others (82.9 percent) and even more frequently by those who killed other relatives (90.0 percent). In these cases, victim precipitation was a significant factor and was exacerbated by the victims' use of alcohol before their deaths, particularly in the deaths of significant others.

In all but one instance in which an offender killed a relative other than her offspring, the situation was emotionally charged. In a typical example, a twenty-seven-year-old woman killed her fifty-four-year-old father:

> According to an eye witness, the offender had been drinking wine on the Saturday the slaying took place. For three weeks she had been staying at her father's girlfriend's house with them. Her father who was self-employed as a automobile repairman was working on a car in the backyard. During an argument with her father, the offender cursed him and called his deceased mother (her grandmother) a "no good bitch." Her father grabbed her by the hair and told her to never do that again. She agreed, but when he let her go, she said she would kill him and went in the house. The victim went back to his work on the car engine and was bending over the motor when his daughter came up behind him and stabbed him in the back of the neck with a butcher knife. (Mann, in press)

The influence of emotionality on these groups is also seen in the solitary nature of the offense. Spontaneity in committing the homicide is suggested by the finding that these groups were significantly more likely to be unaided when they killed a loved one. On the other hand, a mother who killed her offspring tended not to commit the crime alone; a significant other usually was her helpmate.

The number of wounds (single or multiple) did not distinguish killers of other relatives and significant others from the women who killed their children, but the choice of weapons was a distinguishing factor. Not surprisingly, 82.4 percent of the mothers drowned, strangled, suffocated, or beat their offspring to death; the other two groups, whose victims were adults, used guns and knives predominantly in the homicides. The women who killed their adult progeny also used these weapons.

Criminal Justice Characteristics

Somewhat unanticipated is the finding that no significant differences in criminal justice histories and processing for the crime were found among the three groups of black women who killed their loved ones as defined by the victim/offender relationship. I had expected that the younger, better-educated mothers would be less likely to have been involved in the criminal justice system than the women in the "significant others" and "other relatives" groups. It is true that the majority (64.7 percent) of the mothers who killed their children had no previous arrest records and that three-fourths had no histories of arrest for violent offenses. In regard to criminal histories, however, they were not significantly different from the other groups, who were more likely to have been involved in the criminal justice system. As table 8–6 shows, the women who killed other relatives had had more exposure to the system than either the filicide offenders or those whose homicides involved significant others.

Even though mothers who killed their children were less likely than the offenders to have had a prior arrest record or a history of arrest for violent offenses, they were only slightly less likely to receive a prison sentence. Again, those whose homicide victims were other relatives were sanctioned more severely by incarceration (55.6 percent) and by the mean length of prison sentence (10.6 years). Filicide offenders received the shortest sentences (3.8 years); those who killed significant others fall roughly between the other two groups (6.8 years).

It is difficult to reconcile the harsher treatment of the black women who killed relatives who were not their children. Because only five cases were involved, I examined carefully the data on each of the homicides. Two of the five offenders had prior records, both of which included violent offenses. The victim in one instance was the offender's

Table 8–6
Criminal Justice Characteristics by Victim/Offender Relationship
(in percentages)*

| Characteristic of: | Victim/Offender Relationship | | | Significance |
	Significant Other (n = 122)	Child (n = 17)	Other Relative (n = 11)	
Offender violent history				
Yes	30.4	25.0	44.4	NS
No	69.6	75.0	55.6	
Offender prior record				
Yes	49.5	35.3	55.6	NS
No	50.5	64.7	44.4	
Final disposition				
Prison	37.4	31.3	55.6	NS
No prison	62.6	68.8	44.4	
Prison time (mean yrs.)	(6.8)	(3.8)	(10.6)	NS
5 years or less	53.5	60.0	40.0	
More than 5 years	46.5	40.0	60.0	

* Does not include missing cases.

brother; in the other, an in-law. The other victims of women who had no arrest histories were the killer's father, son-in-law, and stepson. Guns were the weapons of choice in three of the homicides; knives were used in two. In all five cases in which the offenders received prison sentences, the victims were men and an argument was involved.

Intense arguments and violent rage were exhibited both by victims and offenders in the cases in which relatives were killed. An argument or a fight, self-defense or defense of others, anger, or the rationale that the homicide was justifiable account for 90.9 percent of the reasons why these women killed persons close to them. Similar motives were cited by most of the women (82.9 percent) who killed their significant others. Thus one reasonably could assume that there was some provocation for the homicide. In contrast, only 41.2 percent of the mothers whose victims were primarily their infant children expressed such emotionality during their homicidal act.

Summary and Discussion

Black females who kill today are similar to those described in previous studies that addressed this subgroup of our society. They continue to kill those closest to them, most commonly a husband, a lover, a relative, or a child.

In an effort to understand this tragic phenomenon, two different analyses were undertaken. I used cross-tabulations to compare the study group—black women whose victims were significant others, their children, or other relatives—with a contrast group of the remaining offenders in the larger data base. A second comparison included analyses by victim/offender relationship.

With the exception of significant differences between the study group and the contrast group on offender's age and maternal status, a profile of the black women who killed their loved ones (the study group) resembles that of other black female homicide offenders (the contrast group) more than it differs. Members of the study group are older and more frequently are mothers, but do not differ from the contrast group killers in years of education or in employment status. The victims of the two groups, however, differ significantly. Women who killed persons close to them chose victims who tended to be under twenty-five years of age, black, and male. On the other hand, victims in the contrast group were more likely to be over twenty-five years old; although predominantly black and male, they also included Hispanics, whites, and other females.

As found in earlier studies, victims in close interpersonal relationships tended to precipitate their own deaths; these homicides usually were committed by a lone female offender in a highly emotional encounter. In contrast, the black women who killed strangers, acquaintances, and friends were more likely to have been drinking before the homicide, to have had accomplices, and to have given significantly fewer emotional reasons for the crime. The criminal justice background of the latter group helps to explain these differences. These women were more likely to have been arrested and have more histories of arrest for violent offenses than the women whose victims were close to them. Finally, women who killed loved ones were less likely to receive prison sentences; if they were sent to prison, they were given shorter sentences than the slayers in the contrast group.

In the comparisons by victim/offender relationship, I found a number of significant differences among the women who killed significant others, their children, or other relatives. Black women who killed their children were younger and were less likely to have criminal histories; subsequently, they were less likely to be sent to prison and received shorter sentences than the other two groups.

Although black women who killed significant others and relatives were different from the child killers, there were numerous parallels. Both groups were in their early thirties; their victims were mostly men in their late thirties; all participants in the homicides had been drinking; the victims provoked their deaths, which were committed by the offenders alone; and a gun or a knife was the weapon of choice. The criminal justice histories and final dispositions of these women were not distinguished significantly from those of the women who killed their children, but both of the latter groups more frequently had prior records, had been arrested previously for violent crimes, received prison sentences for the murders, and received longer sentences. These characteristics were more typical of the women whose victims were other relatives. Generally black females who kill today, like those in the past, are not treated harshly by the criminal justice system: Fewer than half go to prison, and even a smaller proportion receive prison sentences for killing a loved one (37.9 percent); at most they are sentenced to only a few years.

Further investigation is needed to discover how black women who kill are processed by the criminal justice system. Why were the filicide offenders treated more leniently? Is a child's life of less value than an adult's, particularly that of a female child? Conversely, is a male's life considered by the criminal justice system to be more valuable? Unfortunately, the answers to these questions cannot be answered from the data available in this research because they are found in the deliberations and decisions of the criminal courts who tried these defendants. Even so, the direction of future research on women who kill their loved ones now can be set for other social scientists.

The findings of this study suggest strongly that many changes are needed in the black community. These changes must eliminate poor education, unemployment, poverty, and the many other indicators of social disorganization contributing to the anger and violence that lead black women to kill their children and others whom they love. Black genocide undoubtedly will continue until effective policy changes are implemented.

Notes

1. Although the current nomenclature for Americans of African descent is *Afro-American, black* is used in this chapter for the sake of consistency with the book title and with the other contributors' use of the term.

2. The generic term *woman* is used throughout the chapter, although the offender group included four teenagers (thirteen, fifteen, seventeen, and nineteen years of age).

3. *Homicide*, the killing of one human being by another, is the most appropriate term for the action studied here. The homicide files examined in this research used *murder, homicide,* and *criminal homicide* interchangeably and are reported similarly here. See Wilbanks (1982, p. 153) for a description of this semantic problem.

4. This nomenclature is used merely to differentiate the groups. Clearly one's child, sibling, or parent is also a significant other in the sociological sense.

5. This category included husbands, former husbands, common-law and former common-law husbands, heterosexuals, and the homosexual lovers.

6. Contrary to popular jokes and cartoons, it was found in the few cases involved that the offender's in-laws were considered close family members; they are included here as such.

7. The exploratory nature of the research and the preponderance of nominal variables are treated most effectively by a nonparametric method of statistical measurement; in this case, chi-square.

8. To conserve space, I did not include tabular frequencies for any of the subgroups discussed here.

9. "Emotional" motives include self-defense, defense of others, being under the influence of some substance, psychological reasons (e.g., mental illness), PMS (although no cases of premenstrual syndrome were found), emotional reasons (e.g., anger, jealousy), a domestic quarrel or fight, senselessness, and justifiable. The "other" category contains innocence, accident, another's fault, multiple reasons, and economic reasons (e.g., robbery or insurance).

10. Darnell Hawkins (1986) developed a hypothetical prototype to measure the devaluation of black life in homicide prosecutions, but it was not available when this research was undertaken.

9

Patterns of Marital Homicide: A Comparison of Husbands and Wives

Ann Goetting

Most Americans view the family as a center for warmth, affection, acceptance, and happiness that serves as a refuge from the more competitive, stressful, and violent outside world. This image remains intact in spite of the fact that for over a decade now, research and the media have demonstrated the "underside" (Adler, 1981) of domestic life. It has become clear that the home is a dangerous place; more violence occurs there than outside its doors (Pagelow, 1984). Perhaps we cling to notions of the idealized family with good reason. Maybe the image of wise and devoted husbands and wives lovingly nurturing one another and their attractive, courteous, obedient, and charming children through the typical stages of the life cycle provides us with an important source of comfort (Pagelow, 1984). Or perhaps, as is suggested by Steinmetz and Straus (1974), this myth of domestic tranquility plays a critical role in the maintenance of the social institution of the family by encouraging individuals to marry, to stay married, and to have children. Whatever causes the persistence of this ideology, we should recognize that it may not occur without cost, for it likely has served to limit the objective analysis of family violence (Steinmetz and Straus, 1974). It is only through such analysis that we may become freed to understand and perhaps ultimately prevent such violence.

The purpose of this study is to contribute to the very limited data based on one form of family violence in the United States, that is marital homicide, which involves the killing of a person by his or her spouse. In 1984 marital homicide accounted for nearly half of intrafamily homicide, making it the most frequent type of intrafamily victim-offender relationship (Straus, 1986). This research is intended to update sociological knowledge on the subject, and to extend current information by introducing additional variables. What remains the most important sociological inquiry into marital homicide, Wolfgang's (1956)

Reprinted with permission from *Journal of Comparative Family Studies* XX (3), 341–54.

Philadelphia study, is now dated by over three decades. More recent efforts focus exclusively on homicidal wives (Browne, 1986; 1988; Bunyak, 1986; Mann, 1988; Totman, 1978). The concerns addressed by this study relate to the general contextual nexus of marital homicide as well as to specific gender-based comparisons. What kinds of people kill their spouses? When, where and under what circumstance do they act? What weapons do they select? What motivational forces come into play? Is the fatal act typically offensive or defensive? Is alcohol involved? Are there witnesses? Does the offender flee the scene? What legal dispositions are associated with this behavior? Finally, do husbands and wives differ from one another on these factors? Wolfgang (1956) discovered gender to be a critical determinant of weapon selection, room of offense, victim precipitation, and legal disposition. Do these correlates hold true in the 1980s in a different Midwestern city?

Research Methods

The subjects selected for this study include the total population of eighty-four arrestees,[1] twenty-eight male and fifty-six female,[2] accused of having killed their spouses (both legal and common-law) in the city of Detroit, Michigan, during 1982 and 1983 (except those attributed to the negligent use of a vehicle). An important limitation of the study lies in its lack of generalizability; its subjects are drawn from an urban, predominantly black population with an inordinately high homicide rate. In fact, in 1987, its third consecutive year for ranking highest in the nation, Detroit reported 54.6 homicides per 100,000 inhabitants. The eight-four cases constituting this study population account for 11.2 percent of all closed homicide cases in that city during those two years. Data collection took place in June 1986 in the offices of the Homicide Section of the Detroit Police Department. Police-recorded information regarding each case, including the Investigator's Report, Interrogation Record, and Witness Statements, was electronically copied for subsequent perusal.

The data were tabulated and, when feasible, comparisons were made with the total population of Detroit arrestees for homicides committed during 1982 and 1983, and with previous homicide studies employing general populations and offenders. Since the proportion of homicide arrestees who are accused of having killed spouses remains between 8 and 9 percent (U.S. Department of Justice, 1981–85), this means that the comparisons employed should have, according to the laws of probability, utilized populations and samples constituting approximately 91 percent members who are not offenders against spouses. Clearly the comparisons applied for this study are less than ideal on two counts: (1) the comparison groups are not totally mutually exclusive (i.e., the other-than-offender-against-spouse groups actually contain some offenders against spouses) and (2) except when 1982 and 1983 Detroit data are available, the comparison groups are not geographically and temporally comparable. Throughout the analyses, notable differences between male and female subjects are acknowledged. Population characteristics and gender differences are summarized in table 9–1.

The information reported herein is presented through use of a three-part organizational scheme: demographic and social characteristics of offenders and victims, circumstances of offense, and arrest disposition.

Table 9–1
Summary of Population and Subpopulation (by Gender) Characteristics

Characteristics	(Sub) Population Size[1]	Number	Percent	Mean
Demographic and Social Characteristics				
Offender: Black	84	76	90.5	
Women	56	54	96.4	
Men	28	22	78.6	
Victim: Black	84	77	91.7	
Women	28	22	78.6	
Men	56	55	98.2	
Offender: Age	84			35.5 years
Women	56			34.1 years
Men	28			38.3 years
Victim: Age	84			37.9 years
Women	28			34.8 years
Men	56			39.4 years
Offender: Lived in family setting	80	76	95.0	
Women	54	52	96.3	
Men	26	24	92.3	
Offender: Residing with spouse	84	73	86.9	
Women	56	51	91.1	
Men	28	22	78.6	
Offender: Child(ren)	73	59	80.8	
Women	53	43	81.1	
Men	20	16	80.0	
Offender: Completed 12 years school	63	33	52.4	
Women	45	22	48.9	
Men	18	11	61.1	
Offender: Unemployed	72	53	73.6	
Women	50	39	78.0	
Men	22	14	63.6	
Offender: Welfare recipient	33	22	66.7	
Women	28	20	71.4	
Men	5	2	40.0	

continued

Table 9–1 continued

Characteristics	(Sub) Population Size[1]	Number	Percent	Mean
Offender: No residential telephone	74	18	24.3	
Women	52	14	26.9	
Men	22	4	18.2	
Offender: Arrest record	53	30	56.6	
Women	35	18	51.4	
Men	18	12	66.7	
Circumstances of Offense				
Motive: Domestic discord	84	79	94.0	
Women (O)[2]	56	53	94.6	
Men (O)	28	26	92.9	
Method: Gunshot	84	49	58.3	
Women (V)[3]	28	18	64.3	
Men	56	31	55.4	
Method: Stabbing	84	27	32.1	
Women (V)	28	4	14.3	
Men (V)	56	23	41.1	
Single-victim/Single-offender	84	81	96.4	
Women (O)	56	55	98.2	
Men (O)	28	26	92.9	
Victim precipitation	55	33	60.0	
Women (O)	45	32	71.1	
Men (O)	10	1	10.0	
Location: Residence	84	75	89.3	
Women (O)	56	51	91.1	
Men (O)	28	24	85.7	
Location: Bedroom	69	27	39.1	
Women (O)	49	15	30.6	
Men (O)	20	12	60.0	
Time: Weekend	82	49	59.7	
Women (O)	56	34	60.7	
Men (O)	26	15	57.7	
Time: 8 P.M.–1:59 A.M.	81	34	42.0	
Women (O)	55	25	45.5	
Men (O)	26	9	34.6	
Offender: Alcohol	31	27	87.1	
Women	21	18	85.7	
Men	10	9	90.0	
Victim: Alcohol	33	31	93.9	
Women	26	25	96.2	
Men	7	6	85.7	
Audience	82	32	39.0	
Women (O)	55	23	41.8	
Men (O)	27	9	33.3	
Fled scene	77	21	27.3	
Women	51	8	15.7	
Men	26	13	50.0	
Arrest Disposition				
Denied warrant	78[3]	23	29.5	

Table 9–1 continued

Characteristics	*(Sub) Population Size*[1]	*Number*	*Percent*	*Mean*
Women	54[3]	20	37.0	
Men	24[3]	3	12.5	
Convicted of murder or manslaughter	53[4]	33	62.3	
Women	34[4]	16	47.1	
Men	19[4]	17	89.4	
Prison sentences	38[5]	27	71.1	
Women	21[5]	12	57.1	
Men	17[5]	15	88.2	

1. Number of subjects for which information was available
2. O = offenders; V = victims
3. Number of subjects at risk of prosecution
4. Number of subjects processed by court
5. Number of subjects convicted

Analyses

Demographic and Social Characteristics of Offenders and Victims

Race. Research repeatedly has verified that homicide offenders and their victims in the United States are disproportionately black. Detroit provides no exception to this generalization, and neither do the men and women who kill their spouses in that city. In 1980, 63 percent of the Detroit population was black (U.S. Bureau of the Census, 1984). Of all arrestees for homicides committed in Detroit during 1982 and 1983, 89.1 percent were black, and 81.9 percent of victims were black (U.S. Department of Justice, 1981–85). Information on the offenders against spouses in that population indicated that 90.5 percent (seventy-six) of them and 91.7 percent (seventy-seven) of their victims were of that racial category. Three of the offenses under observation here were interracial: In two cases a white woman killed her black husband, and in the remaining case a black woman killed her white husband.

Age. The study population of offenders ranged in age between eighteen and eight-two years, with a mean of 35.5. Their victims showed approximately the same age range, with a mean of 37.9 years of age. As might be expected the victims of the women generally were older than they, while the victims of the men generally were younger than their slayers. The killers and victims under observation here were slightly older than the general population of arrested killers and slain victims in

Detroit during 1982 and 1983. Those mean arrestee and victim ages were 31.5 and 35 years, respectively.

Residential Mode and Parental Status of Offender. Nearly all (95 percent, or seventy-six) of the eighty killers who reported residential mode were living in a family setting; all except eleven (86.9 percent) of the total population were residing with their victimized spouses at the time of the offense. Nearly 81 percent (fifty-nine) of the seventy-three offenders for whom data were available acknowledged at least one living child.

Social Class Indicators of Offender. Just over half of the sixty-three offenders for whom information on formal education was available had completed at least twelve years of school. Over 20 percent (thirteen) were educated beyond that level. These data reflect a relatively low level of formal education when compared with the general United States population at the same point in time.[3] Employment information was available for seventy-two of the arrestees; nearly three quarters (73.6 percent, or fifty-three) of whom were unemployed, one of them having retired and another currently collecting disability compensation.

These data on education and unemployment, in conjunction with the facts that two-thirds (twenty-two) of the thirty-three subjects for whom information was available were welfare recipients, and 24.3 percent (eighteen) of the seventy-four for whom data were recorded reported having no residential telephone,[4] are congruent with other studies suggesting that homicide offenders are concentrated in the lower social classes (Bensing, Jackson, and Schroeder, 1960; Swigert and Farrell, 1978; Wolfgang, 1958).

Arrest Record of Offender. Homicide records indicate that 56.6 percent (thirty) of the fifty-three offenders for whom data were available had been arrested at least once prior to the offenses that precipitated them into the study population. While this is a crude measure of criminal history, since it fails to delineate the particular charges and dispositions associated with arrests, it does suggest that a high proportion of the spouse killers under observation here are likely to have had criminal backgrounds. Available research indicates a basic consistency when comparing this particular category of offender with general populations of homicide offenders on this dimension. Wolfgang (1958) reports 64 percent and Swigert and Farrell (1978) report 56 percent of their homicide offender populations as having had previous arrests.

Circumstances of Offense

Homicidal Motive. Most marital homicides occur in the context of domestic discord. The typical scenario involves an argument or a physical or verbal confrontation, perhaps over sexual indiscretion, money, or the threat of terminating the relationship. In such cases, the death blow usually is the culminating event in a long history of interpersonal tensions entrenched in violence. It is struck in the urgency of passionate anger; the fatal outcome commonly is realized with shock and disbelief. Often the offender had not intended to go so far. Homicidal marriages appear to be strongly ambivalent in nature, and the deadly act seems to dissipate hateful sentiments on the part of the offender, leaving a sense of despair at the loss of a loved one (Browne, 1987).

All but five (94 percent) of the cases under consideration here conform to this general description. One exception involved a woman who beat to death her husband with a baseball bat as he was beating their son. Two other cases were premeditated and motivated by insurance benefits. In one such case, a forty-year-old woman and her eighteen-year-old boyfriend conspired to kill her twenty-nine-year-old husband for the freedom to have a baby together as well as for insurance benefits. The boyfriend beat the husband to death with a baseball bat, arranging the scene to appear as though the death had resulted from a drug-related robbery. She was convicted of manslaughter, and he of first degree murder; both were sentenced to prison. In the other premeditated incident, a twenty-six-year-old woman beat and shot to death her estranged husband of the same age after having secured several insurance policies on his life without his knowledge. Three months before the fatal incident, the offender had commented to her mother and sisters that she was going to make them rich, and that she planned to buy a Mercedes Benz. Though at the wake she had to be pulled away from the coffin as she exclaimed, "All I want to do is tell him that I was sorry to do it," she never formally admitted her guilt, and was acquitted. Finally, two exceptional cases were accidental shootings. In one case, a forty-year-old white man shot his thirty-three-year-old common-law wife in the face with a double-barrel shotgun as she entered the doorway to the basement where he and a friend were handling the weapon and discussing it in the context of an upcoming hunting trip. The offender was sentenced to one to two years in prison for careless and reckless use of a firearm: death resulting. The other accidental incident involved a seventy-three-year-old white man who shot to death with a handgun his seventy-two-year-old wife as their home was being burglarized by seven young (age fifteen to twenty-two years) black males. For some unknown reason the lights in the house went out during the burglary, which caused the old man to mistake his wife for a burglar. The killer was not charged with a criminal offense, but was instead employed by the state as a witness.

Homicidal Method. Firearms are the most common means of inflicting death in this country. Between 1968 and 1978 the proportion of homicides committed with firearms varied between 63 and 65.7 percent (Riedel, Zahn, and Mock, 1985). In Detroit during 1982 and 1983, 65.8 percent of the 1138 reported homicides were shootings. Another 17.8 percent were stabbings, 11.4 percent were beatings, .7 percent were burnings, and 4.2 percent were conducted by some other means (U.S. Department of Justice, 1981–85). The distribution of homicidal methods associated with the victims of marital homicide in Detroit during those years differs from that associated with the general population of victims primarily in that a somewhat lower proportion of the spouses (58.3 percent, or forty-nine) died of gunshot wounds, and a much higher proportion (32.1 percent, or twenty-seven) were stabbed. Five victims (5.6 percent) were beaten to death, three (3.6 percent) with blunt instruments, and two (2.4 percent) through the use of hands and/ or feet as weapons; and another three (3.6 percent) were strangled or suffocated. Distributions of methods vary distinctly by gender. A somewhat lower proportion of husbands than wives died of gunshot wounds, and a much higher proportion (nearly triple) were stabbed. This is consistent with Wolfgang's (1956) observation that wives were more than twice as likely as husbands to use cutting instruments, attributing that difference to "cultural tradition": Because of their domestic role (i.e., involving food preparation), women are more accustomed to using knives than are men (Wolfgang, 1958). Additionally, all beatings using hand and/or feet and all strangulations or suffocations were inflicted on wives.

Number of Victims and Offenders. Almost all homicides are one-on-one incidents, with a higher concentration among domestic killings. Detroit provides no exception to this generalization, and neither do the men and women who kill their spouses in that city. In Detroit during 1982 and 1983, 87.9 percent of the 578 homicides for which information is available involved a single victim and a single offender. Another 10.6 percent of those offenses were single-victim/multiple offender; 1.4 percent of those offenses were multiple-victim/single offender; and the remaining .2 percent were multiple-victim/multiple offender (U.S. Department of Justice, 1981–85). All except three (96.4 percent) of the homicides against spouses occurring in that city during those years were one-on-one. Two of the exceptional incidents, both perpetrated by men, involved a single offender, one with two victims (a wife and their eighteen-year-old daughter), and the other with three (a common-law wife, her ten-year-old son, and their eight-year-old son). The third case involved the woman and her boyfriend who conspired to kill her husband for insurance benefits.

Victim Precipitation. The concept of victim precipitation originated with von Hentig in the 1940s, who observed that "the victim shapes and molds the criminal" and that "the victim assumes the role of a determinant" (von Hentig, 1948, 383–85 cited in Wolfgang, 1958, 245–46). The actual term *victim precipitation* was later coined by Wolfgang (1958), and is applied to those offenses in which the victim is the first in the homicide drama to use physical force directed against his subsequent slayer.

Information on victim precipitation could be gleaned from 1982 and 1983 Detroit police records for fifty-five homicides perpetrated against spouses. Sixty percent (thirty-three) of these cases were victim precipitated. This proportion is high when compared with data from studies of general homicide populations, which report victim precipitation to characterize between 22 and 37.9 percent of deadly encounters (Curtis, 1974; Voss and Hepburn, 1968; Wolfgang, 1958). This discrepancy can be explained by the predominance of homicidal wives in the study population (forty-five of the fifty-five subjects for whom information was available were wives). It has been established that a relatively high proportion of spousal homicides perpetrated by women are victim precipitated (Wolfgang, 1956; Wilbanks, 1983), and the wives under observation here conform to that generalization (71.1 percent of their offenses were of that nature).

Spatial Considerations. A survey of homicide research suggests that between 42 and 53 percent of homicides occur at a private residence (Pokorney, 1965; Riedel, Zahn, and Mark, 1985; Swigert and Farrell, 1978; Wolfgang, 1958). Consistent with Wolfgang's (1956) study, the present Detroit data suggest, as might be expected, that marital homicides are far more likely to occur in that setting than are the general population of homicides. Over 89 percent (seventy-five) of the killings in this study were accomplished in a home: 78.6 (sixty-six) occurred at the common residence of the offender and victim, 8.3 percent (seven) at the residence of the offender, 1.2 percent (one) at the residence of the victim and another 1.2 percent (one) at the residence of a friend. Additionally, eight offenses (9.5 percent) took place on public streets, and one (1.2 percent) at the place of business of the victim.

Over 39 percent (twenty-seven) of the sixty-nine offenses committed at a private residence for which information was available occurred in a bedroom; again, this closely approximates the 35 percent reported by Wolfgang (1956). Another 21.7 percent (fifteen) took place in the living room. Approximately 10 percent (seven) occurred outside the actual residence (usually on the porch or in the yard) and in the kitchen, 7.2 percent (five) in the dining room, 4.3 percent (three) in a hallway, 2.9 percent (two) each in a bathroom and an "other" room, and 1.4 percent (one) in the basement. Like the husbands observed in the Wolfgang (1956) study, those under observation here were twice as likely to kill in a bedroom as were the wives. Only one of the six offenses occurring in the kitchen was perpetrated by a husband, and all seven of the outdoor incidents were perpetrated by wives.

Temporal Considerations. Clearly there is a temporal order inherent in violent behavior. While the tempo of homicide varies slightly according to season, it varies markedly by days of week and hours of day. Homicide is a leisure-related activity, and is closely associated with periods typically devoted to recreation.

For 1982 and 1983 combined, the frequency distribution of all Detroit homicides over the twelve months indicates a general overall stability except for slight increases during August–September (the hot season) and December–January (the holiday season), and a discernable dip in April (the introduction to spring) (U.S. Department of Justice: 1982–85). Except for a moderate increase during January and February, the marital homicides in that city during those years displayed no apparent seasonal fluctuations. Their frequencies over the ten or perhaps twelve months appear to be randomly distributed, with a high of 13.1 percent in January to a low of 4.8 percent in May and October.

Relative to days of week, the research population of marital homicides conformed closely to the norm. Data are consistent in indicating that homicide is concentrated during weekends, peaking on Saturdays (Bensing, Jackson, and Schroeder 1960; Voss and Hepburn, 1968; Wolfgang, 1958), and these husbands and wives provide no exception to that generalization. Nearly 60 percent (forty-nine) of the eighty-two killings in this study for which information was available occurred on Fridays, Saturdays, and Sundays (the days of the three highest frequencies), which clearly is in line with the range extending between 56.6 and 84 percent reported by studies using general populations of offenders. The subjects conformed less closely to hourly norms. Wolfgang (1958) and Pokorney (1986) provide the only two sources of information on homicide that effectively can be compared with data describing the Detroit killers on the subject of time of offense.[5] The two studies are consistent with one another in indicating that approximately half of homicides occur between 8:00 P.M. and 1:59 A.M., and another quarter occur between 2:00 P.M. and 7:59 P.M. Basically congruous with these general homicide populations, the spouses under observation here executed 42 percent (thirty-four) of the eighty-one homicides for which information was available between 8:00 P.M. and 1:59 A.M., and 28.4 percent (twenty-three) between 2:00 P.M. and 7:59 P.M. The remaining 29.6 percent (twenty-four) of the cases apparently were evenly distributed throughout the remaining hours of the day.

Alcohol Consumption. Available information suggests that alcohol consumption contributes to the homicide drama (Collins, 1981; Wolfgang,

1958; MacDonald, 1961; Riedel, Zahn, and Mock, 1985; Wolfgang, 1958) and to marital violence (Frieze and Browne, 1989; Leonard and Jacob, 1988). The information gleaned from witness statements for this study of homicidal spouses is limited in that data were available for just over a third of the subjects. But these data suggest that alcohol may have played a vital role in many of the incidents. At least 32.1 (twenty-seven) of the total population of offenders had been drinking prior to the homicide, as had at least 36.9 percent (thirty-one) of their victims.

Audience and Offender's Response. Thirty-nine percent (thiry-two) of the eighty-two victims for whom data were recorded received their fatal blows before witnesses. Most (67.5 percent, or fifty-two) of the seventy-seven offenders for whom information was available remained at the homicide scene until investigators arrived; only 27.3 percent (twenty-one) fled to avoid detection. Another four (5.2 percent), all men, committed suicide at the scene. This gender differential relating to suicide among spouse-killers is consistent with other research (Daly and Wilson, 1988). Furthermore, it is interesting to note that more than three times the proportion of men than women fled the scene.

Arrest Disposition

Prosecuting Attorney. Prosecuting attorneys are recognized as yielding weighty influence in the determination of criminal processing outcomes. They are allowed much discretion in their decisions as to what criminal charges, if any, will be filed against arrestees in court. Of the seventy-eight spouse killers for whom information was available who were at risk of prosecution (excluding the four suicides), 29.5 percent (twenty-three) were denied warrant for criminal charge by the prosecutor. This proportion is congruent with the estimated 30.4 percent of the general population of homicide arrestees for that city during 1983 who enjoyed similar denial,[6] suggesting an absence of prosecutorial bias toward this category of offender. Nearly three times the proportion of women as men who were at risk were denied warrant, which is not surprising in light of the fact that such a high proportion of incidents perpetrated by women were victim precipitated. Additionally, the notion of chivalry may enter in here; most studies of felony defendants have found that women are more likely to be released prior to trial than are their male counterparts (Gruhl, Welch, and Spahn 1984).

Court. Court dispositions associated with the fifty-three arrestees who were processed by the Court (excluding the subject never taken into custody, the four suicides, and one subject who skipped bond) indicate

that 62.3 percent (thirty-three) were convicted of a misdemeanor including careless discharge, intentionally pointing a firearm without mal-
ice, and careless and reckless use of a firearm: death resulting (high
misdemeanor); and 28.3 percent (fifteen) were acquitted. Of the thirty-
eight convicted arrestees, 71.1 percent (twenty-seven) received prison
sentences: three for life, and the rest for a mean minimum of 7.7 years.
A total of twenty-six of the thirty-three convicted of murder or manslaughter (78.8 percent) were sentenced to incarceration. One woman
convicted of a misdemeanor received a prison sentence of fifteen days.
Again, with court disposition, leniency toward women is suggested.
Consistent with the observations of Wolfgang (1956), a much lower
proportion of women than men who were processed by the court were
convicted of murder or manslaughter. Also, a much lower proportion
of convicted women were sentenced to incarceration. This apparent
leniency directed toward women by the court system is incongruent
with the discrimination applied to them as described by Browne (1988).

Discussion

The construction of a statistical profile describing the population of
eighty-four men and women arrested for killing their spouses in the
predominantly black city of Detroit, Michigan, during 1982 and 1983
yields the image of a black man or woman in his or her middle thirties
who lives in a family setting. He or she is an undereducated, unemployed parent with an arrest record, whose finale in a series of heated
arguments or confrontations with his or her spouse culminated in a
defensive fatal gunshot in a bedroom or the living room of their residence on a weekend.

The findings reported herein are totally consistent with those derived from Wolfgang's (1956) Philadelphia study conducted over thirty
years ago. This fact suggests that a robust and predictable pattern of
circumstances surrounds marital homicide. It also verifies that the marital homicide experience differs significantly by gender: For the homicidal husband the act is nearly always offensive; for the wife it is usually
defensive. This supports the popular contention that marital homicide,
regardless of who inflicts the fatal blow, typically is a reflection of wife
abuse (Browne, 1986; Mann, 1988; "Wives Face Bigger Risk in Spouse
Killings," 1989). In the words of Russell (1982): "The statistics on the
murder of husbands, along with the statistics on the murder of wives,
are both indicators of the desperate plight of some wives, not a sign
that in this one area, males and females are equally violent" (p. 299).
Previous research indicates that homicide does not occur without
warning—nonlethal violence precedes domestic homicide (Straus,

1986). Abused women have been warned, yet they remain in a violent situation hoping for improvement. Consistent with other studies (Gelles and Cornell, 1985), the wives involved here along with witnesses to the incidents, usually children and other family members, seemingly accepted the situation as normal or at least tolerable. Even more disheartening is the suggestion that such violence inflicted in the context of a romantic relationship is in some cases perceived as a sign of love (Henton et al., 1983), and therefore perhaps even encouraged of the participants by one another.

Clearly there is a critical need for effective intervention and support agencies to accommodate the needs of women victimized by domestic violence. Help must be provided to prevent the kinds of fatal incidents depicted in this study. Police should be trained specifically in domestic concerns, and urged to view reported cases of domestic conflict in a more serious light (Pagelow, 1984). Additionally, it is believed by some that they need to respond more effectively (Elliott, 1989; Gelles and Straus, 1989; Gillespie, 1989).

Available evidence suggests that continued domestic violence against women may be reduced by police arrests (Sherman and Berk, 1984). Langen and Innes's (1986) Analysis of National Crime Survey (NCS) data indicate that simply reporting such violence may decrease the likelihood and severity of subsequent assaults. Only an estimated 14.4 percent of incidents of domestic violence against women are brought to police attention (Kantor, Kaufman, and Straus, 1987). The most common reason offered by 1978 through 1982 NCS female respondents for not reporting domestic violence was that the woman considered the incident a private or personal matter (Langen and Innes, 1986). These women need to be dissuaded from that perspective, and encouraged to seek formal intervention.

Notes

1. Actually, five subjects are not arrestees: One was charged by the prosecuting attorney for a felony killing, but was never taken into custody, and four others committed suicide at the scene. For the purpose of this study, however, these five offenders are not distinguished from the arrestees.

2. This finding of a relatively high proportion of wife/husband versus husband/wife homicides among this predominantly black population is consistent with the results of three studies (Block, 1985; Plass and Straus, 1987; "Wives Face Bigger Risk in Spouse Killings," 1989) that discovered a higher number of female than male spouse killers among blacks, but a lower number among whites (and in Block's study, Latin Americans). Plass and Straus suggest that white women, because of greater economic and social-emotional dependency on their husbands, may be more vulnerable to being victims of wife beating—and homicide—than are black women.

3. In March 1982, 70.9 percent of the noninstitutionalized United States population aged twenty-five and older had completed four years of high school. In 1983 that proportion increased to 72.1 percent (U.S. Bureau of the Census, 1984–85).

4. This proportion is high when compared with the estimated 10.4 percent of Detroit residences reportedly having no telephone service in January 1986 (Cross, 1986).

5. Only those two studies utilized a coding scheme for hour of offense similar to that employed for the present study.

6. This estimate was computed by dividing the number of warrants issued by the Office of Wayne County Prosecuting Attorney in 1983 for murder and manslaughter in the city of Detroit (296) (Smith, 1985) by the total number of 1983 arrests for murder and manslaughter recorded by the Homicide Section of the Detroit Department of Police (425); by then transforming that quotient (.696) to a percentage by multiplying by 100 (69.6 percent—this represents the proportion of arrestees who were issued warrants); and by subtracting that percentage from 100 (30.4 percent). The estimate is vulnerable to error to the extent that some arrestees may have died before the preliminary hearing or may have been issued a warrant for a crime other than murder or manslaughter. Those cases would be incorrectly counted as having been denied a warrant, artificially inflating the true proportion of dismissals.

Part VI
Preventing Violence

10

Clinical Care Update: Preventive Strategies for Dealing with Violence among Blacks

Carl C. Bell

In regular medicine if a patient goes to a doctor to be treated for a rat bite, the physician cleans the bite, dresses it, gives antibiotics, and gives a tetanus shot. The physician practicing social medicine would give our imaginary patient the same treatment but would go a step further; he would arrange for someone to go into the patient's community and set rat traps. A similiar distinction is made between general psychiatry and community psychiatry, and this distinction highlights one of the main principles of the community psychiatrist's mission—community development being the art of helping a community achieve a social and interpersonal milieu that promotes an optimum level of mental health (Freed, 1967; 1972). This aspect of community psychiatry takes on an even greater significance when the community being served is a lower socioeconomic, minority community because of the conditions found in such communities that can impair the overall mental health of the community's individuals, families, and groups. This chapter will illustrate the principle of community development, the role of one psychiatrist in community development, and its importance to deprived minority communities by describing a community psychiatry approach to the problem of black-on-black homicide.

The Problem

Black-on-black homicide is the leading cause of death in black males fifteen to thirty-four. Black males have a chance of being murdered ten times more than white males, and black females have a chance of being murdered five times more than white females. More specifically, black males have a 1-in-21 chance and white males have a 1-in-131 chance of

Reprinted with permission from *Community Mental Health Journal* 23 (3), 217–28.

becoming homicide victims; black females have a 1-in-104 chance and white females have a 1-in-369 chance of being homicide victims. Two-thirds to three-fourths of those murdered will know their murderer as family, friends, or acquaintances. Thus, a majority of black-on-black murder occurs in the interpersonal context, and, since it is estimated that for every one murder there are about one hundred assaults (Koop, 1985), it is apparent that there exists a significant amount of violence in black interpersonal relationships. Black-on-black murder is simply a measurable tip of the iceberg of black interpersonal violence. The focus on the problem of black-on-black murder should not be taken as a denial of the problem in society in general. In fact, although black males experience the highest rate of homicide and have the greatest absolute increase in homicide, homicide rates have been increasing more dramatically for Hispanic males when compared with black males (University of California at Los Angeles and Centers for Disease Control, 1985). Further, for society at large, husbands caused their wives more injuries requiring medical treatment than car accidents, rapes, and muggings combined. The black-on-black murder problem is simply a discrete, epidemilogic phenomenon that allows itself to be addressed by a community, much like Tay-Sachs disease.

The phenomenon of violence in the black community can be viewed from several different perspectives. For example, from the victim's perspective, the black child who witnesses her parent being murdered will undergo a major psychic trauma that will seriously affect her mental health. Parents who are informed of the grisly death of their offspring will have to mourn the loss of that offspring in addition to learning how to cope with the stress of knowing the horrendous manner of their child's death—the combination of both possibly leading to symptoms of depression and posttraumatic stress disorders (Rynearson, 1986). I recall the case of a black elderly woman whose daughter had been killed by her daughter's boyfriend during a domestic quarrel. The perpetrator of the murder, in a state of rage, repeatedly stabbed the mother of his child in front of the child, who was seven years old at the time. The grandmother of the child (my patient) came to the Community Mental Health Council complaining of a prolonged grief reaction over the loss of her daughter, which had developed into a major depressive disorder. The patient also had signs and symptoms of post-traumatic stress disorder characterized by intrusive fantasized thoughts of the horrible scene of her daughter's death, sleep-onset insomnia, irritability, an exaggerated startled response, withdrawal from her usual activities, and symptoms of panic attacks. Further, the patient was "saddled" with the care of her grandson, which was an issue of great psychological ambivalence as the patient had raised nine children and had looked forward to her "golden years" as a time for her as opposed to a dependent child. Yet, at the same time, the patient felt a great deal of responsibility for her grandson. The case was also complicated by the grandmother and her grandson both suffering the loss of the homicide victim. In one way this allowed the grandmother to identify with the grandson and be more responsive to him, but since the grandson resembled his father (the murderer), there was also a significant amount of anger being directed at the grandson. Lastly, the grandson had problems of school failure, nightmares, and excessively aggressive behavior, which indicated the grandson was also having difficulties adjusting to his mother's death (as well as the loss of his father due to incarceration) and needed treatment. Individuals who are assaulted in a family context such as child abuse or spouse abuse are likely to develop a variety of psychiatric symptoms including suicide attempts, psychophysiologic disorders, anxiety disorders, and interpersonal difficulties (Stark and Flitcraft, 1982; Okun, 1986). From the offender's perspective, we see the majority of black-on-black murder occurring in the context of "crimes of passion or rage" as opposed to felony homicides, those occurring during the commission of a felony such as armed robbery. Such out-of-control emotional states are often at the base of spousal abuse and domestic violence prior to becoming a homicide. In a study of family homicide in Kansas City in 1977, it was found that in 85 percent of the cases the police had been called to the home of the victim five times or more before the murder in 50 percent of the cases studied (Police Foundation, 1977). Often such rageful behavior is regretted after the violent episode and a cause of psychic pain for the abuser. As such it may encourage a batterer to engage in batterer's counseling, which may have a positive outcome (Okun, 1986).

The etiology of the problem of black-on-black murder can be approached in at least three different manners—all of which have merit. From a biologic perspective it is suspected that at the base of a large number of interpersonal violent episodes is a diagnosis of intermittent explosive disorder for which acquired central nervous system damage (perinatal trauma, head trauma, infection, etc.) is a significant predisposing factor (American Psychiatric Association, 1979). Clearly, epidemiologic studies show lower socioeconomic groups are more predisposed to having head injuries (Jennett and Teasdale, 1981), and more specifically, blacks have more such occurrences than whites; an example being head trauma from freefalls (Ramos and Delany, 1986) or auto accidents (Clark, 1965). In Lewis, May, and Jackson's work (1985), which outlined the biopsychosocial characteristics of children who would later go on to murder, head injury from falls from roofs and car accidents was present in two-thirds of their sample. In another study, Dr. Lewis and her colleagues (Lewis, Pincus, and Feldman, 1986) found that the fifteen murderers on death row studied for psychiatric, neurological, and psychoeducational characteristics all had extensive histories and evidence for head injury. These findings, along with the high prevalence of coma in black subjects (Bell, 1986), suggest that acquired biological causes (as opposed to genetic biological causes) may be partially at the root of the disproportionately high levels of black-on-black murder; more research in this area needs to be done to shore up these preliminary hypotheses.

Other acquired biological causes of violence have been linked to alcohol abuse, which has been shown to deplete serotonin levels in the brain, serotonin being an important neurotransmitter in the regulation of aggression in animals. One study found that impulsive violent offenders with antisocial or intermittent explosive personality disorders and impulsive arsonists had low levels of the major metabolite of serotonin in their cerbrospinal fluid (Linnolia, 1986). In addition to acquired biologic causes of violence (which stem from noxious environmental surroundings), other psychological issues such as stress from inadequate socioeconomic milieus and self-deprecation ascribed to racist attitudes incorporated from the majority culture also play a role in the generation of violence among blacks. Finally, situational sociologic factors can encourage violence, such as the establishment of a gang among idle youth. A review of the literature on the etiology of violence tends to emphasize the psychological and sociological factors as opposed to biologic factors, and this has been due to the lack of ownership medicine has with regard to violence—an error that I have been trying to correct.

Action to Be Taken

Consciousness Raising

Community psychiatrists seeking to alleviate the pathogenic phenomenon of black-on-black violence can do so from several preventive medicine standpoints, namely primary, secondary, and tertiary intervention (Allen, 1981). However, in order to intervene on these levels much community development groundwork must be accomplished as often services are not available, or the established black institutions, such as black colleges, civil rights organizations, the black church, or beauty parlor/barber shops, may need some support and guidance to adequately address the issue. In order to begin to develop community institutions and support systems into vehicles that will prevent black-on-black murder, a great deal of public awareness and education must be done.

In Chicago, the Community Mental Health Council, Inc. (CMHC) got involved in the issue of black-on-black murder at my request because I felt, being a community mental health agency serving a black community, CMHC would be remiss if it didn't deal with the psychic impact of murder on blacks in the community. In addition, I felt CMHC had an obligation to prevent this course of stress among blacks. My own personal experiences of growing up black in the inner city and personally witnessing events of interpersonal violence among blacks served to strengthen my convictions. CMHC began this process by having a series of call-in radio programs on black-on-black violence. CMHC gathered together an array of professionals who had demonstrated expertise in the study of murder, interpersonal violence, rape, child abuse, suicide, spousal abuse, violence in the media, and so on and went on the radio once a week for twelve weeks during a regularly scheduled talk show. I was responsible for three of the shows: the first one on black-on-black murder; a second one regarding biologic, psychologic, and sociologic causes of violence; and the third on the prevention of violence. The response from the community was good although opinions about the topic of black-on-black violence varied. A lot of misconceptions about the sources of violence became apparent. For example, a number of callers thought police were responsible for most of the black homicide victims. Some advocated a "head in the sand" approach as they felt to attend to the issue would only cast blacks in a bad light. For example, one caller felt that, by attributing murders to head injury in perpetrators, blacks could be said to be biologically inferior—an old racist argument. I answered that some, not all, murderers may have had a head injury play a role in their murderous rage, and head injury was an acquired (not inherited) biologic factor in violence; thus I was not providing grounds for support of blacks being racially predisposed to violence. Still others said to raise this issue would fuel racist stereotypes that most blacks are violent. I countered such objections by noting the fact that statistics on black-on-black violence were easily accessible from various public sources so we really were not exposing a well-hidden secret. Further, if blacks did not do something about the problem of violence in our community no one else would. The important thing was that the issue of black-on-black violence had been raised, people in the black community were discussing the issue, and we facilitated the involvement of a number of black professionals in the issue. The group of guests on the program formed an advisory board to CMHC on how to address the issue of violence in the black community. It continues to function.

CMHC also became involved with the black-on-black Love Campaign sponsored by the American Health and Beauty Aids Institute (a consortium of black hair care products companies), which was designed to fight black-on-black crime. By being advisor to the campaign, I was able to bring into focus two separate issues related to black-on-black crime. One was the issue of black-on-black robbery, burglary, felony homicide, and so on—a great deal of which is stranger crime often committed by habitually criminal types. This issue was a major concern of the business people, law enforcement officials, ex-offender representatives, and so on. The other issue was more near and dear to the black health professionals, that of black-on-black murder—the majority of which is not committed by criminal types, but rather family and friends or acquaintances in an interpersonal context. Clearly, these two foci deserved different approaches to alleviate the problem. The "criminal" black-on-black crimes needed to address issues of violent interpersonal dynamics—spousal abuse, child abuse, and so on—areas that concerned home life and not street life. Of course the overall motto of the campaign, "Replace black-on-black Crime with black-on-black Love," was directed to both foci and emphasized respect, discipline, and self-esteem (Stengel 1985). The black-on-black Love Campaign's major public education activity is "No Crime Day," which is a city-wide effort. Chicago's media, politicans, police department, judicial officials, business leaders, clergy, hair care establishments, health care professionals, and many, many more are involved in making the "No Crime Day" a reality. Some successes have been gained; for example each year the event receives more support from community leaders who have influence on the black community, and there is increasing media coverage of the event. More successes and affect will be realized as "No Crime Day" continues to establish a track record of influence and accomplishment.

Another effort of CMHC's involved raising consciousness of the problem of Black-on-Black murder by selling "Stop Black-on-Black Murder" T-shirts. As I found myself faced with the problem of how to draw attention to this sensitive issue, I decided to advertise the problem on T-shirts, which hopefully could be worn by health care professionals. Using a crude drawing done by a public aid volunteer for CMHC's radio series, I developed and refined the concept into the "Stop Black-on-Black Murder" design. I used my influence on CMHC to get them to finance the first batch of 125 T-shirts. Three months later, I had personally given away (in exchange for a five dollar donation to CHMC—to cover the cost of the shirts and mailing) over one thousand T-shirts to physicians, congressmen, celebrities, mayors of major cities, and so on. This effort received national attention, and the effort was reported in American Medical News—the American Medical Association's national newspaper (Staver, 1986). At the National Medical Association's 1986 Annual Meeting, I organized the plenary session to focus on black-on-black murder. This session was reported on the front page of the *New York Times* along with a picture of me selling T-shirts, which resulted in a national electronic media coverage of the problem and its solutions. As CMHC's executive/medical director, I continue to bring the issue of black-on-black murder into public awareness by making presentations to professional organizations and giving lectures on the subject around the country. These efforts have been helpful as several of my psychiatric and nonpsychiatric black physician colleagues have heard my message and have begun to engage in activities designed to prevent black-on-black murder.

All of these public awareness–consciousness raising efforts enlighten the public to the problem of black-on-black murder as well as the problem of interpersonal violence present in the black community. This enlightenment made the work of the community development to prevent black-on-black murder easier as the black community was helped to become receptive to the idea of intervening in the problem.

Primary Prevention Strategies

In looking to prevent all violent behaviors, CMHC started surveying three of CMHC's catchment area schools regarding children's attitudes and experience with violence. This survey of 538 second, fourth, sixth, and eighth graders revealed that about one-sixth had witnessed parents or relatives fighting. A striking number of children had had first-hand encounters with violence: 31 percent of the children had seen someone shot, 34 percent had seen a person stabbed, and 84 percent had seen someone "beaten-up." Further, there were indications that families with frequent violence in the home were associated with the presence of violent attitudes and behaviors in the children of those families. Armed with this knowledge, CMHC arranged for about seventy children and their parents to go to a retreat to discuss violence and its prevention in an effort to develop strategies to reduce family violence. It was found that several of these children knew of a murder that occurred in an interpersonal context and several of the mothers had been abused, either as children or spouses. Most left the retreat with a better understanding of the problem, some strategies to avoid violence, and, with the aid of a CMHC facilitator, the women formed a support group to help with their having been victims of violence. The establishment of such social networks for families at risk for violence has been shown to reduce isolation and lack of support thus reducing abusive potential of such families.

Preventing Elderly Abuse

The Surgeon General's Source Book on Violence (Koop, 1985) points to the growing problem of elderly abuse occurring in this country. Depending on the support system, caring for the elderly can be quite a taxing task. With this in mind, CMHC opened its doors and allowed the establishment of an Alzheimer's Disease Family Support Group. In addition, an Elderly Respite Care Service was established that was run by volunteers. These two support networks work at educating families about the care of the elderly. Furthermore, they allow family members the opportunity to take a break from elderly care, which is a useful strategy in preventing elderly abuse. Similarly, the Family Systems Program at CMHC makes outreach efforts in its catchment area to troubled families who may be at risk of interpersonal violence that could result in murder. Parenting classes, family orientation to support services in the community, family therapy, and group family therapy all allow for the opportunity to prevent family violence before it begins.

Other primary intervention strategies include vocational programs that help patients start patient businesses, and activities for community residents that offer an alternative to involvement in gang or illegal activities that may lead to violence. A center that develops a boys' club, be it a judo team (a self-defense sport) or a boy scout chapter, will be developing its community by offering an alternative to gangs. I know from personal experience—from teaching martial arts for nearly fifteen years—I have done more to constructively influence the lives of young black males away from violent tendencies by teaching karate than I have as a psychotherapist.

Finally, as it has been suggested that central nervous system damage (such as perinatal trauma and head injury) may predispose some individuals to violence, efforts to improve infant care and to prevent children from having freefalls from windows by requesting secure window screens are in order by lobbying for better health care and housing (Freed, 1967).

Secondary Prevention

The secondary prevention of black-on-black murder, that is, the identification and treatment of individuals who have been perpetrators or victims of violence but not to the extent of murder, can be done with an already existing community mental health center's patient population. At CMHC all patients are given a victim's screening form designed to identify potential future victims or perpetrators of violence that could result in a murder. Several studies have noted how often abused women are not attended to by general medical practitioners and as a result often wind up in the mental health care system (Stark and Flitcraft, 1982). It has also been pointed out that a number of women who murder their husbands do so in self-defense to prevent another beating. I directed the development of the screening form at CMHC to be designed to identify these cases before the violence escalated and resulted in a murder. Once identified the victim can be serviced in CMHC's Victims Assistance Service; for example, an abused spouse can be helped with getting aid from the criminal justice system to prevent continued abuse. This approach to violence intervention by community mental health centers has been advocated by others (Attorney General's Task Force, 1984; Lystad, 1986) and has been shown to get results. Counseling is also available to cope with the problem of being a victim of spousal or child abuse. A liaison relationship with a woman's shelter also aids in placing women at risk for immediate violence in a safe environment. Through CMHC's work with the community's clergy, a number of ministers have become more sensitive to the issue of family violence and are seeking to also provide services to reduce violence in families such as shelter and counseling.

Community hospital emergency rooms also offer an excellent vehicle for case finding of victims or perpetrators of violence. In CMHC's catchment area, Jackson Park Hospital's emergency room staff participated in Chicago's "No Crime Day" by the whole staff wearing "Stop Black-on-Black Murder" T-shirts for twenty-four hours and handing out fact sheets on black-on-black murder to all of their patients and their families. This effort was well received by the black community and the patients who visited the emergency room that day. In educating the community that day, the emergency room staff at Jackson Park Hospital were also enlightened. As a result, it was easier for me to request that the staff familiarize themselves with the acquired biologic causes of violence (Bell, 1986; 1987) and to begin to look for such situations as Lion, Bach-y-Rita, and Ervin (1968; 1969) did in their emergency room work. It was from this work that the concept of episodic dyscontrol syndrome was refined and later developed into DSM-III's intermittent explosive disorder. Similarly, Lewis, Moy, and Jackson's (1985) five criteria for potentially differentiating homicidal adolescents from nonhomicidal adolescents (neuropsychiatric impairment, nonschizophrenic psychotic symptoms that occur intermittently, a history of extreme violent behavior, family members who have had psychotic symptoms, and being witness or victim of violence in their families) could be screened for, and high-risk patients could be offered counseling similar to the therapy Lion, Bach-y-Rita, and Ervin (1970) offered their cohort. In addition, newer pharmacologic agents such as propranolol, carbamazepine, trazadone, and lithium have been shown to have some value in reducing explosively violent behavior in some patients (Bell, 1987). Thus, armed with the new information that there are medically treatable acquired biologic factors that may predispose an individual to violence, physicians were more willing to intervene by identifying and treating potential perpetrators of violence. In addition to the now-accepted role of emergency room physicians' identification and intervention of child abuse, the Jackson Park Hospital emergency room staff are being asked to perform a similar function regarding spouse abuse and habitual victims and perpetrators of fighting (which has been shown to be associated with greater chances of being involved in a murder either as a victim or perpetrator) (Rose, 1981; Dennis, Kirk, and Knuckles, 1981). Finally, by realizing a connection between head injury and the potential for future violence, prospective studies can be designed to provide follow-up for victims of head injury who present to the emergency room for treatment in order to determine if there is a relationship.

The community psychiatrist can also become involved in community groups, state legislative action, and policy-making institutions to aid in the secondary prevention of black-on-black murder. When I first began to advocate awareness I was initially received with skepticism, but once the publicity about my efforts began, people began to get interested and began to listen to the common sense in my thoughts. For example, by securing a position on the board of the National Commission on Correctional Health Care, I can advocate for national correctional health care standards that seek to reduce black-on-black violence by taking a public health approach to the problem. Specifically, since it's apparent that individuals with intermittent explosive disorder may be prone to be arrested for interpersonal violence, it would make sense for correctional health care professionals to screen for this disorder on a regular basis. Such a case has been made for tuberculosis and regular screening has increased the finding of tuberculosis cases four fold. As tuberculosis kills fewer black males than black-on-black murder, a policy to routinely ask jail inmates about symptoms of intermittent explosive disorder is in order, and with treatment and a treatment referral on release from the correctional facility, there might well be a reduction in black murders. The health promotion standard of the National Commission's Correctional Health Care Standards suggests inmates be educated about diabetes, hypertension, and so on. It seems a similar inclusion regarding the education about black-on-black murder, child abuse, spouse abuse, and so on could be equally useful to help inmates understand other factors that cause morbidity and mortality.

Last, community psychiatrists can give support of legislative action and criminal justice policy such as outlined in the *Attorney General's Task Force* (1984). Due to an invitation from the Congressional Black Caucus, I went to Washington, D.C., during their annual meeting and did just that. Pilot projects in cities in which the police can arrest men if they see evidence of a wife having been assaulted (e.g., a fresh black eye in the midst of a domestic violence call), when the state's attorney presses charges, and the witness (victim) is subpoenaed for testimony have been shown to reduce the recurrence of family violence (Attorney General's Task Force, 1984; Lystad, 1986).

Tertiary Prevention of Postvention

This type of prevention would unfortunately occur after the fact of a black-on-black murder, and, although a black life would be unchangeably lost, a reduction of the sequelae from the murder is still in order. Mention has already been made of the stress and separation dynamics that occur in a murder victim's relatives. A survey of a community mental health center's patient population will usually reveal a startling number of black patients who have lost relatives or friends as a result of black-on-black murder. Being a family member of a homicide victim is an issue for psychotherapy that should be looked for and addressed.

Although countertransference problems often preclude appropriate services to offenders of black-on-black murder (such as revulsion, anger, overidentification, etc.), Lewis, Moy, and Jackson's work (1986) on murderers on death row aptly points out the significant occurrence of neuropsychiatric impairment in this population, impairment that was never considered in the sentencing of the inmate to death. This work, while being considered by some as outside of the community psychiatrist's purview due to the mistaken notion a correctional facility does not constitute a type of community, yields significant clues valuable for the primary and secondary prevention of black-on-black murder and is worthy of consideration. In addition, the study of people who have murdered yields important diagnostic and treatment issues necessary to deal with the released offender. Thus, closer to home for the traditional community psychiatrist is the release of inmates who have committed murder and who have served their time or were found "not guilty by reason of insanity," and who were returned to the community. Often these patients need aid in adjusting back into society or treatment for chronic mental illness.

Conclusions

Work as a community psychiatrist can be rewarding for a psychiatrist who has an interest in practicing social medicine to improve a community's milieu in such a way as to promote optimum mental health for the residents living in the community. This approach can be especially rewarding if the community is an unserved or underserved, lower socioeconomic, minority community. By using the community psychiatry principle of community development, the community psychiatrist can help the community mature in such a way that needed primary, secondary, and tertiary preventive medicine intervention vehicles can be established to meet the specific problems of the community. While this chapter describes the experience of working in a black community, the principles can be generalized to other minorities. For instance, a community psychiatrist can become involved in inhalant abuse in the Mexican-American community; another can become involved in the adaptation of refugees; and another can practice in a multiethnic setting. In practicing community psychiatry in this fashion one person can make a significant difference.

11
The Need for Cultural Competencies in Child Protective Service Work

Robert L. Pierce
Lois H. Pierce

Considerable time and effort have been devoted to the task of trying to understand why some parents and close friends engage in sexual activities with children, while others do not. Certainly among the myriad of social problems to confront this society in the 1970s and 1980s, none seems more complex and overwhelming than these encounters. Although it is no longer unusual to read about these escapades in local newspapers, open conversations about them come about less frequently. On the other hand, prime-time television has produced dramas like "Something about Amelia" and "To a Safer Place," in an effort to enlighten and educate the public about unsavory parents who sexually misuse children. Another reminder of these sexual liaisons emerged from the recent publicity surrounding the Morgan case in the District of Columbia and the McMartin day-care fiasco in California. Each situation forced the American public to grapple with these seldom talked about sexual liaisons, and perhaps in more important ways, they brought home the message that we are frightfully naive about the spectrum of human sexuality.

Public reaction to these sexual exploits and others like them often ranges from violent confrontation to total indifference. For example, recently within the authors' community, the public's impatience with an alleged sexual abuse offender erupted into a fatal confrontation between the suspect and the victim's father, uncle, and a family friend. Admittedly, public awareness is a critical step in understanding these encounters, but most clinicians would agree that mere recognition without competent and effective interventive and treatment strategies is of little use to either the victims or their offenders.

Unfortunately, one area that is frequently missed when examining effective intervention is that of how ethnicity affects treatment. Undoubtedly competent child protective service (CPS) workers and the treatment they provide black children and their families lie at the heart of successful interventions. However, the CPS and/or child abuse literature is relatively mute regarding question about the race of either worker or client and the results that may have on intervention.

Although numerous treatment strategies have been proposed (Sgroi, 1982; Faller, 1988; Mayhail and Norgard, 1983; Conte and Berliner, 1981; Lanyon, 1986), few have incorporated the variable of race and/or ethnicity in their application. This omission exists even in light of the fact that black children and their families have been overrepresented in national tabulations of official child abuse and neglect reports since the inception of those reports (Hampton, Gelles, and Harrop, 1989; Hampton, Daniel, and Newberger, 1983; Hampton and Newberger, 1985; American Association for Protecting Children, 1986; Hampton, 1987). Additionally, despite the documentation in the broader social work literature calling for ethnic and racially sensitive practice approaches (Pinderhughes, 1989; Lum, 1986; McGoldrick, Pearce, and Giordano, 1982), the extent to which these strategies have filtered down and through child protective services work (CPS), and, more generally, child welfare services, is questionable. For example, in the national survey of child welfare in-service trainers, it was found that 63 percent of the trainers surveyed mentioned that their agency had no program plan to train workers to serve ethnic and racial groups (Vinokur and Gray, 1981). Hence, Conte's (1987) observation that there are virtually no guidelines for clinical practice in the area goes unchallenged.

These findings are disturbing particularly in light of the fact that reports of child sexual abuse are on the increase (American Association for Protecting Children, 1987), and many of these "multi-problem families are not being served or given adequate attention" (Kamerman and Kahn, 1989, 33). Given this predicament treatment is most likely misdirected, idiosyncratic, and based on weak or no theory at all. The net result seems to be that scores of black children and their families are subjected to a wide assortment of theories of treatment and people whose decisions may or may not be in their best interest.

It is the thesis of this chapter that in order to effectively treat sexually abused black children and their families, child protective services and the broader child welfare system must do more than simply identify and catalogue individual and family problems. To be more sensitive and responsive to the needs of black children, these systems must acknowledge both structural and individual barriers that effectively operate to provide less than adequate care to these children and their families.

To help understand how this can be done this chapter will (1) describe very generally the context of child welfare services and its response to black children and their families, (2) describe several worker attributes or characteristics that are compatible with racially sensitive practice, (3) identify several key areas of CPS work that lend themselves to racially sensitive practice strategies, and (4) discuss several recommendations that show promise of more successful interventions on behalf of black children and their families.

The Context of Child Welfare

Any effort to apply a racial perspective to current treatment methods for sexually abused children and their families encounters first the agency context in which treatment is being offered. Although all social service agencies have a responsibility to act on behalf of sexually abused children, CPS agencies (traditional child welfare programs) have the explicit and delegated responsibility in most jurisdictions to intervene in such situations (Kadushin and Martin, 1988).

Treatment of black children and their families does not occur within a vacuum nor within rigid boundaries of traditional agency philosophies or therapies. Rather, as Cross et al. (1989) point out, a "culturally competent system of care for minority children is made up of culturally competent institutions, agencies, and professionals" (p. 19). Such a system "values diversity, has the capacity for cultural self-assessment, is conscious of the dynamics inherent when cultures interact, has institutionalized cultural knowledge, and has developed adaptations to diversity" (p. 19). Because these five elements operate at every level of the system, they therefore buttress a variety of practice approaches. In this regard attitudes are unbiased, policies are impartial and practice is based on accurate perceptions of behavior (Cross et al., 1989).

It follows then that effective clinical practice with black families must occur within a culturally competent organizational context in which there is a healthy respect for and commitment to "policies that enhance services to diverse clientele" (Cross et al., 1989, 17). However, institutional recognition of the importance of cultural variation among clients goes beyond policy concerns to include issues such as (1) the equal distribution of resources among staff and clients served, and (2) monitoring staffing patterns and behaviors (Boyd-Franklin, 1989). Unfortunately this multisystems approach (Boyd-Franklin, 1989) to treating problem behavior is more the ideal for CPS work than the reality.

Even the most casual examination of child welfare intervention and practice with black children and their families reveals a rather tragic picture of insensitivity and cultural disregard. The overwhelming nature of the service and the conflicting organizational climate in which child welfare services operate strongly suggest that these agencies really lack the capacity to help, in a meaningful way, minority children or their families. Hence, problems are seemingly exacerbated rather than eliminated.

The predicament is a difficult one particularly since today, as compared with years past, the climate within most child welfare agencies is dominated by workers responding to child abuse and neglect reports. In fact Kamerman and Kahn (1989) recently observed that the increased demand for child protective services has driven out all other child welfare services to the extent that CPS work is the dominant social service program in most public agencies. As a result, and for reasons that are not totally clear, black children are overrepresented in CPS caseloads and in out-of-home placement (foster care) arrangements (Black Child Development [BCDI], 1989), suggesting at a minimum that rather than being treated, black children are being "warehoused" with little chance or hope of being reunited with their families (Children's Defense Fund [CDF], 1989). Yet, despite the evidence, reports of abuse continue to climb (Kamerman and Kahn, 1989), and black children continue to be placed.

Questions about the effectiveness of child welfare intervention and treatment services, particularly for black children, have been with us for some time. Skeptics like Billingsley and Giovannoni (1972) observed nearly two decades ago that historically child welfare programs were never conceived of nor intended to serve black children. This neglect, which is based in racism, results in (1) services that do not address the special concerns of black children, (2) black children who are not treated equitably in the system, and (3) efforts to change the situations that are fragmented and abortive (Billingsley and Giovannoni, 1972). Chestang (1978) also observed that the "persistence of insensitivity and, in some cases, negative attitudes on the part of staff in traditional agencies" account for the lack of focus on the service needs of minorities" (p. 186). Moreover, the organizational climate within traditional public child welfare agencies is typically adversarial, responsive only to involuntary clients, and unfortunately offered to more clients than these agencies are financially or structurally capable of serving (Bolton and Bolton, 1987; Kamerman and Kahn, 1989).

Now that public child welfare agencies are driven by child abuse and neglect reports, the organizational thrust revolves around child maltreatment interventions that are legalistic and emphasize investigatory and risk assessments work as opposed to treatment (Kamerman and Kahn, 1989). Hence CPS activities in most jurisdictions operate within statutory requirements surrounding the investigatory process that typically stipulates that cases of abuse must be investigated within twenty-four hours after a report is received and substantiated (verified) within thirty days. Among the host of activities CPS workers are expected to initiate and or accomplish within this time frame, some of the more important tasks include (1) ensuring the safety of the victim, (2) identifying and isolating the offender(s), (3) determining the degree to which the nonoffending caretaker is capable of protecting the victim, (4) accurately diagnosing the effect of the abuse, (5) determining the type and level of treatment needed, (6) orchestrating collateral contacts with other supportive systems, and (7) initiating court action if that focus is indicated. Certainly, considerable knowledge and skill in all aspects of CPS work is a major prerequisite if these tasks are to be accomplished with any degree of competency. However, because these tasks are carried out within public child welfare agencies, where resources are inadequate and programs poorly funded, the agreed-on notion of "starting where the client is," somehow gets lost in the process.

Boyd-Franklin (1989) holds that the organizational climate plays a vital role in creating the environment in which workers can feel free to learn to treat black children and their families. The literature reveals however, that the notion of treatment has as many interpretations as there are professionals involved in the process. For example, it is not uncommon for a given case of sexual abuse to fall into the institutional domain of doctors, police, probation officers, lawyers, the public agency, teachers, day-care providers, and the judicial system. Despite all the professional attention, there is still considerable distrust and competition among professionals. Turf issues, overlapping diagnosis, and redundant interviewing of victims are just a few of the concerns that complicate and influence treatment, thus precluding consideration of more racially focused interventions.

The Worker

Along with institutional commitment and support of racial and cultural diversity, there is also the need to consider the racial identities of the "helper" and "client" including the extent to which these identities facilitate or impede effective culturally sensitive practice. This simply means the ability of the helper or worker to "balance his/her perceptions of universal norms, specific group norms, and individual norms in (1) differentiating between normal and abnormal behaviors, (2) considering etiologic factors, and (3) implementing appropriate interventions" (Lopez et al., 1989, 370). Pinderhughes (1989) contends that this ability is characterized by "flexibility, openness, warmth, and empathy, which signals a way of thinking that is marked by a tolerance and acceptance of difference" (19). But some investigators have noticed that the expectation of accepting differences creates the biggest struggle for therapists (Lopez et al. 1989). In fact, these same investigators noted that white therapists have a tendency to "normalize or minimize their judgments of pathology when taking cultural factors into account" (370). In CPS work this would be akin to workers pursuing a less aggressive stance toward treatment including a pronounced reluctance to orchestrate appropriate treatment and legal action when called for. Therefore, when working with minorities understanding the context of the worker-client relationship is key to successful interracial counseling (McGoldrick, Pearce, and Giordano, 1982; Lum, 1989; Davis and Proctor, 1989). More pointedly, it is the fulcrum of interracial helping (Davis and Proctor, 1989).

This is a significant finding particularly when considered against data describing staff make-up within the child welfare system. For example, according to the national survey by the National Child Welfare Training Center (1982), 80 percent of the child welfare workers and 78 percent of child welfare supervisors are white, suggesting the very real likelihood that black clients will most likely be served by white workers who are in turn supervised by white supervisors.

Add to this the propensity of white clinicians to misdiagnose (Adebipe, 1981), distance themselves (Pinderhughes, 1989), minimize the importance of racial or cultural factors (Proctor and Davies, 1989), or simply blot out the patient's blackness, the rehabilitative progress of sexually abused black children and their families can be seriously compromised. However, some white clinicians attempt to avoid this pitfall and ascribe to a posture that Cooper (1973) describes as a color-blind perspective or approach to helping, adhering to the notion that we treat everyone the same. Couched in this approach however, is the tendency of white workers to reject the social reality of black clients and their life experiences. What follows, then, are a series of questions about the accuracy and relevance of the total intervention plan, including the assessment, diagnosis process, and subsequent decisions about treatment goals, methods, and outcomes.

By emphasizing the racial sensitivity of the worker there is no intent to relegate to a secondary level the skills level of the worker. Certainly the practice competencies of the worker are key elements in successful helping relationships, regardless of the race of the client(s). Workers must have the necessary training and clinical skills to work competently with sexually abused children. There is no compromise or substitute for these worker attributes. Pinderhughes (1989) notes, however, that being a competent and effective clinician with black and other minority families requires the additional requisite of being sensitive to racial issues and clear and positive about one's own cultural identity (black or white), including how this awareness, or lack of it, affects treatment. The process of self-exploration and the active use of self in person-to-person therapeutic situations demands a willingness to explore long-held values, perceptions, and stereotypes about black people that have had an impact on one's personal and clinical frame of reference and approach to treatment (Pinderhughes, 1989; Boyd-Franklin, 1989).

Thus, providing therapy to troubled sexually abused black children and their families is a unique personal as well as clinical experience that extends beyond skilled treatment techniques to include interactions between worker and client. In these situations the demands are heavy on the therapist to be sensitive and responsive to the "totality" or "multisystem" (Boyd-Franklin, 1989) environment of the client, and a significant part of that environment includes the adult-child sexual encounter. While these experiences and their disclosure generate in most workers moral outrage and disgust, successful worker interventions with black children and their families must begin with a willingness of the worker to participate in the client's social context empathetically and sensitively. Thus, "knowledge about the client's culture adds a critical dimension to the helping process" (Cross et al., 1989, 34).

All workers should never be expected to achieve a comprehensive understanding of minority cultures. However, having the ability and motivation to know what, who, and how to ask for information about specific cultural issues is indeed a desirable goal (Cross et al., 1989). Wilson's (1982) (cited in Cross et al., 1989) conceptualized worker attributes that were essential for work with culturally diverse environments as:

1. a personal style that is flexible, accepts ethnic differences between people and reflects true genuineness and accurate empathy.
2. a willingness to articulate and challenge personal values and stereotypes about one's own ethnicity and that of others, including ways in which these perceptions conflict with the needs of minority clients.
3. a willingness to work with clients who are culturally different and a commitment to work toward changing racism and poverty.
4. confronting feelings about being identified with a field that has excluded people of color.

One might ask, Why spend so much time emphasizing the importance of race? Is not the aim of good clinical practice to simply treat those needing services regardless of race? The answer is yes. But there is more. First, perhaps, because it's necessary. If we look at the child welfare system in general and CPS specifically, we notice that the number of black children involved in these systems is not decreasing. As noted earlier, despite all the efforts of the child welfare, juvenile justice, and child mental health systems, black and other minority children are still overrepresented in most service categories. Second, since the greater proportion of child welfare workers and supervisors are white, it increases the likelihood of black and other minority children not being served appropriately or adequately (Cross et al., 1989; Kamerman and Kahn, 1989). Third, projections for the year 2000 indicate an increase in the number of poor minority children in this country (Children's Defense Fund, 1989). Consequently, the racial imbalance between child welfare staff and client population present conditions that have serious implications for appropriate intervention and treatment. Fourth, the fact that the child welfare system was designed and programmatically arranged to address problems of needy white and not needy black children and their families strongly suggests that it may well be time to reconceptualize the mission and purpose of these programs. While these public services were originally conceptualized to be helpful, public expectations and new economic and political pressures frequently have the effect of making the child welfare system more destructive than helpful to children and families in need.

The Child Protective Service Arena

There is no question that today child protective service workers see, and supposedly treat, some of the most serious problems that affect children, particularly those who have been sexually and physically abused. However, because abused children seldom self-refer, they are almost completely dependent on CPS workers to discover their predicament, protect them from further abuse, interpret the severity of their presenting problem, and decide the type and method of treatment best suited for the victim and his or her family. However, as Kamerman and Kahn (1989) observed, since CPS work has become more legalistic and investigatory than treatment focused, very few children, particularly black and other minorities, are receiving the therapeutic services they so desperately need (Johnson, 1981).

The authors take the position that regardless of the maltreatment scenario, the approach to black children and their families must be culturally specific, and span attitudes, policy, and practice. Certainly, employing cross-cultural considerations across these domains in no way absolves nonoffending parents from fulfilling their responsibility, nor exempts perpetrators from guilt. When used, the approach, whether with the victims or perpetrators, has the advantage of empowering a dysfunctional family system, and thus builds a foundation of trust and respect, two precursors to effective intervention and treatment. In this regard, the worker "starts where the client is," and thus increases the likelihood of generating considerably more information about the problematic situation.

Despite the variety of factors that mitigate against more worker-client contact in CPS work (the involuntary and sporadic nature of client-agency contacts, staffing patterns of intake and treatment workers, high caseloads, and minimal training) maintaining a culturally relevant stance across all points of worker-client contact is a must. Thus, the following skills will help clinicians construct a more accurate picture of clients and their presenting situation. However, it should be made clear very early that treatment goals for black clients should be "consistent with the goals for all patients" (Carter, 1979, 1007), which include facilitating the ability of clients to make independent decisions, improving self-esteem, and increasing self-reliance (Carter, 1979).

Culturally competent skills are bidirectional in that they are buttressed by (1) a clear understanding of racial and ethnic dynamics of the client, and (2) the clinician's understanding, "comfort and security about their own cultural identity, including their power needs and responses" (Pinderhughes, 1989, 198). This requires, at a minimum, an ability to discuss openly with one's peers the meaning and significance of racial and ethnic differences including their effect on perceptions of clients. Currently, CPS training focuses primarily on client racial or ethnic differences and leaves totally neglected cultural dynamics among staff. Pinderhughes (1989) noted that "it is very difficult for white people to confront other white people about their racial stereotypes" (200). Without this clarity of one's cultural base, the worker-client situation can become confused and inactive.

Foremost among intervention and treatment strategies with abused black children and their families is the need to develop skills that acknowledge there is no such thing as "the black family." As Boyd-Franklin (1989) noted, "black people in this country are not a monolithic group" (p. 6). Therefore, differences and variations exist between as well as among black individuals, groups, families, and communities. Moreover, an individual child's disorder results from problematic transactions between persons and their environments including the conditions that breed them (Myers and King, 1983). In this context, behaviors can be influenced just as much by geography, social class (Willie, 1988), or race (Davis and Proctor, 1989) as by intrapsychic factors (Spurlock, 1985). Thus, it would do well for the unsuspecting CPS worker to discard stereotypes that serve to categorize or lump all black families together, and "evaluate each patient and his or her family as an individual and unit" (Spurlock, 1985, 168).

Interviewing techniques that are reflective of the worker's understanding of powerlessness and empowerment as they relate to black and other minority clients should be used. In contrast to other client-worker contacts, the initial interview in CPS work is mandated by law, and its primary purpose is to gather information so as to establish the presence or absence of abuse. The process involves (1) gathering data that reveals or points to the identities of the victim and the perpetrator, (2) ensuring the victim(s)' safety by isolating the offender, (3) determining the appropriateness of initiating court action against the offender, (4) assessing the degree to which the nonoffending parent/caretaker is capable of protecting the victim, and if indicated, (5) filing a petition with the juvenile court to have the child removed from the home. Given these responsibilities, one has very little choice but to characterize CPS work as legalistic and investigatory. However, despite the focus, there is a need to uncover the strengths as well as weakness or pathology in the client's behavior. For example the nonperpetrating mother in sexual abuse situations, who must work in order to make ends meet, may be unjustly blamed for not protecting her child from an abusive paramour. Labeling this woman as a willing participant in her child's abuse may reinforce negative thoughts of herself and stifle any resiliency or thoughts of self-improvements. The clinician should not convey the thought that having a male in one's life is pathological or that having babies is a favorite pastime of black AFDC clients. Pinderhughes (1989) notes that when clinicians insist on working with clients from a stereotyped perspective it provides self-protection and further exploits clients.

Although a child's personal distress from being in these adult-child sexual encounters may be inferred from a given referral, clinicians need skills in accurately diagnosing the presenting problem. However, given the spectrum of these adult-child sexual encounters and their effects, it seems that a critical first step in treatment is to identify, as best possible, the resulting constellation of dysfunctional behaviors and/or emotions that prevent a child's optimal functioning. Whether one decides to interview the child victim alone or with his or her family to get this information will depend on the child's age and cognitive abilities and the willingness of the caregiver to permit the interview. But if our aim is treatment, then we need to know the children within the cultural context in which they live, including the recognition of how culture affects the presenting behaviors they exhibit as a result of their abuse. Moreover, because the emotional and behavioral effects of these sexual encounters can manifest themselves at different stages of a child's development, or be totally masked by traumas caused by other overwhelming experiences (Emery, 1989), the crucial question for clinicians becomes, What traumatic experience are we treating? And, does the experience of one traumatic event take treatment precedence over another?

For example, children living in poverty, those from divorcing and/ or alcoholic families, and sexually abused children reportedly exhibit depression, low self-esteem, feelings of loss, and are capable of expressing both inner- and outer-directed forms of aggression (Wolkind and Rutter, 1985; Mrazek and Kempe, 1981; Sgroi, 1982). Kazdin (1989) stipulates further that a child's dysfunctioning cannot be easily separated from the web of parental dysfunctioning and family interaction patterns. Given the evidence, it seems totally inappropriate to anchor treatment approaches to any single contributing factor. Being so narrowly focused can seriously jeopardize treatment and its outcome.

Agency encounters with black and other minority clients are a function of the times. The increased incidence of minority children in CPS caseloads supports the need for a multilevel systems approach that is committed to and well grounded in cultural competence. Thus, agency administrators and managers have the responsibility to create, interpret, and implement policy that is consistent with the belief system of the clients and communities being served (Cross et al., 1989). Administrators should develop job descriptions that require cultural competence, employ program evaluations that tap recipient's perspectives of service delivery, and most importantly require vendors (contracted therapists) to meet certain cultural competence requirements (Cross et al., 1989).

Recommendations

The following recommendations, which are adopted from the work of Cross et al. (1989), are not intended to be complete or an exhaustive list. Rather, the examples are given to prompt thinking and to spark dialogue within the child welfare system, which, despite its mission to respond to all children, is systematically failing thousands of black and other minority children.

1. The child welfare system must sanction and in some cases mandate the incorporation of cultural knowledge into all levels of policy formulation and service delivery.

2. Inherent in the cultural competency model of service delivery is the notion that the family is the preferred point of intervention. Hence, services must be geared toward preserving the integrity of the family.

3. The child welfare system's interventions must acknowledge that culturally competent services begin with a recognition that clients are viewed within the context of their own cultural group, including their experiences of being part of that group.

4. Culturally competent child welfare services are matched with the needs of a given client population. Thus, service delivery is a unique aspect of culturally sensitive practice.

5. Child welfare systems must acknowledge the strength as well as the weakness of minority communities. Thus, cultural competence expands the notion of self-determination to the community. It is only when the community assumes ownership of its problems that culturally relevant solutions will be generated.

6. Despite the claim that we are a child-centered country, there is little integration of services across systems supposedly responsible for their care. Different goals and philosophies of care within and between state governments contribute to a fragmented and inconsistent approach to the range of problems that confront our children. Hence, there is a need to consolidate bureaucracies and redesign their focus so as to realize a more systematic approach to the needs of all children.

In summary, few would disagree with the position that learning the right lessons from the current condition of the child welfare system is our greatest challenge. However, most child advocates would agree that the system needs our immediate attention. Unquestionably, given the current plight of thousands of needy black and other poor and minority children in this country, the system needs an unambiguous and consistent approach to intervention. The approach should be accountable to the American public but free from partisan politics so that its policies and regulations are truly child centered.

References

Adebimpe, V. (1981). Overview: White norms and psychiatric diagnosis of black patients. *The American Journal of Psychiatry, 138*, 279–85.

Adler, E. S. (1981). The underside of married life: Power, influence, and violence. In Lee H. Bowker (ed.), *Women and Crime in America*. New York: Macmillan.

Allan, C., and Brotman, H. (1981). *Chartbook on Aging in America*. Washington, D.C.: White House Conference on Aging.

Allen, N. H. (1981). Homicide prevention and intervention. *Journal of Suicide and Life Threatening Behavior, 11*, 167–79.

Allen, W. (1978). Class, culture, and family organization: The effects of class and race on family structure in urban America. *Journal of Comparative Family Studies, 10*, 301–13.

Altemeier, W. A., III, Vietze, P. M., Sherrod, H. M., Falsey, S., and O'Connor, S. (1979). Prediction of child maltreatment during pregnancy. *Journal of the American Child Psychiatry, 18*, 205–18.

American Association for Protecting Children. (1985). *Highlights of Official Child Neglect and Abuse Reports, 1983*. Denver: American Humane Association.

———. (1986). *Highlights of Official Child Neglect and Abuse Reports, 1984*. Denver: American Humane Association.

———. (1987). *Highlights of Official Child Neglect and Abuse Reports, 1985*. Denver: American Humane Association.

American Association of Retired Persons. (1987). *Minority Affairs Initiative*. Washington, D.C.: AARP–Andrus Foundation.

American Humane Association. (1979). *National Analysis of Official Child Neglect and Abuse Reports, 1977*. Denver: American Humane Association.

American Psychiatric Association. (1979). *Dianostic and Statistical Manual of Mental Disorders* (3d ed.). Washington, D.C.: American Psychiatric Association.

Asbury, J. (1987). African-American women in violent relationships: An exploration of cultural differences. In Robert Hampton (ed.), *Violence in the Black Family: Correlates and Consequences*. Lexington, Mass.: Lexington Books.

Ashenbrenner, J. (1975). *Lifelines: Black Families in Chicago*. New York: Holt, Rinehart and Winston.

Attorney General's Task Force. (1984). *Attorney General's Task Force Report on Family Violence*. Washington, D.C.: U.S. Department of Justice.

Bard, M., and Zacker, J. (1976). How police handle explosive squabbles. *Psychology Today*, 71–74, 113.

Baron, L., and Straus, M. A. (1988). Cultural and economic sources of homicide. *Sociological Quarterly, 29*, 371–90.

Beck, A. T. (1970). *Depression:. Causes and Treatment*. Philadelphia: University of Pennsylvania Press.

Bell, C. C. (1986). Coma and the etiology of violence, part 2. *Journal of the National Medical Association, 78*, 1139–67.

———. (1987). Coma and the etiology of violence, part 2. *Journal of the National Medical Association, 79*, 79–85.

Bell, C. C., Thompson, B., Shorter-Gooden, K., Shakoor, B., Dew, D., Hughley, E., and Mays, R. (1985). Prevalence of coma in black subjects. *Journal of the National Medical Association, 77*, 391–95.

Bensing, R. C., Jackson, P. B., and Schroeder, O., Jr. (1960). *Homicide in an Urban Community*. Springfield, Ill.: Charles C. Thomas.

Berliner, L. (1987). The frequency of interpersonal violence: What do the studies tell us? *Journal of Interpersonal Violence, 2*, 223–24.

Billingsley, A. (1968). *Black Families in White America*. Englewood Cliffs, N.J.: Prentice-Hall.

———. (1969). Family functioning in the low-income black community. *Casework, 50*, 563–72.

Billingsley, A. and Giovannoni, J. (1972). *Children of the Storm: Black Children and American Child Welfare*. New York: Harcourt, Brace and Jovanovich.

Blau, Z. S. (1981). *Aging in a Changing Society*. New York: Franklin Watts.

Block, C. R. (1981). Black Americans and the cross-cultural counselling and psychotherapy experience. In J. Marsella and P. Pedersen (eds.), *Cross-Cultural Counselling and Psychotheraphy*. New York: Pergamon.

———. (1985). *Lethal Violence in Chicago over Seventeen Years: Homicides Known to the Police 1965–1981*. Chicago: Criminal Justice Information Authority.

Bolton, F., and Bolton, S. (1987). *Working With Violent Families*. Newbury Park, Calif.: Sage.

Boundouris, J. (1971). Homicide and the family. *Journal of Marriage and the Family 33*, 667–77.

Bowker, L. H. (1983). *Beating Wife Beating*. Lexington, Mass.: Lexington Books.

———. (1984). Coping with wife abuse: Personal and social networks. In Albert R. Roberts (ed.), *Battered Women and Their Families*. New York: Springer.

Boyd-Franklin, N. (1989). *Black Families in Therapy: A Multisystems Approach*. New York: Guilford Press.

Boyer, E. L. (1974). Breaking up the youth ghetto. In D. W. Dyckman (ed.), *Lifelong Learners—A New Clientele for Higher Education*. San Francisco: Jossey-Bass.

Browne, A. (1986). Assault and homicide at home: When battered women kill. In Michael J. Saks and Leonard Saxe (eds.), *Advances in Applied Social*

Psycology, 3. Durham, N.C.: Family Research Lab, University of New Hampshire.

———. (1987). *When Battered Women Kill.* New York: Free Press.

———. (1988). Family homicide: When victimized women kill. In Vincent B. Van Hasselt, Randall L. Morrison, Alan S. Bellack, and Michel Hersen (eds.), *Handbook of Family Violence* (pp. 271–89). New York: Plenum.

Bunyak, J. R. (1986). Battered wives who kill: Civil liability and the admissibility of battered women's syndrome testimony. *Law and Inequality, 4*(3), 606–36.

Bureau of the Census. (1983). *America's Black Population, 1970 to 1982: A Statistical View.* Series P10/POP83. Washington, D.C.: U.S. Government Printing Office.

Burgdorf, K. (1980). *Recognition and Reporting of Child Maltreatment.* Rockville, Md.: Westat.

———. (1981). *Recognition and Reporting of Child Maltreatment.* Rockville, Md.: Westat.

Butler, R. N., and Lewis, M. L. (1983). *Aging and Mental Health.* St. Louis: Mosby.

Cannon, M., and Locke, B. (1977). Being black is detrimental to one's mental health: Myth or reality? *Phylon, 38,* 408–28.

Carter, J. (1979). Frequent mistakes made with black patients in psychotherapy. *Journal of the National Medical Association, 71,* 1007–9.

Cazenave, N. A. (1979). Family violence and aging blacks: Theoretical perspectives and research possibilities. *Journal of Minority Aging, 4,* 99–108.

———. (1981). *Elder Abuse and Black Americans: Incidence, Correlates, Treatment, and Prevention.* Presented at the annual meeting of the National Council of Family Relations, Milwaukee, October 13–17.

Cazenave, N., and Straus, M. (1979). Race, class network embeddedness and family violence: A search for potent support systems. *Journal of Comparative Family Studies, 10,* 281–99.

Center on Budget and Policy Priorities. (1988). *Still Far from the Dream: Recent Developments in Black Income, Employment, and Poverty.* Washington, D.C.: Center on Budget and Policy Priorities.

Chestang, L. (1978). The delivery of child welfare services to minority group children and their families. In A. Kadushin (ed.), *Child Welfare Strategy in the Coming Years.* U.S. Department of Health, Education, and Welfare, Office of Human Development Services, Administration for Children, Youth and Families, Children's Bureau (DHEW Publication No. [OHDS] 78-30158). Washington, D.C.: U.S. Government Printing Office.

Children's Defense Fund (1989). *A Vision for America's Future.* Washington, D.C.: The Children's Defense Fund.

Clark, K. (1965). *Dark Ghetto.* New York: Harper and Row.

Cohen, A., and Daro, D. (1987). Is treatment too late? What ten years of evaluative research tells us. *Child Abuse and Neglect, 11,* 433–42.

Cohn, A. H. (1987). How do we deal with research findings? *Journal of Interpersonal Violence, 2,* 228–32.

Cole, K. E., Fisher, G., and Cole, S. R. (1968). Women who kill. *Archives of General Psychiatry 19,* 1–8.

Collins, J. J. (1981). *Drinking and Crime: Perspectives on the Relationships*

190 • *Black Family Violence*

between Alcohol Consumption and Criminal Behavior. New York: The Gilford Press.

Comer, J. (1985). Black violence and public policy: Changing directions. In Lynn A. Curtis (ed.), *American Violence and Public Policy*. New Haven: Yale University Press.

Conte, J. (1987). Child sexual abuse. In *Encyclopedia of Social Work*, Eighteenth Edition. Washington, D.C.: The National Association of Social Workers.

Conte, J. and Berliner, L. (1981). Sexual abuse of children: Implications for practice. *Social Casework, 62,* 601–606.

Cook, T., and Campbell, D. (1979). *Quasi-experimentation*. Chicago: Rand McNally.

Cooper, S. (1973). A look at the effect of racism on clinical work. *Social Casework, 54,* 76–84.

Covey, H. C. (1983). Higher education and older people: Some theoretical considerations. *Educational Gerontology, 9*(1), 1–14.

Cross, C. (1986). Media Relations Manager, Michigan Bell Telephone Company, Detroit, Telephone communication, July.

Cross, T., Bazron, B., Dennis, K., and Isaacs, M. (eds.). (1989). *Towards a Culturally Competent System of Care: A Monograph on Effective Services for Minority Children Who Are Severely Emotionally Disturbed*. Washington, D.C.: Georgetown University Child Development Center.

Cuellar, I., Harries, L. C., and Jasso, R. (1980). An acculturation scale for Mexican normal and clinical populations. *Hispanic Journal of Behavioral Science, 3,* 199–271.

Curtis, L. A. (1974). *Criminal Violence*. Lexington, Mass.: Lexington Books.
———. (1975). *Violence, Race, and Culture*. Lexington, Mass.: Lexington Books.

Daly, M. and Wilson, M. (1988). *Homicide*. New York: Aldine De Gruyter.

Dancy, J., Jr. (1977). *The Black Elderly, a Guide for Practitioners*. Ann Arbor: Institute of Gerontology, University of Michigan/Wayne State University.

Daro, D. (1985). *Half Full and Half Empty: The Evaluation Results of Nineteen Clinical Research and Demonstration Projects*. Paper presented to the 7th National Conference on Child Abuse and Neglect, Chicago, November.

Davis, L. and Proctor, E. (1989). *Race, Gender and Class: Guidelines for Practice with Individuals, Families and Groups*. Englewood Cliffs, N.J.: Prentice Hall.

Dennis, R. E., Kirk, A., and Knuckles, B. N. (1981). *Black Males at Risk to Low Life Expectancy: A Study of Homicide Victims and Perpetrators*. Project funded by NIMH Grant #1 R01 MH 36720. Rockville, Md.: Center for Studies of Minority Group Mental Health.

Dexter, L. A. (1958). A note on selective inattention in social science. *Social Problems, 6,* 176–82.

Dietrich, K. N., Starr, R. H., Jr., and Weisfeld, G. E. (1983). Infant maltreatment: Caretaker-infant interaction and developmental consequences at different levels of parenting failure. *Pediatrics, 72,* 532–40.

Dobash, R., and Dobash, R. (1981). Social science and social action: The case of wife beating. *Journal of Family Issues, 2,* 439–70.

Dobson, J. (1981). Conceptualization of black families. In H. McAdoo (ed.), *Black Families*. Beverly Hills: Sage.

Edye, D. P., and Rich, J. A. (1983). *Psychological Distress in Aging: A Family Management Model*. Rockville, Md.: Aspen.

Egeland, B., Jacobvitz, D., and Papatola, K. (1987). Intergenerational continuity of abuse. In Richard J. Gelles and Jane B. Lancaster (eds.), *Child Abuse and Neglect: Biosocial Dimensions*. Hawthorne, N.Y.: Aldine de Gruyter.

Egeland, B., Jacobvitz, D., and Sroufe, L. A. (1988). Breaking the cycle of abuse. *Child Development, 59,* 1080–88.

Egeland, B., and Vaugh, B. (1981). Failure of "bond formation" as a cause of abuse, neglect, and maltreatment. *American Journal of Orthopsychiatry, 51,* 78–84.

Elbow, M. (1982). Children of violent marriages: The forgotten victims. *Social Casework, 63,* 465–71.

Elliot, D. S. (1989). Criminal justice procedures in family violence crimes. In Lloyd Ohlin and Michael Tonry (eds.), *Family Violence*. Chicago: The University of Chicago Press.

Emery, R. (1989). Family Violence. *American Psychologist, 44,* 321–28.

Empey, L. T. (1978). *American Delinquency*. Homewood, Ill.: Dorsey.

Evans, L., Acosta, F., Yamamoto, J., and Hurwicz, M. (1986) Patient requests: Correlates and therapeutic implications for Hispanic, black and Caucasian patients. *Journal of Clinical Psychology, 42*(1), 213–21.

Fagen, J., Stewart, D., and Hansen, K. (1983). Violent men or violent husbands? Background factors and situational correlates. In David Finkelhor, Richard Gelles, Gerald Hotaling, and Murry Straus (eds.), *The Dark Side of Families: Current Family Violence Research*. Beverly Hills: Sage.

Faller, K. (1988). *Child Sexual Abuse: An Interdisciplinary Manual for Diagnosis, Case Management, and Treatment.* new York: Columbia University Press.

Famularo, R., Barnum, R., and Stone, K. (1986). Court-ordered removal in severe child maltreatment: An association to parental major affective disorder. *Child Abuse and Neglect, 10,* 487–92.

Farley, W. R. (1984). *Blacks and Whites Narrowing the Gap*. Cambridge, Mass.: Harvard University Press.

Ferguson, E. J. (1978). *Protecting the Vulnerable Adult: A Perspective on Policy and Program Issues in Adult Protective Services*. Ann Arbor: Institute of Gerontology, University of Michigan/Wayne State University.

Finley, J. P. (1884). Tornado predictions. *The American Meteorological Journal, 1,* 85–88.

Fischer, J. (1969). Negroes and whites and rates of mental illness: Reconsideration of a myth. *Psychiatry, 32,* 428–46.

Fleiss, J. L. (1981). *Statistical Methods for Rates and Proportions*. New York: John Wiley & Sons.

Floyd, J. (1984). Collecting data on abuse of the elderly. *Journal of Gerontological Nursing, 9*(2), 11–15.

Flynn, J. P. (1977). Recent findings related to wife abuse. *Social Casework, 58,* 13–20.

Formby, W. A. (1985) Homicides in semi-rural southern environments. *American Journal of Criminal Justice, IX*(2).

Freed, H. M. (1967). The community psychiatrist and political action. *Archives of General Psychiatry, 17,* 129–34.

———. (1972). Subcontracts for community development and service. *American Journal of Psychiatry, 129,* 568–73.

Freed, H. M., Schroeder, D. J., and Baker, B. (1972). Community participation in mental health services: A case of fractional control. In L. Miller (ed.), *Mental Health in Rapid Changing Society.* Jerusalem, Israel: Jerusalem Academic Press.

Frieze, I. H., and Browne, A. (1989). Violence in marriage. In Lloyd Ohlin and Michael Tonry (eds.), *Family Violence.* Chicago: The University of Chicago Press.

Frisbie, W. P. (1986). Variation in patterns of marital instability among Hispanics. *Journal of Marriage & Family, 48,* 99–106.

Garbarino, J. (1981). An ecological approach to child maltreatment. In L. Pelton (ed.), *The Social Construction of Child Abuse and Neglect.* New York: Human Sciences Press.

Garbarino, J. and Ebata, A. (1987). The significance of ethic and cultural differences in child maltreatment. In Robert Hampton (ed.), *Violence in the Black Family: Correlate and Consequences* (pp. 21–38). Lexington, Mass.: Lexington Books.

Gelfand, D. M. (in press). The effects of maternal depression on children. *Clinical Psychology Review.*

Gelfand, D., and Fandetti, D. (1986). The emergent nature of ethnicity: Dilemmas in assessment. *Social Casework, 66*(4), 542–50.

Gelles, R. J. (1974). *The Violent Home: A Study of Physical Aggression between Husbands and Wives.* Beverly Hils: Sage.

———. (April 1975). The social construction of child abuse. *The American Journal of Orthopyschiatry, 43,* 363–71.

———. (October 1978). Violence toward children in the United States. *American Journal of Orthopsychiatry, 48,* 580–92.

———. (1979). *Family Violence.* Beverly Hills: Sage.

Gelles, R. J. (1980). Violence in the family: A review of research in the seventies. *Journal of Marriage and the Family, 42,* 873–86.

———. (1982). Problems in labeling and defining child abuse. In Raymond Starr, Jr. (ed.), *Child Abuse Prediction: Policy Implications.* Boston: Ballinger.

———. (1985). Family violence. In Ralph Turner (ed.), *Annual Review of Sociology.* Palo Alto: Annual Reviews.

———. (1987). Community agencies and child abuse: Labeling and gatekeeping. In Richard J. Gelles (ed.), *Family Violence.* Newbury Park, CA: Sage.

———. (1988). Violence and pregnancy: Are pregnant women at greater risk of abuse? *Journal of Marriage and the Family, 50,* 841–47.

———. (October 1989). Child abuse and violence in single parent families: Parent-absent and economic deprivation. *American Journal of Orthopsychiatry, 59,* 492–501.

———. (1990). *Poverty and Violence Towards Children.* Paper presented at the annual meetings of the Society for the Study of Social Problems, Washington, D.C.

Gelles, R. J., and Cornell, C. P. (1985). *Intimate Violence in Families*. New-bury Park, Calif.: Sage.

Gelles, R. J., and Straus, M. A. (1979). Determinants of violence in the family: Towards a theoretical integration. In W. R. Burr, R. Hill, F. I. Nye, and I. L. Reiss (eds.), *Contemporary Theories about the Family* (vol. 1). New York: Free Press.

———. (1988). *Intimate Violence: The Causes and Consequences of Abuse in the American Family*. New York: Simon and Schuster.

Gelles, R. J., Straus M. A., and Harrop, J. (1988). Has family violence de-creased? A response to J. Timothy Stocks. *Journal of Marriage and the Family, 50*, 286–91.

Gibbs, D. L., Silverman, I. J., and Vega, M. (1977). *Homicides Committed by Females in the State of Florida*. Presented at the annual meeting, American Society of Criminology. University Press.

Gil, D. (1970). *Violence against Children: Physical Abuse in the United States*. Cambridge: Harvard University Press.

Gillespie, C. K. (1989). *Justifiable Homicide: Battered Women, Self-Defense and the Law*. Columbus: Ohio State University Press.

Giordano, N. H., and Giordano, J. A. (1984). Elder abuse: A review of the literature. *Social Work, 29*, 232–36.

Giovannoni, J., and Billingsley, A. (1970). Child neglect among the poor: A study of parental adequacy in families of three ethnic groups. *Child Wel-fare, 49*(4), 196–204.

Goetting, A. (1987). Homicidal wives: A profile. *Journal of Family Issues, 8*(3), 332–41.

Goldberg, W. G., and Tomlanovich, M. C. (1984). Domestic violence victims in the emergency department: New findings. *Journal of the American Med-ical Association 251*, 3259–64.

Gondolf, E. (1988). The effect of batterer counseling on shelter outcome. *Jour-nal of Interpersonal Violence, 3* (no. 3, September), 275–89.

Goodman, L. A., and Kruskal, W. H. (1959). Measures of association for cross classifications. II: Further discussion and references. *American Statistical Association 54*, 123–63.

Greenblat, C. (1983). A hit is a hit . . . Or is it: Approval and tolerance of the use of physical force by spouses. In David Finkelhor, Richard J. Gelles, Gerald T. Hotaling, and Merry A. Straus (eds.), *The Dark Side of Fami-lies: Current Family Violence Research*. Beverly Hills, Calif.: Sage.

Griffin, L. W., Gottesman, L. E., and Slamon, J. (1979). *Protective Service Study: A Comparison of Protective Service Delivery Systems in Pennsylva-nia*. Philadelphia: Philadelphia Geriatric Center.

Gruhl, J., Welch, S., and Spahn, C. (1984). Women as criminal defendants: A test for paternalism. *Western Political Quarterly, 37* (September), 456–67.

Haeuser, A. A. (1985). *Social Control over Parents' Use of Physical Punish-ment: Issues for Cross National Child Abuse Research*. Paper presented at the United States–Sweden Joint Research Seminar on Physical and Sexual Abuse of Children, Satra Bruk, Sweden.

Hampton, R. L. (1986). Race, ethnicity, and child maltreatment: An analysis of cases recognized and reported by hospitals. In Robert Staples (ed.), *The*

Black Family: Essays and Studies (Third Edition). Belmont: Wadsworth.

———. (1987). Violence against black children: Current knowledge and future research needs. In Robert L. Hampton (ed.), *Violence in the Black Family: Correlates and Consequences*. Lexington, Mass.: Lexington Books.

Hampton, R. L., Daniel, J. H., and Newberger, E. H. (1983). Pediatric social illnesses and black families. *Western Journal of Black Studies, 7*, 190–97.

Hampton, R. L., and Gelles, R. J. (1988). *Physical Violence in a Nationally Representative Sample of Black Families*. Paper presented at the annual meeting of the National Council of Family Relations.

Hampton, R. L., Gelles, R. J., and Harrop, J. W. (1989). Is violence in black families increasing? A comparison of 1975 and 1985 national survey rates. *Journal of Marriage and the Family, 51*, 969–80.

Hampton, R. L., and Newberger, E. H. (1985). Child abuse incidence and reporting by hospitals: The significance of severity, class, and race. *American Journal of Public Health, 75* (1), 56–60.

Hanushek, E., and Jackson, J. (1977). *Statistical Methods for Social Scientists*. New York: Academic Press.

Hare, N. (1979). The relative psychosocial economic suppression of the black male. In W. D. Smith (ed.), *Reflections of Black Psychology*. Washington, D.C.: University Press.

Hawkins, D. F. (1986). Black and white homicide differentials: Alternatives to an inadequate theory. In D. F. Hawkins (ed.), *Homicide among Black Americans*. New York: University Press.

———. (1987). Devalued lives and racial stereotypes: Ideological barriers to the prevention of family violence among blacks. In R. L. Hampton (ed.), *Violence in the Black Family: Correlates and Consequences*. Lexington, Mass.: Lexington Books.

Henton, J., Cate, R., Koval, J., Lloyd, S., and Christopher, S. (1983). Romance and violence in dating relationships. *Journal of Family Issues, 4* (September), 467–82.

Herrenkohl, E. C., Herrenkohl, R. C., and Toedler, Lori. (1983). Perspective on the intergenerational transmission of abuse. In David Finkelhor, Richard J. Gelles, Gerald Hotaling, and Murray A. Straus (eds.), *The Dark Side of Families: Current Family Violence Research*. Newbury Park, CA: Sage.

Herrenkohl, R. C., Herrenkohl, E. C., and Egolf, B. P. (1983). Circumstances surrounding in occurrence of child maltreatment. *Jounal of Consulting and Clinical Psychology, 51*, 424–31.

Hershorn, M., and Rosenbaum, A. (1985). Children of marital violence: A closer look at the unintended victims. *American Journal of Orthopsychiaty, 55*, 260–66.

Herskovits, M. J. (1958). *The Myth of the Negro Past*. Boston: Beacon.

Hewitt, J. B., and G. A. Rivers. (1986). *The Victim-Offender Relationship in Convicted Homicide Cases: 1960–1984*. Presented at annual meeting of Academy of Criminal Justice Sciences.

Hill, R. B. (1971). *The Strengths of Black Families*. New York: Emerson Hall.

Hill, R. B., and Shackleford, L. (1975). The black extended family revisited. *Urban League Review*, 18–34.

Hofeller, K. H. (1982). *Social, Psychological, and Situational Factors in Wife Abuse*. Palo Alto, CA: R. and E. Research.

Hollingshead, A., and Redlich, F. (1958). *Social Class and Mental Illness: A Community Study*. New York: Wiley.

Hornung, C. A., McCullough, B. C., and Sugimoto, T. (1981). Status relationships in marriage: Risk factors in spouse abuse. *Journal of Marriage and the Family*, 43, 675–92.

Hotaling, G., and Straus, M. (eds.). *The Dark Side of Families: Current Family Violence Research*. Beverly Hills: Sage.

Hudson, W. W. (1982). *The Clinical Measurement Package: A Field Manual*. Homewood, Ill.: Dorsey.

Hwalek, M. A., and Sengstock, M. C. (1986). Assessing the probability of abuse of the elderly: Toward development of a clinical screening instrument. *Journal of Applied Gerontology*, 5(2), 153–73.

Jackson, J. J. (1980). *Minorities and Aging*. Belmont, Calif.: Wadsworth Publishing.

Jaffe, P., Wolfe, D., Wilson, S., and Zak, L. (1985). Children of battered women: The relation of child behavior to family violence and maternal stress. *Journal of Consulting Clinical Psychology*, 53, 657–65.

———. (1986). Similarities in behavioral and social maladjustment among child victims and witnesses to family violence. *American Journal of Orthopsychiatry*, 56, 142–46.

Jennett, B., and Teasdale, G. (1981). *Management of Head Injuries*. Philadelphia: F. A. Davis.

Johnson, C. (1981). Child sexual abuse: Case handling through public social agencies in the southeast of the USA. *Child Abuse and Neglect*, 5, 123–28.

Johnson, C. F., and Showers, J. (1985). Injury variables in child abuse. *Child Abuse and Neglect*, 9(2), 207–16.

Johnson, W., and L'Eperance, E. (1984). Predicting the recurrence of child abuse. *Social Work Research and Abstracts*, 21–26.

Jorgensen, S. R. (1977). Societal class heterogamy, status striving, and perception of marital conflict: A partial replication and revision of Perlin's Contingency Hypothesis. *Journal of Marriage and the Family*, 43, 679–92.

Kadushin, A. and Martin, J. (1988). *Child Welfare Services*. New York: Macmillan.

Kammerman, S. and Kahn, A. (1989). *Social Services for Children, Youth and Families in the United States*. New York: Columbia University School of Social Work, Annie E. Casey Foundation.

Kantor, G., Kaufman and Straus, M. A. (1987). *Stopping the Violence: Battered Women, Police Utilization and Police Response*. Paper presented at the annual meeting of the American Society of Criminology, Montreal, November.

Kaplan, S., Pelcovitz, D., Salzinger, S., and Ganeles, D. (1983). Psychopathology of parents of abused and neglected children and adolescents. *Journal of the American Academy of Child Psychiatry*, 22(3), 328–44.

Katz, M. H., Hampton, R. L., Newberger, E. H., Bowles, R. T., and Snyder, J. C. (1986). Returning children home: Clinical decision making in cases of child abuse and neglect. *American Journal of Orthopsychiatry, 56*(2), 253–62.

Kaufman, J., and Zigler, E. (1987). Do abused children become abusive parents? *American Journal of Orthopsychiatry, 57,* 186–92.

Kazdin, A. (1989). Developmental psychotherapy: Current research issues and directions. *American Psychologist, 44,* 180–87.

Keefe, S. (1982). Help-seeking behavior among foreign-born and native-born Mexican Americans, *Social Science Medicine, 16,* 1467–72.

Kempe, C. H., Silverman, F., Steele, B., Droegemueller, W., and Silver, H. (1962). The battered child syndrome. *Journal of the American Medical Association, 181,* 17–24.

Koop, C. E. (1985). *Surgeon General's Workshop on Violence and Public Health: Source Book.* Washington, D.C.: National Center on Child Abuse and Neglect.

Kravits, J., and Schneider, J. (1975). Health care need and actual use by age, race, and income. In 0. Anderson, R. Anderson, and J. Kravits (eds.), *Equity in Health Services.* Cambridge, Mass.: Ballinger.

Langan, P. A., and Innes, C. (1986). Preventing domestic violence against women. University of Michigan: CJAIN (Bulletin of the Crimimal Justice Archive and Information Network, Fall).

Lanyon, R. (1986). Theory and treatment in child molestation. *Journal of Counseling and Clinical Psychologist, 54,* 176–82.

Lassiter, R. T. (1987). Child rearing in black families: Child-abusing discipline. In Robert L. Hampton (ed.), *Violence in the Black Family: Correlates and Consequences.* Lexington, Mass.: Lexington Books.

Lazare, A., Eisenthal, S., Wasserman, L., and Harford, T. (1975). Patient requests in a walk-in clinic. *Comparative Psychiatry, 16,* 467–77.

Leonard, K. E., and Jacob, T. (1988). Alcohol, alcoholism and family violence. In Vincent B. Van Hasselt, Randall L. Morrison, Alan S. Bellack, and Michael Heersen (eds.), *Handbook of Family Violence.* New York: Plenum Press.

Lewis, D. K. (1975). The black family: Socialization and sex roles. *Phylon, 36*(3), 221–37.

Lewis, D. O., Moy, E., and Jackson, L. D. (1985). Biosocial characteristics of children who later murder: A prospective study. *American Journal of Psychiatry, 142,* 1161–67.

Lewis, D. O., Pincus, J. H., and Feldman, M. (1986). Psychiatric, neurological, and psychoeducational characteristics of 15 death row inmates in the United States. *American Journal of Psychiatry, 143,* 838–45.

Linnolia, M. (1986). Alcohol abuse linked to brain changes causing violence. *Behavior Today Newsletter, 17,* 6–7.

Lion, J. R., and Bach-y-Rita, G. (1970). Group psychotherapy with violent outpatients. *International Journal of Group Psychotherapy, 20,* 185–91.

Lion, J. R., Bach-y-Rita, G., and Ervin, F. R. (1968). The self-referred violent patient. *Journal of the American Medical Association, 205,* 503–05.

———. (1969). Violent patients in the emergency room. *American Journal of Psychiatry, 125,* 1706–10.

Liu, William T. and Yu, Ellen D. (1985). Asian–Pacific American elderly:

Mortality, differentials, and health status in the use of health services. *Journal of Applied Gerontology*, 4(1), 35–64.

Lockhart, L. (1985). Methodological issues in comparative racial analyses: The case of wife abuse. *Social Work Research and Abstracts*, 21, 35–41.

———. (1987). A re-examination of the effects of race and social class on the incidence of marital violence: A search for reliable differences. *Journal of Marriage and the Family*, 49, 603–10.

Lockhart, L., and White, B. (1989). Understanding marital violence in the black community. *Journal of Interpersonal Violence*, 4(4), 3–4.

Longfellow, C., Zelkowitz, P. and Saunders, E. (1981). The quality of mother-child relationships. In D. Belle (ed.), *Lives in Stress: Women and Depression*. Beverly Hills, CA: Sage.

Lopez, S., Grover, K., Holland, D., Johnson, M., Kain, C., Kanel, K., Mellins, C., and Rhyne, M. (1989). Development of culturally sensitive psychotherapists. *Professional Psychology: Research and Practice*, 89, 369–76.

Lum, D. (1986). *Social Work Practice and People of Color: A Process-Stage Approach*. Monterey, Calif.: Brooks/Cole Publishing Company.

Lystad, M. (ed.). (1986). *Violence in the Home: Interdisciplinary Perspectives*. New York: Brunner/Mazel.

MacDonald, J. M. (1961). *The Murderer and His Victim*. Springfield, Ill.: Charles C. Thomas.

McAdoo, H. P. (1978). Factors related to stability in upward mobility black families. *Journal of Marriage and the Family*, 40, 762–78.

———. (1981). *Black Families*. Beverly Hills: Sage.

McClain, P. D. (1982–83). Black females and lethal violence: Has time changed the circumstances under which they kill? *Omega*, 13(1), 3–25.

McDonald, G. W. (1980). Family power: The assessment of a decade of theory and research, 1970–1979. *Journal of Marriage and the Family*, 42(4), 881–94.

McGoldrick, M., Pearce, J., and Giordano, J. (1982). *Ethnicity and Family Therapy*. New York: Guilford Press.

McKinlay, J. (1975). The help seeking behavior of the poor. In J. Kosa and I. Zola (eds.), *Poverty and Health: A Sociological Analysis* (2nd edition). Cambridge, Mass.: Harvard University Press.

McNeeley, R. L., and Robinson-Simpson, G. (1988). The truth about domestic violence: A falsely framed issue. *Social Work*, 32, 485–90.

Magura, S., and Moses, B. (1986). *Child Maltreatment Rating Scales*. New York: Child Welfare League of America.

Mann, C. R. (1988). Getting even? Women who kill in domestic encounters. *Justice Quarterly*, 5(1), 33–51.

———. (in press). Maternal filicide of preschoolers. In Anna F. Kuhl (ed.), *Dynamics of the Victim-Offender Interaction*. Cincinnati: Anderson.

Manual, R. C. (1982). *Minority: Sociological and Social Psychological Issues*. Westport, Conn.: Greenwood.

Marascuilo, L. A., and McSweeney, M. (1977). *Nonparametric and Distribution-free Methods for the Social Sciences*. Monterey, Calif.: Brooks/Cole.

Martin, H. P., and Beezely, P. (1977). Behavioral observation of abused children. *Developmental Medicine and Child Neurology, 19,* 373–87.

Mayer, A. J., Joyce, T., Simmons, P. E., and Cook, W. J. (1977). The graying of America. *Newsweek, 89* (February 28), 50–65.

Mayhall, P., and Norgard, K. (1983), *Child Abuse and Neglect: Sharing Responsibility.* New York: John Wiley & Sons.

Millier, D. A. (1981). The sandwich generation: Adult children of aging. *Social Work, 26,* 419–23.

Morash, M. (1986). Wife beating. *Criminal Justice Abstracts, 18*(2), 252–71.

Moynihan, D. (1965). *The Negro Family: The Case for National Action.* Washington, D.C.: Department of Labor.

Mrazek, P., and Kempe, C. (eds.). (1981). *Sexually Abused Children and Their Families.* New York: Pergamon Press.

Myers, H., and King, L. (1983). Mental health issues in the development of the black American child. In G. Powell, J. Yamamoto, A. Romero, and A. Morales (eds.), *The Psychosocial Development of Minority Group Children.* New York: Brunner/Mazel Publishers.

Myers, J. E., and Shelton, B. (1987). Abuse and older persons: Issues and implications for counselors. *Journal of Counseling and Development, 65* (March), 376–80.

Nalepka, C., O'Toole, R., and Turbett, J. P. (1981). Nurses' and physicians' recognition and reporting of child abuse. *Comprehensive Pediatric Nursing, 5,* 33–44.

National Black Child Development Institute. (1989). *Who Will Care When Parents Can't: A Study of Black Children in Foster Care.* Washington, D.C.: National Black Child Development Institute, Inc.

National Center On Child Abuse and Neglect. (1988). *Study Findings: Study of National Incidence and Prevalence of Child Abuse and Neglect: 1988.* Washington, D.C.: U.S. Department of Health and Human Services.

Neighbors, H. (1984). Professional help use among black Americans: Implications for unmet need. *American Journal of Community Psychology, 12*(5), 551–65.

Neighbors, H., and Jackson, J. (1984). The use of informal and formal help: Four patterns of illness behavior in the black community. *American Journal of Community Psychology, 12*(6), 629–44.

Nelson, K. G. (1984). The innocent bystander: The child as unintended victim of domestic violence involving deadly weapons. *Pediatrics, 73,* 251–52.

Newberger, E. H., and Bourne, R. (1978). The medicalization and legalization of child abuse. *American Journal of Orthopsychiatry, 48,* 593–607.

Newberger, E. H., Reed, R., Daniel, J. H., Hyde, J., and Kotelchuck, M. (1977). Pediatric social illness: Toward an etiologic classification. *Pediatrics, 60,* 178–85.

O'Brien, J. (1971). Violence in divorce-prone families. *Journal of Marriage and the Family, 33,* 692–98.

Okun, L. (1986). *Woman abuse—Facts replacing myths.* Albany, N.Y.: State University of New York Press.

Pagelow, M. D. (1984). *Family Violence.* New York: Praeger.

Pallone, S. R., and Malkemes, L. C. (1984). *Helping Parents Who Abuse Their Children: A Comprehensive Approach for Intervention.* Springfield, Ill.: Charles C. Thomas.

Parke, R. D., and Collmer, C. W. (1975). Child abuse: An interdisciplinary analysis. In E. M. Hetherington (ed.), *Review of Child Development Research,* 5, 509–89.

Pascoe, J., Hebbert, V., Perl, T., and Loda, F. (1981). Violence in North Carolina families referred to a child protection team. *North Carolina Medical Journal,* 42, 35–37.

Peters, M. F. (1981). Parenting in black families with young children: A historical perspective. In Harriette P. McAdoo (ed.), *Black Families.* Beverly Hills: Sage.

Petersen, R. (1980). Social class, social learning and wife abuse. *Social Service Review,* 54, 390–406.

Pianta, R., Egeland, B., and Erickson, M. F. (1989). The antecedents of maltreatment: Results of the Mother-Child Interaction Research Project. In D. Cicchetti and V. Carlson (eds.), *Child Maltreatment: Theory and Research on the Causes and Consequences of Child Abuse and Neglect.* New York: Cambridge University Press.

Pierce, R., and Pierce, L. (1987). Child sexual abuse: A black perspective. In Robert Hampton (ed.), *Violence in the Black Family: Correlates and Consequences.* Lexington, Mass.: Lexington Books.

Pinderhughes, E. (1989). *Understanding Race, Ethnicity and Power: The Key to Efficacy in Clinical Practice.* New York: Macmillan.

Plass, P. S., and Straus, M. A. (1987). *Intra-Family Homicide in the United States: Incidence, Trends and Differences by Region, Race and Gender.* Paper presented at the Third National Family Violence Research Conference, University of New Hampshire, Durham, N.H., July.

Pokorney, A. D. (1986). A comparison of homicides in two cities. *Journal of Criminal Law, Criminology and Police Science,* 56(4), 479–87.

Polansky, N. A., Hally, C., and Polansky, N. F. (1976). *Profile of Neglect: A Survey of the State of Knowledge of Child Neglect.* U.S. Department of Health, Education, and Welfare. Social and Rehabilitation Service. (DHEW Publication No. 620–167/2260.) Washington, D.C.: U.S. Government Printing Office.

Police Foundation. (1977). *Domestic Violence and the Police: Studies in Detroit and Kansas City.* Washington, D.C.: Police Foundation.

Ramos, S. M., and Delany, H. M. (1986). Freefalls from heights: A persistent urban problem. *Journal of the National Medical Association,* 78, 111–15.

Rathbone-McCuan, E. (1980). Elderly victims of family violence and neglect. *Social Casework,* 61, 296–304.

Riedel, M., and Lockhart-Riedel, L. (1984). *Issues in the Study of Black Homicide.* Presented at annual meeting, American Society of Criminology.

Riedel, M., Zahn, M. A., and Mock, L. F. (1985). *The Nature and Patterns of American Homicide.* U.S. Department of Justice, National Institute of Justice. Washington, D.C.: U.S. Government Printing Office.

Riedel, M., Zahn, M. A., and Mock, L. F. (1985). *The Nature and Patterns of American Homicide*. U.S. Department of Justice, National Institute of Justice. Washington, D.C.: U.S. Government Printing Office.

Robins, L. N., Helzer, J. E., Croughan, J., and Ratcliff, K. S. (1981). National Institute of Mental Health Diagnostic Interview Schedule: Its history, characteristics, and validity. *Archives of General Psychiatry, 38,* 381–89.

Rose, H. M. (1981). *Black Homicide and the Urban Environment*. United States Department of Health and Human Services, National Institute of Mental Health. Washington, D.C.: U.S. Government Printing Office.

Roy, M. (1977). *Battered Women*. New York: Van Nostrand Reinhold.

———. (1982). Four thousand partners in violence: A trend analysis. In Marie Roy (ed.), *The Abusive Partner*. New York: Van Nostrand Reinhold.

Russell, D. E. H. (1982). *Rape in Marriage*. New York: MacMillan.

Rynearson, E. K. (1986). Psychological effects of unnatural dying on bereavement. *Psychiatric Annals, 16,* 272–75.

Sack, W. H., Mason, R., and Higgins, J. E. (1985). The single-parent family and abusive child punishment. *American Journal of Orthopsychiatry, 55,* 252–59.

Sampson, R. J. (1987). Urban black violence: The effect of male joblessness and family disruption. *American Journal of Sociology, 93*(2), 348–82.

Schechter, S. (1982). *Women and Male Violence: The Visions and Struggles of the Battered Women's Movement*. Boston: South End Press.

Schene, P. (1987). Is child abuse decreasing? *Journal of Interpersonal Violence, 2,* 225–27.

Schneider, C., Helfer, R., and Pollock, C. (1972). The predictive questionnaire: A preliminary report. In C. Kempe and R. Helfer (eds.), *The Battered Child*. Chicago. Chicago University Press.

Schumm, W. R., Bollman, R. S., Jurich, A. P., and Martin, M. J. (1982). Adolescent perspectives on family violence. *Journal of Social Psychology, 117,* 153–54.

Seelbaugh, W. C. (1978). Correlates of aged parents filial responsibility, expectations, and realizations. *Family Coordinator, 27,* 341–50.

Sgroi, S. (1982). *Handbook of Clinical Intervention in Child Sexual Abuse*. Lexington, Mass.: Lexington Books.

Sherman, L., and Berk, R. A. (1984). The specific deterrent effects of arrest for domestic assault. *American Sociological Review, 49,* 261–72.

Showers, J., and Bandman, R. L. (1986). Scarring for life: Abuse with electric cords. *Child Abuse and Neglect, 10,* 25–31.

Shupe, A., Stacey, W. A., and Hazelwood, L. R. (1986). *Violent Men, Violent Couples*. Lexington, Mass.: Lexington Books.

Silverman, R. A., and Kennedy, L. W. (1988). Women who kill their children. *Violence and Victims, 3*(2), 113–27.

Smith, B. (1985). Assistant Administrator, Office of Wayne County Prosecuting Attorney. Personal communication, January 17.

Smyer, M. A., and Gatz, M. (1983). *Mental Health and Aging—Programs and Evaluations*. Beverly Hills: Sage.

Snyder, J. C., and Newberger, E. H. (1986). Consensus and differences among hospital professionals in evaluating child maltreatment. *Violence Victims*, 1, 125–39.

Sokolovsky, J. (1985). Ethnicity, culture, and aging: Do differences really make a difference? *Journal of Applied Gerontology*, 4(1), 6–17.

Spanier, G., and Glick, P. (1980). Mate selection differentials between blacks and whites in the United States. *Social Forces*, 58, 707–25.

Spearly, J., and Lauderdale, M. (1983). Community characteristics and ethnicity in the prediction of child maltreatment rates. *Child Abuse and Neglect*, 7, 91–105.

Sprung, G. M. (1989). Transferential issues in working with older adults. *Social Casework*, 70(10), 597–602.

Spurlock, J. (1985). Assessment and therapeutic intervention of black children. *Journal of the American Academy of Child Psychiatry*, 24, 168–74.

Stack, C. (1974). *All Our Kin: Strategies for Survival in the Black Community*. New York: Harper and Row.

Staples, R. (1976a). Race and family violence: The internal colonialism perspectives. In Lawrence Gary and Lee Browns (eds.), *Crime and Its Impact on the Black Community*. Washington, D.C.: Howard University.

———. (1976b). *Introduction to Black Sociology*. New York: McGraw-Hill.

———. (November 1985). Changes in black family structure: The conflict between family ideology and structural conditions. *Journal of Marriage and the Family*, 47, 1005–15.

Stark, E., Flitcraft, A. (1982). Medical therapy as repression: The case of the battered woman. *Health and Medicine*, 29–32.

———. (1988). Women and children at risk: A feminist perspective on child abuse. *International Journal of Health Services*, 18, 97–118.

Starr, R. H., Jr. (1982). A research-based approach to the prediction of child abuse. In R. H. Starr, Jr. (ed.), *Child Abuse Prediction: Policy Implications*. Cambridge, Mass.: Ballinger.

Staver, S. (1986). M.D. Stresses physician role in stopping murder. *Am Medical News*, July 31.

Steinmetz, S. (1977). *The Cycle of Violence: Assertive, Aggressive, and Abusive Family Interaction*. New York: Praeger.

Steinmetz, S. K. (1978). Battered parents. *Society*, 15, 54–55.

Steinmetz, S. K., and Straus, M. A. (1974). *Violence in the Family*. New York: Harper and Row.

Stengel, R. (September 1985). When brother kills brother. *Time*, 126, 32–36.

Steur, J., and Austin, E. (1980). Family abuse of the elderly. *Journal of the Geriatrics Society*, 28, 372–75.

Stocks, J. T. (1988). Has family violence decreased? A reassessment of the Straus and Gelles data. *Journal of Marriage and the Family*, 50, 281–85.

Straus, M. A. (1977). Wife beating: How common and why? *Victimology*, 2, 443–58.

———. (1979). Measuring intrafamily conflict and violence: The conflict tactics (CT) scales. *Journal of Marriage and the Family*, 41, 75–88.

———. (July 1981). *Re-evaluation of the conflict tactics scale*. Paper presented at the National Conference for Family Violence Researchers, University of New Hampshire, Durham, N.H.

———. (1986). Domestic violence and homicide antecedents. *Bulletin of the New York Academy of Medicine, 62,* 446–65.

———. (1990). The Conflict Tactics Scale and its critics: An evaluation and new data on validity and reliability. In Murray A. Straus and Richard J. Gelles (eds.), *Physical Violence in American Families: Risk Factors and Adaptations in 8,145 Families.* New Brunswick, N.J.: Transaction Books.

Straus, M., and Gelles, R. (1986). Societal change and change in family violence from 1975–1985 as revealed by two national studies. *Journal of Marriage and the Family, 48,* 465–79.

———. (1988). Violence in American families: How much is there and why does it occur? In Elam W. Nunnally, Catherine Chilman, and Fred Cox (eds.), *Troubled Relationships.* Newbury Park, CA: Sage.

———. (eds.). (1990). *Physical Violence in American Families: Risk Factors and Adaptations in 8,145 Families.* New Brunswick: Transaction Books.

Straus, M., Gelles, R., and Steinmetz, S. (1980). *Behind Closed Doors: Violence in American Families.* Garden City, NY: Doubleday.

Surgeon General's Workshop on Violence and Public Health Report. (1985). Washington, D.C.: Department of Health and Human Services.

Sutherland, E. H., and Cressey, D. L. (1978). *Criminology.* Philadelphia: J. B. Lippincott.

Suval, E. M., and Brisson, R. C. (1974). Neither beauty nor beast: Female criminal homicide offenders. *International Journal of Criminology and Penology, 2,* 23–34.

Swigert, V. L., and Farrell, R. A. (1978). Patterns in criminal homicide: Theory and research. In Peter Wickman and Philip Whitten (eds.), *Criminology* (pp. 91–202). Lexington, Mass.: Lexington Books.

Szegedy-Maszak, M. (1989). Whose to judge? *New York Times Magazine,* 28–29.

Taylor, M. C., and Hammond, P. V. (1987). See how they run: Battered women in shelters in the old dominion. In Robert L. Hampton (ed.), *Violence in the Black Family: Correlates and Consequenses* (pp. 107–19). Lexington, Mass.: Lexington Books.

Taylor, R. (1986). Receipt of support from family among black Americans: Demographic and familial differences. *Journal of Marriage and Family, 48,* 67–77.

Taylor, R. J., and Chatter, L. M. (1986). Patterns of informal support to elderly black adults: Family, friends, and church members. *Social Work, 31*(6), 432–38.

Thomas, A., and Sillen, S. (1976). *Racism and Psychiatry.* Secaucus, N.J.: Citadel.

Torres, S. (in press). A comparative analysis of wife abuse among Anglo-American and Mexican-American battered women: Attitudes, nature and extent, and response to the abuse. *Victimology.*

Totman, J. (1978). *The Murderess: A Psychological Study of Criminal Homicide.* San Francisco: R. & E. Research Associates.

Turbett, J. P., and O'Toole, R. (1980). *Physicians recognition of child abuse.* Paper presented at the annual meeting of the American Sociological Association, New York.

Turner, C. (1972). Some theoretical and conceptual considerations for black family studies. *Black Scholar*, 2, 13–27.

University of California at Los Angeles and Centers for Disease Control. (1985). *The Epidemiology of Homicide in the City of Los Angeles 1970–79*. Atlanta: Department of Health and Human Services, Public Health Service, Centers for Disease Control.

U.S. Bureau of the Census. (1971). *1970 Census of Population*. Washington, D.C.: Bureau of the Census, U.S. Department of Commerce.

———. (1981). *1980 Census of Population*. Washington, D.C.: Bureau of the Census, U.S. Department of Commerce.

———. (1984). *County and City Data Book: 1983* (10th ed.) Washington, D.C.: U.S. Government Printing Office.

———. (1984–85). *Statistical Abstract of the United States*, unpublished data.

———. (1987). *Statistical Abstract of the United States: 1986* (106th ed.). Washington, D.C.: U.S. Government Printing Office.

U.S. Department of Health and Human Services. (1981). *Study Findings: National Study of the Incidence and Severity of Child Abuse and Neglect*. DHHS Publication No. (OHDS) 81–3025.

U.S. Department of Justice, Federal Bureau of Investigation. (1981–85). Uniform Crime Reports. Unpublished data.

———. (1986). *Crime Reports: Crime in the U.S., 1985*. Washington, D.C.: U.S. Department of Justice.

U.S. Select Committee on Aging. (1980). *Elder Abuse*. Washington, D.C.: U.S. Government Printing Office.

Vinokur, D. and Gray, S. (1983). *Attitudes and Evaluation of In-Service Training by Child Welfare Trainers*. (profile four). Ann Arbor: National Child Welfare Training Center, The University of Michigan School of Social Work.

von Hentig, H. (1948). *The Criminal and His Victim*. New Haven, Conn.: Yale University Press.

Voss, H. L., and Hepburn, J. R. (1968). Patterns of criminal homicide in Chicago. *Journal of Criminology and Police Service*, 59, 499–508.

Walker, L. (1979). *The Battered Woman*. New York: Harper and Row.

———. (1984). *The Battered Woman Syndrome*. New York: Springer.

Warren, D. (1981). *Helping Networks: How People Cope with Problems in the Urban Comunnity*. Notre Dame, Ind.: University of Notre Dame Press.

Wauchope, B. A., and Straus, M. A. (1990). Physical punishment and physical abuse of American children: Incidence rates by age, gender, and occupational class. In Murray A. Straus and Richard J. Gelles (eds.), *Physical Violence in American Families: Risk Factors and Adaptations in 8,145 Families*. New Brunswick, N.J.: Transaction Books.

Weiner, M. B., Brok, A. J., and Snadowsky, A. M. (1987). *Working with the Aged* (2d ed.). Norwalk, Conn.: Appelton-Century-Crofts.

Widom, C. S. (1989). The cycle of violence. *Science*, 244, 160–66.

Williams, O. J. (1988). Abuse of adults and elders. In L. W. Griffins (ed.), *A Guide for Adult Protective Services*. Morgantown, W.V.: West Virginia University Press.

———. (October 1989). *Enhancing the black batterers' participation in bat-*

terers' treatment programs. Presented at 1989 Conference, National Association of Social Work, San Francisco.

————. (1989). Spouse abuse: social learning and attribution and intervention.
Journal of Health and Social Policy, 1(2).

Willie, C. (1988). *A New Look at Black Families*. New York: General Hall,
Inc.

Weis, J. G. (1989). Family violence research methodology and design. In Lloyd
Ohlin and Michael Tonry (eds.), *Family Violence* (pp. 117–62). Chicago:
The University of Chicago Press.

Weisheit, R. A. (1984). Female homicide offenders: Trends over time in an
institutionalized population. *Justice Quarterly,* 1(4), 471–89.

Weissman, M., Paykel, E., and Klerman, G. (1972). The depressed woman as a
mother. *Social Psychiatry,* 7, 98–108.

White, B. W. (1981). Black women: The resilient victims. In Ann Weick and
Susan Vandirer (eds.), *Women, Power, and Change*. Washington, D.C.:
National Association of Social Workers.

White, E. C. (1985). *Chain, Chain, Change*. Seattle: Seal Press.

Wilbanks, W. (1982). Murdered women and women who murder: A critique of
the literature. In N. H. Rafter and E. A. Stanko (eds.), *Judge, Lawyer,
Victim, Thief: Women, Gender Roles, and Criminal Justice*. Boston:
Northeastern University Press.

————. (1983). The female homicide offender in Dade County, Florida. *Criminal Justice Review,* 8(2), 9–14.

Wilson, M. N., Cobb, D., and Dolan, R. T. (1987). Raising the awareness of
wife battering in rural black areas of central Virginia: A community outreach approach. In Robert L. Hampton (ed.), *Violence in the Black Family: Correlates and Consequences*. Lexington, Mass.: Lexington Books.

Wives Face Bigger Risk in Spouse Killings. (1989). *Wall Street Journal* (May 9),
B1.

Wolfe, D. (1985). Child abusive parents: An empirical review and analysis.
Psychological Bulletin, 97(3), 462–82.

Wolfgang, M. E. (1956). Husband/wife homicides. *Journal of Social Therapy,*
2, 263–71.

————. (1958). *Patterns in Criminal Homicide*. Montclair, N.J.: Patterson
Smith.

Wolkind, S., and Rutter, M. (1985). Sociocultural factors. In M. Rutter and L.
Hersov (eds.), *Child and Adolescent Psychiatry: Modern Approaches*. Boston: Blackwell Scientific Publications.

Wolking, S., and Rutter, M. (1985). Sociocultural factors. In M. Rutter and L.
Hersov (eds.), *Child and Adolescent Psychiatry: Modern Approaches*. Boston: Blackwell Scientific Publications.

Wolock, I., and Horowitz, B. (1977). *Factors relating to levels of child care
among families receiving public assistance in New Jersey*. Final report to
the National Center on Child Abuse and Neglect DHEW Grant 9-C-418.

Wood, W., and Sherrets, S. (1984). Requests for outpatient mental health
services: A comparison of whites and blacks. *Comprehensive Psychiatry,*
25(3), 329–34.

Zuravin, S. (ed.). (1988a). Child abuse, child neglect, and maternal depression:

Is there a connection? In National Center on Child Abuse and Neglect, *Child Neglect Monograph: Proceedings from a Symposium*. U.S. Department of Health and Human Services, Office of Human Development Services. Clearinghouse on Child Abuse and Neglect Information, Washington, D.C.

Zuravin, S. (1988b). Child maltreatment and teenage first births: A relationship mediated by chronic sociodemographic stress? *American Journal of Orthopsychiatry, 58*(1), 91–103.

Zuravin, S. (1990). Unpublished paper.

Index

About the Contributors

Carl C. Bell is executive director of the Community Mental Health Council, Chicago, Illinois.

Edward De Vos is a senior scientist, Education Development Center, Inc., Newton, Massachusetts.

Ellen Fisher is affiliated with the Austin Center for Battered Women, Austin, Texas.

Richard J. Gelles is a professor of sociology and anthropology, the University of Rhode Island, and lecturer on pediatrics (sociology), Harvard Medical School, Boston, Massachusetts.

Ann Goetting is professor of sociology, Western Kentucky University, Bowling Green, Kentucky.

Edward W. Gondolf is professor of sociology at Indiana University of Pennsylvania, Indiana, Pennsylvania, and is a research fellow at the Western Psychiatric Institute and Clinic, University of Pittsburgh, Pittsburgh, Pennsylvania.

Linner Griffin is an assistant professor, School of Social Work, East Carolina University, Greenville, North Carolina.

John Harrop is an assistant research professor of psychiatry and human behavior, Brown Medical School, and program manager, Center for Alcohol and Addiction Studies, Brown University, Providence, Rhode Island.

Lettie L. Lockhart is an associate professor, School of Social Work, The University of Georgia, Athens, Georgia.

Coramae Richey Mann is professor of criminal justice, Indiana University, Bloomington, Indiana.

J. Richard McFerron is director of academic computing services, Indiana University of Pennsylvania.

Linda McKibben is an assistant professor, department of pediatrics, Tufts University School of Medicine, Boston, Massachusetts.

Eli H. Newberger is an assistant professor of pediatrics, Harvard Medical School, and director, Family Development Study, Children's Hospital Center, Boston, Massachusetts.

Lois H. Pierce is an associate professor of Social Work, University of Missouri—St. Louis, St. Louis, Missouri.

Robert L. Pierce is an associate professor, The George Warren Brown School of Social Work, Washington University, St. Louis, Missouri.

Raymond H. Starr, Jr. is an assistant professor, department of psychology, University of Maryland at Baltimore.

Oliver J. Williams is an assistant professor, Graduate School of Social Work, University of Minnesota, Minneapolis, Minnesota.

Susan J. Zuravin is an assistant professor of social work, School of Social Work and Community Planning, University of Maryland at Baltimore.

About the Editor

Robert L. Hampton, Ph.D., received an A. B. degree from Princeton University and an M.A. and Ph.D. from the University of Michigan. He is professor of sociology and dean of the college, Connecticut College, New London, Connecticut, a research associate in the Family Development Program, Children's Hospital Center, and lecturer on pediatrics (sociology), Harvard Medical School, Boston, Massachusetts. He has published extensively in the field of family violence including an earlier book entitled *Violence in the Black Family: Correlates and Consequences* (1987, Lexington Books). His research interests include interspousal violence, family abuse, community violence, stress and social support, and institutional responses to violence.